DRINKING OCCASIONS

International Center for Alcohol Policies
Series on Alcohol in Society

DRINKING OCCASIONS:
Comparative Perspectives on Alcohol and Culture

Dwight B. Heath, Ph.D.
Department of Anthropology
Brown University
Providence, RI, USA

BRUNNER/MAZEL
Taylor & Francis Group

USA	Publishing Office:	BRUNNER/MAZEL
		A member of the Taylor & Francis Group
		325 Chestnut Street
		Philadelphia, PA 19106
		Tel: (215) 625-8900
		Fax: (215) 625-2940
	Distribution Center:	BRUNNER/MAZEL
		A member of the Taylor & Francis Group
		47 Runway Road, Suite G
		Levittown, PA 19057-4700
		Tel: (215) 269-0400
		Fax: (215) 269-0363
UK		BRUNNER/MAZEL
		A member of the Taylor & Francis Group
		27 Church Road
		Hove
		E. Sussex, BN3 2FA
		Tel: +44 (0) 1273 207411
		Fax: +44 (0) 1273 205612

DRINKING OCCASIONS: Comparative Perspectives on Alcohol and Culture

2 3 4 5 6 7 8 9 0

Printed by Sheridan Books, Ann Arbor, MI, 2000.
Cover design by Nancy Abbott.

A CIP catalog record for this book is available from the British Library.
⊗ The paper in this publication meets the requirements of the ANSI Standard Z39.48-1984 (Permanence of Paper).

Library of Congress Cataloging-in-Publication Data

Heath, Dwight B.
    Drinking occasions : comparative perspectives on alcohol and culture / Dwight B. Heath.
      p. cm. -- (Series on alcohol in society)
    Includes bibliographical references and index.
    ISBN 1-58391-047-6 (alk. paper)
    1. Drinking customs--Cross-cultural studies. 2. Drinking of alcoholic beverages--Cross-cultural studies. I. Title. II. Series.
GT2884 H4 2000
394.1′3--dc21
                                         99-059618
                                            CIP

ISBN 1-58391-047-6 (case)

Dedication

ETOH, alias Ethanol, Alcohol, C_2H_5OH

food, complement to food, and poison,
stimulant to appetite, and aid to digestion,
tonic, medicine, and harmful drug,
elixir, potion, or "a tool of the devil,"
energizer or soporific,
sacrament or abomination,
aphrodisiac or turn-off,
euphoriant, and depressant,
adjunct to sociability or means of retreat,
stimulant or relaxant,
tasty nectar or godawful stuff,
exculpatory, or aggravating, with respect to blame,
god's gift or a curse,
analgesic and anesthetic, disinhibitor or knock-out,
etc., etc.

Contents

Acknowledgments

Every book is a joint enterprise, and that is especially true of this one, because it grew out of a concern for no less than all peoples throughout all of history.

I was lucky to have as teachers Clyde Kluckhohn, who first fired my enthusiasm for anthropology, and George P. Murdock, who taught me rigor in cross-cultural studies. Both of them stressed an ethnographer's duty to observe as faithfully as possible and to report as fully on the context, so that data can be linked with theory and vice versa. In alcohol studies, E. M. Jellinek, Mark Keller, David Pittman, and Charles Snyder encouraged even a newcomer to contribute so that the pool of shared knowledge could be expanded. Robin Room, Linda Bennett, Robert Popham, and Sol Tax exemplified in their own work the mutual relevance of the fields. And, through it all, A. C. has been a steadfast friend and colleague, chasing rainbows when that matters, and working hard in untold ways when that is needed.

A consultantship with International Center for Alcohol Policies gave me the time to write this book. Marcus Grant, Bart Alexander, Gaye Pedlow, and Stephen Whitehead were especially helpful in terms of lending other viewpoints. Shirley Gordon, Bernadette Capelle, Eleni Houghton, Marjana Martinic, and Linda Schmidt helped keep the manuscript manageable, and the confidence of others lent confidence to me.

Dwight B. Heath

Foreword

The main purpose of this book is to describe the variety of drinking occasions that exist around the world. As such, it celebrates the diversity of normal drinking behavior and illustrates the wide range of beneficial drinking patterns. In general, it does not dwell upon drinking problems, alcohol abuse, excessive, reckless or inappropriate drinking, or harmful drinking patterns.

It is therefore important to acknowledge, here in the foreword to the book, that its intention is not to ignore or minimize the adverse health and social consequences of irresponsible drinking. There is, as readers will be well aware, a vast scientific and epidemiological literature that deals with somatic and psychiatric diseases, accidents and injuries, and social and behavioral problems—all associated to a greater or lesser extent with alcohol consumption. Generally, of course, that association is with patterns of consumption that are quite different from those with which this book is mainly concerned, but part of the fascination of the subject of alcohol is its double-edged capacity to induce euphoria and sociability on the one hand, and, on the other, to lead to serious personal and social problems.

This book has been commissioned by the International Center for Alcohol Policies (ICAP), which is a not-for-profit organization supported by 11 major international beverage alcohol companies. ICAP is dedicated to helping reduce the abuse of alcohol worldwide and to promoting understanding of the role of alcohol in society through dialogue and partnerships involving the industry, the public health community, and others interested in alcohol policy. The first three books in this ICAP series on Alcohol in Society are multiauthored volumes dealing with shifting paradigms in alcohol studies.

The current book, written by a single author and focusing more on what might be considered the positive aspects of drinking behavior, deals directly with the challenge of how to define responsibility in the face of the world's many different drinking styles. By concentrating upon descriptions of normal drinking occasions, it is intended to distinguish these as clearly as possible from abnormal or inappropriate occasions. The book is intended to demonstrate how well-integrated with many other aspects of human life normal drinking occasions can be, and to help to differentiate those drinking occasions which are dislocated from benign human interaction and which may therefore be more likely to lead to problems.

Having spent a quarter of a century working on alcohol policy issues, I am amazed at how little attention has been paid to the characteristics of the vast majority of drinking occasions, namely those which lead to feelings of subjective well-being and social cohesiveness. I see this book as an important contribution to this sorely neglected area.

There are, of course, aspects of drinking behavior where the dividing line between normal and abnormal drinking becomes blurred. An obvious example relates to the issue of drunkenness or intoxication. Alcohol is a psychoactive substance, and those choosing to consume it do so in part in order to experience its psychostimulant effects. In addition, a variety of social and even religious occasions are based upon a presumption that those participating will be experiencing exactly those effects. Yet, at the same time, increasing levels of intoxication clearly carry elevated levels of risk to self and others, especially in relation to accident and injury. The challenge for alcohol policy is to create an environment in which the beneficial potential of moderate drinking is maximized and the harmful potential of excessive drinking is minimized.

The substantial literature on the cardioprotective effects of light to moderate drinking is another example. It is abundantly clear that if two drinks a day may benefit a middle-aged man's heart, that does not mean that six drinks a day will confer three times the benefit. It is also abundantly clear that there are categories of individuals who might well be advised to abstain from alcohol for constitutional, medical, occupational or other grounds. This is, indeed, an issue which is touched upon more than once in this book.

I have been privileged to work with Professor Heath during the development of this book and have watched with admiration as his scholarship and encyclopedic knowledge have filled its pages with exactly the kind of information that has never previously been available from a single source. As I have watched, however, I have never for a moment suspected that what he was trying to do was to provide a cover of erudition for the marketing aspirations of the companies that support ICAP. For more than 25 years, he has written about social and psychological benefits of drinking in various societies around the world. Time and again, we confronted the question of how to portray normal drinking behavior without condoning—or even appearing to condone—reckless drinking. Time and again, we have discussed where the boundaries exist and how they can best be mapped.

I mentioned above that I have devoted a quarter of a century to alcohol policy. Professor Heath has devoted an even larger number of years to alcohol studies. I am sure that I speak for him, as well as for myself, when I say that the excitement of this book goes far beyond the richness of the experience from around the world that it contains. This is no anthology of quaint customs and odd drinking habits. It is a serious and sustained attempt to make available, to those interested in alcohol policies, an unbiased account of what actually goes on when people decide to have a drink (or several drinks). As such, it does not ignore alcohol-related problems. What it does is to put them into context. In any assessment of the place of alcohol in society, due weight must be given to the burden of disease and disability associated with it. But weight also needs to be given to its significant contribution to personal and social well-being. This book is intended to help balance the evidence.

Marcus Grant
President
International Center for Alcohol Policies

Introduction

This volume is intended to fill a conspicuous gap between the vast amount of highly specialized scientific and academic writing on the subject (much of which is difficult to find and even more difficult to understand) on the one hand, and a similarly large amount of simple material that is easily accessible to the general reader (but much of which is scant in terms of substantive content).[1] The author has seriously endeavored to make it accurate throughout by including recent authoritative data, and to make it accessible by writing in a style that should be easy to understand. In standard scholarly format, there are citations scattered throughout the text and a substantial list of references at the back of the book. The text can just as well be read and appreciated by anyone who chooses simply to ignore such references, although the sources that are cited should provide reassurance or more details for anyone who wants to pursue a particular topic in more depth.

This is the fourth volume in a series on alcohol in society, sponsored by the International Center for Alcohol Policies (Washington, DC, USA). The first (Grant & Litvak, 1998), a series of essays by specialists from around the world, developed the proposition that the pattern of drinking best predicts whether one will have positive or negative outcomes from drinking. The second (Grant, 1998), by specialists who live and work in developing countries, focused on drinking patterns, problems, and responses that relate to transitions from traditional to modern beverage alcohol there. The third (Peele & Grant, 1999) is a collection of essays by specialists in many disciplines and from many countries, examining the concept of pleasure and how it relates to both alcohol and health. This fourth

---

[1] The opinions expressed in this book are those of the individual author and do not necessarily reflect the views of the sponsors of the International Center for Alcohol Policies (ICAP). The primary goal of this book is a full discussion of the issues and a contribution to the overall body of scholarship. No effort was made to direct the individual author.

volume is the first by a single author and the first that stresses behavior, looking at how people drink, in international and cross-cultural perspective, in an attempt to understand better the varied and contradictory roles that alcohol has played in culture throughout history.

This book is an outgrowth of my nearly 40 years of research on drinking around the world, and about a dozen years of concern about national and international policies as they relate to folk beliefs and behavior. The research has not been done in a sterile laboratory where it is easy to isolate and control variables, but in the real world where people say and do things that the observer must try to interpret but can rarely manipulate. This is not to say that ethnographic or historical research is unscientific. Rather, it is aimed at different levels of understanding. There is a very real sense in which the world itself can be taken as a laboratory, especially if we consider, as subjects of study, populations (rather than individuals), each of which constitutes a natural experiment with its unique history, relation to the environment, and internal dynamics.

Social scientists are well aware that our concerns and approaches differ markedly from those of psychologists, therapists, and many others who also deal with alcohol use and its outcomes. We are well aware that the patterns we discuss both derive from and are expressed in the actions and emotions of specific individuals, but our focus is less on personal uniqueness than on regularities. Most individuals within a given population share emotional and behavioral patterns to a significant degree, even when they differ from—and often even contradict—those that are shared by members of another population. We recognize, too, the idiosyncratic physiology of each human being, and the fact that his or her life experiences are, in some measure, unique. At the same time, we consider it important to examine those ways in which members of one society not only share their experiences but also their expectations, shaped in large part by a world view that differs from that held by members of other societies (Acuda & Alexander, 1998; Levin, 1990).

One might ask why anyone should bother to study social groups or natural communities when there is still so much to be learned about a broad range of phenomena that are so much easier to control and examine. First is the intrinsic interest of populations, how they regulate themselves, how they change over time, how they impact on each participating individual, and how they relate to each other. Next is the fundamental importance that they have in shaping our views of the world, of what's right and what's wrong, what's good to eat (or to do, to think, to wish, and so forth) and what's not. The ways in which populations adjust or adapt in times of adversity or of abundance, and the ways in which they alter their views about time, work, value, and other fundamental aspects of life are endlessly engaging. Then there is always the practical aspect of learning from the experience of others in ways that may be applicable to ourselves. For all of these reasons, social science can be important, even if it doesn't always yield statistically significant numbers, or infallible predictions.

When social scientists talk about norms of belief or behavior, it is not always clear what kinds of norms they have in mind (Harford, Parker, & Light, 1980). In a strictly mathematical sense, a norm is the kind of average that most of us first think about, mathematically discovered by adding the numbers that represent all the different units within a given population and then dividing that sum by the number of units that comprise the total. But there are also nonmathematical norms, such as abstracted or generalized norms *about* behavior, that is the normal, in the sense of what most people say they do, or what they actually do. Anyone concerned about understanding what goes on among a given group of people must also be concerned about prescriptive norms, norms *for* behavior. They comprise the normative or "the ideal" in the sense of what most people say ought to be done, or what they should do. In still another sense, social scientists pay attention to descriptive norms, or norms *from* behavior. They are the real or the actual, in the sense of what people are observed to do, as noted by a relatively objective reporter.

Many books have been written that focus on generalized norms of behavior, summarizing information that had been gathered through social surveys or questionnaires. The elaborate tables, figures, and statistical manipulations that appear in such volumes suggest considerable accuracy and precision. But those who make a living at such work make no secret of the fact that they have little confidence in the accuracy (validity, in the scientific sense) of their own data (Hilton, 1991a; Pernanen, 1974). One of the reasons for their reservations is that heavier drinkers generally understate their consumption, especially those who drink more (Clark, 1991; Hilton, 1991b). Another weakness often cited is that the amount of alcohol that respondents say they drink accounts for only about half of the total sold (Room, 1991b). In many jurisdictions, furthermore, it is recognized that unregistered alcohol may comprise as much as 80% of the total, but cannot be measured because there are no public records of it (Heath, 1998b). In this book, the emphasis will be on this final (descriptive) kind of norm, with occasional mention of prescriptive norms; every effort will be made to distinguish between them in discussion of the context.

For that matter, no reputable physicist can tell you where an object will land even if it's dropped from just a few feet up—unless a number of other variables are specified or controlled, such as wind, movement of other objects, magnetic fields, and so forth. And such hard-core sciences as vulcanology, meteorology, and astronomy fall short on prediction no matter how much they add to our understanding of the universe. Don't confuse numbers with science, and don't interpret a lack of numbers as implying an absence of science.

As the work of a comparative social scientist, this book approaches drinking with a predominantly descriptive orientation, focusing on what people do and what they say. That is very different from a prescriptive approach, which emphasizes what *ought* to be said or done. And it is also very different from an explanatory approach, which tries to provide reasons, explanations, and justification for people's actions. Some of what is described on the part of others may not appear to be pleasant, and some of it is downright dangerous or harmful. Such judgments may be an important part of the clinician's job, or even of concern to an anthropologist who aims to direct the behavior of a group or an individual in a particular way. But the job of observation and description can be hampered by such value judgments and esthetic sensibilities. In this book, the author has no intention of telling people how to drink—or even whether to do so (or not)—but rather aims to let the reader know something about the range of variation that we find, throughout time and space, when we look at drinking as a peculiarly human phenomenon.

Most of the points discussed in this book are not especially technical, although there are always implications that could hold the attention of specialists for months at a time. Much of what is dealt with here has to do with patterns of belief and behavior—what people think, how they feel, and what they do with respect to drinks. There are a few contexts in which specific recommendations are made and the successes and failures of various policies are discussed as they relate to public health and social welfare. But the main concern here is the apparently simple (but really complex) question, "What does it mean to have a drink?"

In simpler times, when journalism was viewed primarily as the relaying of information to a curious and interested public rather than as an attempt to entertain people looking to be distracted, it used to be said that a reporter's job was to answer the straight-forward questions: Who? What? Where? When? How?—and only occasionally, when the human-interest element demanded, to try to describe "Why?" Because this book is concerned mostly with describing the place of beverage alcohol in the world, it is organized in the same way. A single chapter is devoted to each of those questions with respect to people's thinking, talking, and acting about drink. There are also a few additional brief comments pointing to implications and conclusions that may be derived from such a cross-cultural perspective, which is distinctly different from the way most people look at it.

Each chapter begins with a brief introduction and case study, describing the drinking patterns of a particular group of people, with an emphasis on that aspect of drinking that is the focus of the chapter. The description usually includes enough historical and sociocultural context so that meaning and significance should be clear for what might otherwise appear to be merely a bundle of exotic beliefs and practices. With that case study in mind, a reader should be better prepared to appreciate the richness and diversity of other patterns that are more briefly described, sometimes with little in the way of context, in the rest of the chapter. And each chapter concludes with a brief discussion of why the question posed in that chapter's title has some relevance for health, science, or policy.

In an early review of the anthropological literature on drink, this author made the point that "a feature that sets 'alcohol studies' apart from many other topical emphases in behavioral and historical studies is that the majority of the pertinent data and observations have been serendipitous by-products of re-search that had very different foci of concern" (Heath, 1977, pp. 4–5). Strange as it may seem, that was in some respects a strength as well as a weakness, inasmuch as the observers were relatively objective in what they recorded and reported, unencumbered by theoretical preconceptions and the selective vision that sometimes goes with a highly structured conceptual scheme. Of course, it also meant that some potentially important factors may have been insufficiently attended to, or even overlooked, but the richness with which the context was reported often made up for such shortcomings. From about 1970 onward, more social scientists became interested in drinking as a subject of study, and some of them familiarized themselves with work in several fields so that they were better attuned to aspects of drink that had conceptual relevance to colleagues in other disciplines. It is a tribute to the early work that it was sufficiently detailed so that it is still useful for comparative purposes, just as it was originally for providing the germs of middle range theories. More recent work is often more satisfying to those who are looking for specific bits of data, but runs the risk of losing some of the contextual richness that makes ethnography so plausible and gratifying to many.

It has been suggested that "alcohol is the best known and most widely used means of altering human consciousness" (Marshall, 1979b). The holistic approach, by which anthropologists make a sincere effort to understand how parts of any human activity relate to the human enterprise in general, has gone beyond that because alcohol is also used in many settings where its potential to alter human consciousness is irrelevant. Truly, drinking is woven into the very fabric of social existence, for better or for worse (Mandelbaum, 1965). It is important, even in societies where people are supposed not to drink.

As a species, we have developed remarkable technologies and elaborate philosophies, but much of what we do in the course of living through a day, a month, or a year, is pretty much habitual. As such, it is based on what we have seen others do, what we have heard our elders and others approve or recommend, or ways that people we like to admire are apt to behave. Social scientists tend to refer to this ongoing process of learning as "enculturation" or "socialization," and it explains how an undifferentiated infant becomes a functioning member of society. The human animal spends more time in this cultural apprenticeship than other species can afford, with their relatively short life spans and their lower tolerance for dependence on the part of the young.

It has been accurately said that each human being is like no other human being in some respects (as a result of unique genetic and physical composition, life history, social networks, and so forth). Similarly, each human being is like some other human beings in other respects (e.g., range of food preferences, language and gestures, mode of walking, adaptations to weather). At the same time, each human being is like all other human beings in yet other respects (basic needs, susceptibility to injury or disease, range of emotions, and so forth). It is the second of these three categories that most concern the author as a social scientist, and it is the patterns that are socially shared that make up most of which we call culture or the way of life of a given population.

A major portion of this book deals with drinking patterns in modern industrial countries, if only because they are the ones that are most amply documented in the scientific literature on the subject. Ideally, each drinking situation should be understood in its own terms and context, but often sufficient details are not available. Attention is also paid in this book to the relations between drink and culture that prevail in non-Western societies and in developing countries, because they have so often been neglected in discussions of the subject. It would be pointless to try to give evenhanded coverage to every area or people, for the simple fact that much is known about a few, and little is known about so many. Nevertheless, topics that are of theoretical or conceptual significance are dealt with, because of their potential comparative and practical importance, and many minority customs should be of some intrinsic interest. No two persons would write a book the same way on any subject, and a theme as rich and controversial as drinking must yield an idiosyncratic document. The aim is clear and consistent—to portray the many ways in which people have thought about and used beverage alcohol as an integral part of culture.

In order more fully to understand drinking patterns and the various roles that drinking has in cultural context, it is helpful to look at drinking occasions as a specific class of behavior. Chapter 1 analyzes the key question of *when* people drink, showing the wide range of ways in which beverage alcohol fits into the rhythm of lives of individuals, communities, and even countries and cultures. Strong feelings about the propriety of drinking sometimes apply to certain hours of the day, days of each week or month, or even to different seasons. Other norms are relative to whether or not one should be allowed (or expected) to drink at different stages in the life cycle of an individual or of a family. Long-term trends can also be important in historical perspective, just as a more microscopic analysis reveals a variety of drinking occasions that tend to be socially patterned but only minimally regulated. Prohibitions and restrictions on drinking deserve special attention because they reflect strong rejection of the idea that drinking is normal behavior. The chapter concludes with brief discussion of why it matters when people drink (and some policy issues arise in that connection), as well as theoretical and practical concerns. Every occasion has a context, and Chapter 2 shifts the focus to *where* people drink, showing how the setting often affects the meanings and outcomes of drinking. After reviewing the range of living spaces that are used for drinking, the view broadens to include other places within a community and, finally, to encompass places beyond the local community. Again, the chapter ends with some comment on why it matters where people drink, or where they feel that no one should. Any occasion in any setting is shaped, in large part, by the actors, so Chapter 3 turns to *who* drinks. We first look briefly at the ways in which researchers have addressed this question, and then we turn to social categories such as age, gender, education, occupation, class, ethnicity, religion, and other groupings that investigators have found relevant in different populations around the world. The usual question of why it matters is addressed, before Chapter 4 looks at *how* people drink. Etiquette and paraphernalia set a certain frame for any occasion; with reference to drinking, the rhythm of the behavior is especially important, sometimes resulting in excess, which poses a whole new set of issues. The other activities that accompany drinking often influence how one drinks. Again we look at why these matter. In Chapter 5, there is a brief introduction to just *what* it is that people drink, types of drinks, fermented, distilled, fortified, and mixed drinks, and how types of drinks relate to each other. Chapter 6 deals with the sometimes sensitive issue of *why* people drink, or choose not to drink. Medical, religious, esthetic, moral, and other kinds of reasons are briefly examined, as are questions of relevance. Chapter 7 draws upon this broad panorama of human experience to note a few conclusions and implications that derive from such scrutiny of drinking occasions as behavioral keys to the meaning of alcohol in culture. The list of references gives bibliographic information that will be helpful to some readers.

Notably missing from this account is the preponderant emphasis on alcohol*ism* or on specifically problem drinking that occurs in most of what is written about alcohol. That is a deliberate choice that reflects the author's concern to make sense of patterns of belief and behavior that reflect majority choices, that are generally unproblematic for most people most of the time, and that are linked in meaningful ways with other patterns of belief and behavior. It is not a matter of being unaware that a small portion of those who choose to drink in some societies have difficulties, but to turn the focus on the majority who don't. The famous sociologist Selden Bacon (1943) used to say about the need for studying normal drinking, "We'd never learn much about the impact of the automobile if all we paid attention to were accidents."

Chapter 1

To Every Thing
There is a Season:
When Do People Drink?

South Africans, including a uniformed policeman, enthusiastically mark the legalization of alcohol in a *shebeen* (neighborhood bar). Even the repeal of a law can be an occasion for celebratory drinking, particularly among its detractors. © *Alf Kulalo*.

At the same time that few kinds of behavior are more natural and necessary than drinking, there are also few kinds of behavior that are more hedged about by rules, laws, and understandings about when it's to be done or not to be done. Such conventions are clearly social, inasmuch as we find that they vary from one group to another, and they can change, sometimes rapidly and drastically, within a single group. They are also emotionally laden, as reflected in the ways that people feel about them, the intense degree of rancor that can be meted out for a breach of propriety, or the outpouring of warm support that often accompanies the act when it is done in what is locally "the right way," and at a time that is appropriate in terms of the prevailing social code. A brief sampling of the different ways that beliefs about when one may drink will reveal the wide range of variation in that, and also in beliefs about when one should, or even must drink. Similarly, the negative rules—about when one must not drink or should not, or even may not, have affective importance with reference to drinking far beyond what we find with respect to most other behaviors.

Quantitatively oriented epidemiological surveys are the kind of research on drinking that is most often cited when practical or theoretical implications of drinking are being considered. These include matters such as rates of drinking, rates of problems, and risk factors. Often the data are collected in terms of the amounts that respondents drank "the last time they drank," "on a typical day," or "on the last drinking occasion," and they tend to be reported as "per drinking occasion." For that reason, the drinking occasion would appear to be a crucial variable in our understandings about how people relate to drinking and how drinking relates to people. Unfortunately, although those who devise and conduct such surveys may each have a clear idea of what is meant by the term "drinking occasion," few respondents do. To make matters worse, the data that are collected with reference to an entire day are often analyzed and interpreted as if they relate to a single drinking occasion. This results in a significant scientific error, as well as significant amplification of whatever problems are said to be related to alcohol (Room, 1991a and c; 1997).

An open-ended, qualitatively oriented survey recently conducted by the author in several countries indicates an obvious disjuncture between the ways in which most people understand the questions to which they respond, and the theoretical and practical uses to which their responses are later put by the investigators. A qualitatively oriented researcher who is more concerned with meaning and context than with numbers, is apt to find out from the actors themselves when they drink. The responses that they provide give clues as to how they conceptualize time as well as how they view drinking. Our case study in this chapter deals with how contemporary, urban Spaniards talk about the times when they drink. It is remarkable that so many of them indicate drinking occasions that are important to them throughout the entire 24 hours of a day. The rest of the chapter includes a sampling of illustrative material from different cultures around the world with respect to when people drink—or not. There are, of course, different kinds of times that have to be considered. One kind has to do with when, in terms of calendrical chronology: at what time in the day, what day of the week or month, what season or special event, and so forth. Another type of time has to do with when, in terms of people's lives: at what specific age, at what stage in the developmental cycle of the household or family, in relation to age-grades, marital status, parenthood, work, and so forth. A third type of time with which we deal relates to when, in history: long evolutionary cycles within a culture, movements of people and linkages between cultures, war and peace, natural disasters. And, of course, there are numerous occasions in which people drink that fit none of those categories. Our aim is not to be encyclopedic, but to highlight the variability within the human experience as regards this fundamental question about drinking occasions, before we go on to examine other important variables.

Case Study: Spanish Drinking Around the Clock

"In Spain, alcoholic beverages are woven into the cultural fabric of everyday life" (Gamella, 1995). They have always been the major social lubricant and a source of conviviality and sociability. Although social drinking peaks on festival days, such as Corpus Christi, pre-Lenten *Carnaval*, and the local fiestas that mark the anniversary of the patron(ess) of every local community or institution, private rites are also marked by drinking, such as birthdays, Catholic confirmation, 15th-year celebrations marking a girl's coming of age, marriage, and even death and burial. A meal is often considered to be incomplete without wine, which is thought to sharpen the mind, uplift the spirit, strengthen the body, and generally enhance one's health and well-being. Wine is generally available at any grocery store as well as at many gas stations and open markets. Although most people drink each day, drunkenness is generally discouraged and looked down upon as a sign of weakness in a country where men take great pride in their masculinity. In recent years, wine has been losing ground to beer as favored drink, with women and young people accounting for much of that change.

The temporal dimension is important, and drinking that is acceptable at one time may not be at another, even in the same social situation. In hot weather, thirst-quenchers like cold beer, sangria, or diluted wine are popular, whereas straight whiskey, sherry, brandy, or wine are preferred when it is cold. Weekends and holidays tend to be more leisurely for most people, and so entail more drinking. Any fiesta, sacred or secular, is marked by more than usual drinking and a few specific occasions, different in different communities, may involve more than usual drinking by most people. It is important in Spain that one "know how to drink" and not exceed the level of becoming *alegre* (happy, or high, but without impairment).

The combining of food with drink is important, having resulted in the distinctive national tradition of tapas, bite-sized sandwiches or morsels, the quality and variety of which can bring notoriety to a bar. The daily schedule of social life tends to start earlier and to end later than in many other parts of Europe or the rest of the world. The daily round can be conceived as comprising eight distinct periods in relation to food and drink. Although few Spaniards drink during more than half of them, each such period provides a context in which some may drink without prompting comment from those who do not. According to Gamella (1995), metropolitan Spanish drinking routines literally occur around the clock. Breakfast time (7–10 a.m.) may well include one or more glasses of distilled spirits (aguardiente, anisette, or brandy) to energize a laborer, especially in winter. Morning (10–1 p.m.) brings a more substantial breakfast for many, with wine or beer as an accompaniment. Aperitif time (1–2 p.m.) is an occasion for relaxing conversation and socializing with friends and colleagues, often with a beer, liqueur, or glass of wine and a snack before luncheon. Lunchtime (2–3:30 p.m.) often includes the major meal of the day. Traditionally, most of the family may be at home for a lunch that includes at least three courses, accompanied by wine. This is also the time when the day's main newscasts are aired on radio and television. Siesta time (3:30–6 p.m.) may begin with strong coffee and liquor after lunch, followed by a nap or rest. Evening (6–9 p.m.) is a favorite time for drinking, often combined with snacking on tapas. Especially among the young, barhopping at this time entails moving with a group of friends from one bar to another, with social interaction at a premium. Dinnertime (9–11 p.m.) often replicates the pattern of lunchtime, with less food and formality unless people eat away from home, in which event it may be even more elaborate. Night (11 p.m.–7 a.m.) is especially favored by young people as a time away from home, when relaxation, recreation, social and sexual encounters combine with drinking as a focal activity; drunkenness in such a context may be seen as a gesture of independence or a demonstration of wealth.

It would be a mistake to view this sequence as portraying a typical day in the life of an average Spaniard. The important point to be grasped is the acceptability of drink, usually with food, at almost anytime for someone, a degree of accommodation to beverage alcohol that is rare in other parts of the world.

THE CALENDRICAL ROUND

In many societies, a fermented homebrew is a basic staple in the diet and, as such, it is drunk as breakfast and as a refreshing break at almost anytime throughout the day. For the Tonga of Zambia, beer is not so much a complement or supplement to a meal as it is often a meal in itself (Colson & Scudder, 1988). The same can be said of many other populations throughout sub-Saharan Africa (Haworth & Acuda, 1998) or Latin America (Madrigal, 1998).

During a Day

An early morning drink may serve to provide the quick feeling of warmth or to invigorate or waken a worker. Slivovitz (plum brandy) is widely used for this throughout the Balkans, just as brandy or red wine is popular with French truck drivers, farmers, postal workers, shopkeepers, herders, and others whose workday begins earlier than that of most urban white-collar employees.

The familiar pattern of three meals daily, beginning with a morning breakfast, is an alien idea to many, so the rhythms of eating, drinking, and living, are very different around the world. Those who do drink alcohol with or as breakfast tend to do so with fermented homebrews but not with distilled or fortified beverages.

Despite the general rule in North America about not drinking in the morning hours, a few special exceptions have become institutionalized and accepted in recent years. The phenomenon of brunch, a meal later and larger than the usual breakfast and often served in buffet style, may include spirits mixed with orange or tomato juice, or champagne in the scrambled eggs. Code words to disguise such alcohol (Grasshopper, Bloody Mary) insulate people from having to articulate the fact that they are taking alcohol at what would, normally, for them be an inappropriate time. All involved are doubtless aware that some of the food in such a situation is actually ethanol.

In much of the urban industrialized Western world, midday is a significant boundary marker between drinking being inappropriate or permissible. People with higher schooling and larger incomes often routinely have one or more drinks with their noonday meal. In the late 1970s, U.S. President Carter derided "the 3-martini lunch" as emblematic of the hedonistic excesses of newly wealthy and powerful entrepreneurs. There are, however, individuals in finance, journalism, publishing, theater, and other white-collar occupations who consider drinking an integral part of a working lunch, during which considerable constructive talking and dealing often takes place, whether in the U.S. or anywhere else that they may meet with cosmopolitan colleagues.

The traditionally substantial midday meal in Spain (Gamella, 1995), France (Nahoum-Grappe, 1995; Sadoun, Lolli, & Silverman, 1965; de Certau, Giard, & Mayol, 1998), Italy (Cottino, 1995; Lolli, Serriani, Golder, & Luzzatto-Fegiz, 1958; *Osservatorio*, etc., 1998), and other northern Mediterranean countries, included significant quantities of drink, often a liter or more of wine per person. In recent years, both meals and drink are diminishing in many areas, as the pace of life appears to have accelerated. Workers who are on tight schedules, or remote from comfortable places to eat and drink, are less likely to make much of the midday meal as a context for drinking.

Although many North Americans and northern Europeans hold strongly to the view that drinking in the morning is morally wrong and a signal that the drinker is a drunkard, addicted, or will soon have problems, such drinking is acceptable in Chile, Spain, Portugal, Italy, Greece, and in cultures where the drink is viewed as food, or at least as an important part of the diet (Heath, 1995). In general, it is more common for men than women. In many regions of southern Europe, elderly men who are no longer working daily spend large blocks of time in public drinking places, sipping slowly while talking, playing games, or simply enjoying the sun. Austrian housewives, also, sometimes drink small quantities of distilled spirits from time to time throughout the day, when they share a break in their work routine (Thornton, 1987).

It is acceptable to drink lightly with luncheon and or dinner in Australia or Canada, just as it is expected that one do so in the circum-Mediterranean countries. In Chile, China, Spain, or the Azores, it would be normal to offer a drink as a gesture of hospitality at whatever hour a guest arrived. Australians might do so after 2 p.m., or North Americans after 4 p.m. (Heath, 1995).

Although it is generally permissible to drink throughout the rest of the day in most societies, work often takes precedence, and there is a widespread reluctance to combine work with drinking. Certainly, that was not the pattern before the Industrial Revolution, when much of people's work was in their home or someone else's. Since then the risks of accidental injury or of damaging machinery have made it increasingly important to be at peak performance on the job (Fillmore, 1984). No matter what hours that one spends as an employee, it is generally agreed that one shouldn't drink on the job—with some colorful exceptions, such as gamblers, prostitutes, and a few others. It used to be a standard perquisite that brewery workers had free access to a tap of their product, but questions of liability, insurance, and general health have resulted in that having virtually disappeared as an informal tradition.

Interestingly, in the course of doing a general ethnography of an automobile assembly plant in the U.S., an exception was found in that the workplace itself fostered a "drinking subculture," with chronic boredom, lax supervision, easy concealment, and a feeling that to do so was a manly way to defy the management, who were resented for their lives of relative wealth and ease (Ames & Janes, 1987).

Craftsmen, railroaders, sailors, journalists, and early factory workers have all been noted as heavy drinkers in the U.S., both on and off the job (Fillmore, 1990). In a study of sandhogs (tunnel workers) in the U.S., Sonnenstuhl (1996) shows how that occupational group used to build their sense of community around intemperate drinking rituals that created solidarity. Remarkably, and within a single generation, they have transformed to having a temperate subculture in which their group identification is now divorced from heavy drinking.

It is commonplace that a drink or more can serve as a significant marker, symbolizing the shift from work to nonwork or leisure life. Among the Iteso of Kenya (Karp, 1970), this transition may comprise virtually all of the adult males gathering around a large pot of beer, drinking through elaborately decorated straws that each has made, and quietly talking about the cattle they have been herding all day. This takes place in different living-compounds on successive days, after they have penned their herds for the night and before they go to eat dinner at home.

Gusfield (1987) described a similar transition rite on the part of individuals in the U.S., many of whom come directly home from work and immediately have a drink, effectively signaling the change of pace and expectations. Others do not even bother to go home before dramatizing the end of the workday. Some bars advertise "happy hour" or "attitude adjustment hour," with specially discounted prices on drinks for a couple of hours in the late afternoon or early evening.

It is only gradually becoming less common in the U.S. or Australia for factory workers, painting or construction crews, and others who have a sense of camaraderie to go to a nearby bar or tavern after work and to drink for an hour or more. Such behavior clearly marks a psychological boundary for them between work or the job on one hand, and leisure or off-the-job on the other. Where the local custom is to buy rounds, or shouting, with each member of the group buying drinks (usually beer) for all by turns, this may consume considerable amounts of time and money, and may result in the drinking of considerable quantities by each person. A shrewd bartender may encourage his clientele to stay longer by occasionally offering a free drink to everyone, proclaiming "This round is on the house," and knowing that, the longer people stay, the more they will drink (Single & Storm, 1985). Some establishments also provide the convenience of cashing checks, so that one need not rush to the bank on payday; there is the implied expectation that some of the money will be spent there. Talking, horseplay (teasing), playing pool, cards, dice, or dominoes, watching television, listening to recorded music, or any combination of those often adds to the sociability of such an occasion.

Halfway around the world, there is a popular custom that is quite analogous in terms of the functions that it serves, but very different in its formal appearance (Sargent, 1967). Japanese office workers often similarly go out to drink together after work, but their behavior tends to be far more focused. Much of the conversation deals with the day's work, and it is an occasion in which subordinates, who have quietly done as they were told all day, have an opportunity to express their feelings to supervisors. It is not only accepted but even appropriate for a Japanese male to act as if he were slightly drunk after a single drink, and to be voluble and heated after a couple of drinks (usually of sake, beer, or whiskey). In this context, it is expected that any grievances that may have arisen during the day will be aired without reservation, and that no one will take offense at what is said. In fact, the unspoken rule is that what transpires in those afterwork parties is to be forgotten, because no offense was intended and everyone was talking or acting under the influence of alcohol. With such an institutionalized understanding, informal communication may well be more effective than more formal exchanges between the same individuals. An insightful social critic has suggested that a U.S. housewife may justifiably worry that her husband is too social if he comes home late from the office, smelling of drink, whereas her Japanese counterpart may have equal reason for concern if her husband is so antisocial that he comes home early and does not smell of drink.

Blue-collar Hawaiians also tend to enjoy a designated period of time out after work and before returning home. Coworkers eat and drink together, but there is not the airing of grievances that plays so large a role among Japanese office workers.

The cocktail hour, at about the same time, serves much the same function in the lives of some who specifically prefer mixed drinks, or who emphasize socializing as much as drinking (Lolli, 1963). While on a boat, the convention is not to drink before "the sun is below the yard-arm" (i.e., almost sunset), but certainly to have one (or more) then.

Some jurisdictions specify hours before or after which public sales outlets may not serve drinks. In the early 1900s, Australian bars were required to close at 6 p.m., and there was often a frantic rush on the part of drinkers to get as much as possible to carry them into the evening. Such rapid drinking of large quantities triggered nausea and vomiting in many, to the point where it was common for a bar to be tiled on the floor and halfway up the walls, allowing for a quick and easy flushing with a hose after the infamous "six o'clock swill" (Hall & Hunter, 1995).

Many non-Western cultures are blissfully ignorant of what we call clock-time, but they usually recognize segments of the day depending on the height of the sun, position of the moon, what bird-sounds are heard, where shadows fall, and so forth. Rarely do such microunits of time figure in their attitudes toward drink, with the general exception that drinking is more favored and expected after the completion of a day's work away from home. Examples are the leisurely and sociable beer drinking that Kofyar, Tiriki, or Tonga men enjoy together after herding and before returning to their respective families, or the sherry or brandy with which a Spaniard takes leave of his coworkers. Kumiss serves the same purpose for Mongols who have had a hard day of riding, or chicha for Andean market-vendors as they clean up their stalls and prepare to go home.

A drink or more before dinner is commonplace in Europe and North America, especially when eating at a public place. In France or Italy, it can specifically be an aperitif, distilled or fortified. Otherwise, it tends to be wine or a mixed drink—unless the meal is to be one of those that specifically is thought to be appropriate for beer, such as pizza, chili, or barbecue.

The evening meal is often accompanied by more drinks than during any equivalent time-period during the rest of the day. It is not unusual for a different wine to be served with each course, including dessert, and for a drink of distilled spirits such as a liqueur or brandy to conclude the meal. People with a keen appreciation of beer may take care to match specific beers with specific foods in equally elaborate dinners. Although each participant may consume six or more drinks in the course of such a meal, it is rare that anyone shows any effects from doing so, partly because of the food and partly because of the leisurely pace. It is well known to psychologists, and amply proven through a variety of double-blind experiments, that expectation plays a major role in shaping the effects (or lack thereof) that ethanol has on a person's awareness and behavior (Marlatt & Rohsenow, 1980).

The question of whether people drink with meals has an importance quite apart from its relation to clock-time and the daily round. It is a basic biophysiological fact that alcohol ingested on an empty stomach has greater impact on cognitions, perceptions, and capabilities than if one were eating earlier or simultaneously. Similarly, the amount of liquid, fat, or exercise all affect the speed with which ethanol goes through an individual body.

There are many Mongols who drink whiskey with every meal, and some who claim to wake up every night to take a warming drink before going back to sleep (Williams, 1998). Perhaps most common eating-associated drinking of Mongols is the drinking and nibbling that takes place between meals when friends and neighbors may spend hours talking and taking turns at drinking, each using a shot glass and emptying it with a quick draught, after which it is set inverted to show that it is empty.

Another European and North American pattern is that, if an evening meal has included wine or beer, it is often followed by a different kind of drink. A strong spirit or fortified liqueur may be offered after a meal, "to aid digestion" in the Spanish or Italian view. A "nightcap," again usually of spirits, is habitual for many individuals just before retiring.

During a Week

If we shift our focus from the daily cycle, we often find that a weekly or fortnightly cycle has significance too, but in different ways. Many societies observe a sabbath day as a mandatory—and usually welcome—break in the pace of workday routine. The beginning of the Jewish sabbath is marked, anywhere in the world, by a ritual prayer and drinking by all members of the family. The ceremonial closing of the sabbath is similarly marked with a prayer and a drink, and most authorities agree that it doesn't matter whether wine is used or schnapps. A majority of the world's population these days probably observe a weekend with one or two days of relative freedom from other commitments, even if they no longer see the sabbath as sacred. In fact, a weekend is often decidedly secular, with more deliberate seeking of relaxation from regular duties than at other times. This often includes a greater readiness for different kinds of excess than can be comfortably accommodated during the rest of the week. In much of northern Europe until the mid-1800s, workers often joked about "Saint Monday," a holiday they took in defiance of the strict regulation of their other time that was imposed by the owners of factories, mills, and mines, changing the

Begun in the summer of 1880, the light-hearted joy of P.A. Renoir's "Luncheon of the Boating Party" is clearly evident. One need not know the individuals depicted— the artist, his friends, and colleagues—to recognize that, even in the absence of a special occasion, drinking played an important part in their enjoyment. © *The Phillips Collection, Washington, D.C.*

rhythm of life that they had earlier enjoyed as peasants or relatively independent craftspersons (Thompson, 1967).

The weekend tends to be especially sharply marked when payment of wages denotes the start of it, and workers are eager both to enjoy the fruits of their labors and to relax from the heavy or boring routine of work. The Naskapi Indians of northeastern Canada drink on weekends specifically so as not to disrupt the flow of everyday life (Robbins, 1973). In Christian settings, Sunday is marked by church services and Saturday night tends to be a major occasion for socializing and drinking, whether by male-oriented peer groups or by couples meeting with friends and neighbors. For some, such public events as sports, barbecues, or communal dinners provide occasions to leave home; for others, card games, television, or reciprocal visiting make for drinking occasions within the home.

It is similar in Europe and North America that several institutions set aside a couple of hours during the weekly schedule for a regular meeting, with drink, which employees are supposed to attend. Although there is an implicit understanding that one should come, there is usually no specific agenda, occasional absences go unnoticed, and discussions tend to be informal and far-ranging.

The Friday afternoon sherry hour of a college or dormitory was one such that was popular until recent years. Another example is the "brown-bag" luncheon at which members of a hospital, university, or other professional department are invited to bring their own prepared food, but with drinks provided by the institution. The reception that follows a visiting lecturer's presentation is another drinking occasion that seems designed to simulate a nonwork context in what is clearly a work context, whether in academic circles or elsewhere.

Although payday may be fortnightly for some white-collar workers, there are few other special markers for that time-slice and it is rarely demarcated as different from other weekends in terms of drinking.

During a Month

If we shift our focus again, from week to month, it is evident that different segments of a population may be differentially affected. In countries where state welfare or social support payments are made monthly, that payday is likely to be more important to many than is any weekend. Lenin is credited with having enunciated the simple but important law that, as a household's disposable income increases, so do expenditures on nonessentials (by essentials he meant basic food, clothing, and shelter).

Although most people pay some attention to lunar cycles, they do not coincide with months and are often unnamed, with only a few selected for special attention through the year. Contrary to popular expectations, de Castro and Pearcey (1995) found decreased consumption at the time of the full moon.

During a Year

It is when we shift our attention to that yearly round (which varies in terms of enumeration and starting-date, but which is remarkably consistent as a frame of reference for time in the minds of most peoples) that the cyclical nature of drinking becomes most strikingly apparent, both in its opulent detail and in its diversity. In the northern latitudes of Alaska, Levine, Duffy, & Bowyer (1994) found increased consumption during periods of prolonged darkness (winter), although that does not happen in extreme southern latitudes (Mahar, 1999). In southern Scotland, Uitenbroek's (1996) discovery of consumption peaks in August and December may have as much to do with cultural conventions (holidays, gifting, vacations) as with sunlight.

Celebrated with large-scale drinking of kumiss, the birth of colts each spring is a festive occasion for the Yakut of Siberia. Again in the fall as they prepare for winter, a festival that combines eating and drinking brings together extended families and larger groups that live dispersed for most of the year (Shklovsky, 1916). Mongolians and Kazaks drink kumiss at their annual reunion, and almost every step in the progress of courtship and marriage is marked by drinking and gifting of drink to and from relatives of the future bride. The spring harvest is also marked by a multiday ceremony, featuring beer, music, and dance among the Tarahumara of Mexico (Bennett & Zingg, 1935).

For the rural Papago of southwestern U.S. and northern Mexico, an annual midsummer rain ceremony is the major occasion for drinking the cactus wine for which they are noted; it is scarce throughout most of the year, and no one would think of it as something to be enjoyed daily (Waddell, 1979). Among the Azande of Congo, beer dances that occur periodically throughout the year provide the best opportunity to meet a member of the opposite sex in an informal context that might result in lasting friendship or marriage (Evans-Pritchard, 1937).

China is another society in which festivals throughout the year are generally associated with drinking (Xiao, 1995). To be specific, Chinese new year (the Spring Festival) is a time for a special drink that is thought to combine good luck with good health, a concoction featuring cypress leaves and peppers. A festival honoring the dead (April 5) includes families' sharing food and drink with ancestors at their places of burial. The Dragon Boat Festival (5th day of 5th lunar month) features a special liquor to drive away both evil spirits and insects. Mid-Autumn Festival (15th day of 8th lunar month) is celebrated by family reunions held to drink, sing, dance, and watch the full moon (Shen & Wang, 1998). In addition, the Lantern Festival (first full moon of new year) is celebrated with special cordials and sweet dumplings.

Wherever Roman Catholicism is a dominant religion, the annual calendar is punctuated with festive occasions, most of which involve considerable drinking. Such practices usually follow folk custom rather than express church doctrine, but the association is inseparable in the minds and lives of local people. Most famous among these is probably *Carnaval*, the riotous prelude to Lent that is compressed into colorful Mardi Gras in New Orleans, U.S., but that involves a full week of ceaseless partying, dancing, and drinking in Rio de Janeiro, Brazil, and many parts of Spain, Italy, the Caribbean Islands, and elsewhere. Each saint's commemorative day is also marked by celebration wherever that saint is patron, and heavy drinking again is normally an important part of any such a fiesta.

It is curious that St. Patrick's Day is so widely celebrated throughout the U.S. in mid-March, even by many who have no Irish ancestry or affiliation. As a peculiar feature of that tradition, many bars do a brisk business in green-colored draft beer, which would almost certainly be rejected on any other day of the year.

All Saints' Day and All Souls' Day (Oct. 31–Nov.1) are celebrated, especially in Mexico, with lavish spreads of food and drink that are ostensibly shared with the deceased members of a family, often right at the graves. A reflection of that vital and colorful tradition is the growing popularity of parties among adults in the U.S. on Halloween (the night of Oct. 31), while their costumed children visit neighbors to collect candy and other trifles.

Among the Ainu of northern Japan, drink is the ideal sacrifice, other than a bear which can only be offered by the whole community once a year. Singing and dancing accompany drinking by both sexes, in those festivals that last for days at a time (Batchelor, 1892). For the Meo of Laos, the occasions on which drinking is mandatory for all adults include New Year's, weddings, name days, the rice harvest, any animal sacrifice, and funerals (Westermeyer, 1971). Among the Japanese, New Year's Eve is again a special occasion that should be marked by drinking, but so are a leisurely viewing of the moon, a harvest festival, and the initiation of a workman on a new job (Yamamuro, 1958). According to Sargent (1967), the ceremonies connected with house building there should also include drinking by both workmen and prospective tenants.

In the U.S., New Year's Eve is the one occasion on which most people drink—including some of those who are faithful abstainers the rest of the time. Ceremonial meals, such as are commonly served in various countries at Christmas, Easter, Thanksgiving, and other national holidays, are likely to include drinks, even in households where most meals do not. A picnic on Independence Day, an outdoor barbecue, or watching a major sporting event may all be treated as special occasions during the year that are deserving of drink.

Regardless of when they are played, some sports are intimately associated with drinking, and others not. Despite the evident risks, hunting tends more often to be linked with drinking than is fishing, again regardless of the time. Popular concerts tend often to be accompanied by drinking throughout, whereas it is restricted to intermissions during most classical concerts. Although exceptions can be cited for any such generalization, each has some validity as a statement about the patterning of drinking occasions in contemporary Europe and North America, if not elsewhere.

Drinking in Iceland tends to be episodic, especially heavy in relation to specific seasonal events. For young people, there is a series of special holidays in the spring when they gather in enormous numbers to drink, mill about, and generally demonstrate their independence from the older generations. For seamen, there is a big holiday in June that is marked by heavy drinking, although they are careful not to drink at all while at sea. Farmers, by contrast, have their heavy drinking festival as an adjunct to the roundup of sheep and horses that takes place in the autumn (Ásmundsson, 1995).

Many wine-producing communities set aside a specific day or weekend shortly after the hectic harvest season has come to a close, as a time when neighbors visit neighbors to sample the new vintage. Specific wine fairs, regional expositions, or large auctions are other seasonal events that bring significant social as well as economic activity to Beaune in Burgundy, Bordeaux in the region of the same name, Turin, Italy, and cities elsewhere. Oktoberfest in parts of Austria and Germany is a similar community-wide, and sometimes even international, celebration in honor of beer.

In most of the industrialized nations of the world, whether with capitalistic economic systems or not, most paid workers enjoy a week or more of vacation, time without a work commitment during which pay continues. It is a standing joke in France that it is difficult to do any business during the entire month of August because so many people are on vacation. Many U.S. business and industrial workers feel constrained because they enjoy "only" a couple of weeks of such free time, with little attention to the fact that those who work in hospitals, hotels, restaurants, policing, transportation, and other services may have even more demands on their time and energy rather than less during what others consider vacation. Farmers and herders everywhere recognize how difficult it is to take time off, but the pattern of vacation has come to be an integral part of the yearly round for the many whose occupations are not crucial to other living things. And it is commonplace for most people who drink at all to drink at least a little more, and more often, during vacation than during the rest of the year. Seaside resorts cater to this pattern everywhere, and the periodic brief migration of northerners to more benign southern climates has reshaped much of the world. Although such vacations are not always coordinated chronologically, they tend to be important markers in the lives of individuals, signaling more-than-usual drinking occasions.

By contrast, some find the context of work more congenial for drinking than the routine of life at home. Muslim migrant workers who spend nine months each year in Bulgaria often drink heavily throughout that time, and say that they are abstinent during the three months that they spend at home in Turkey or northern Africa (Iontchev, 1998)

As much as many forms of human behavior are shaped to the calendrical round, such a view of time is quite irrelevant to others. Drinking happens to be one of those behaviors that is sometimes affected by days, weeks, months, and seasons, but also by quite different factors. Among such alternative factors, those that are most clearly evident in cross-cultural perspective as shaping when people drink are stages in the life cycle of the individual and of a domestic group.

INDIVIDUAL AND DOMESTIC LIFE CYCLES

Another way of thinking about time has little to do with the official chronology that is generally shared by all members of a given society and relates more to the rhythms of evolution in the lives of individuals and in the lives of domestic units, households, or families. The life cycle of the individual is almost always imbedded in a longer but similarly patterned life cycle, that of the family or domestic group, which similarly has its beginning, maturation, aging, and eventual demise. Because of the importance of that fundamental building block of society, some of the steps or stages are named and publicly celebrated, differently in various societies. As with the individual, such transitions are often marked by the drinking of beer, wine, or spirits. However, life cycle is a far more ambiguous concept than at first appears. In simple terms, it might relate simply to chronology, or developmental stages as an individual progresses from birth to death. But the intricate web of any human society means that much of the importance of each individual is expressed in terms of social relations, and many of the stages that are variously marked in different societies are irreducibly linked to patterns of relationships. Birth may mark a crucial beginning for the individual, but that same event may mark validation of a marriage, expansion of a family, and new roles for every kinsperson. Marriage may unite a couple, but it also is likely to unite extended families. Death may mark an end for the individual, but the family, household, and larger community will continue, although obviously altered in some roles. However convenient it may appear to deal separately with the life cycle of the individual and the life cycle of the domestic group, it would be deceptive to do so.

Coming of age, maturation, or entry into adulthood are variously scheduled and variously marked in different cultures, and such occasions often include drinking. In some societies, the individual is exposed to beverage alcohol throughout the life cycle, beginning before birth and continuing long after death.

One example is the Asante of Ghana, for whom drink is an essential for each of the following key events: birth, naming (on the eighth day), initiation at puberty, many specific stages in the process of courtship and marriage, and the funeral. But links with drinking do not terminate with death; it continues to be important that beverage alcohol is also drunk at ceremonies that are held on the 8th day after death, again on the 15th, 40th, and 80th days, and on the annual anniversary (Akyeampong, 1996). Few populations are so specific about postmortem drinking, largely because the celebrants offer libations that are thought to be drunk by the spirit of the dead person, but many other populations also include most of those occasions for drinking during the life cycle, and some also celebrate others.

Feelings about alcohol are so strong that even the question of whether a fetus is to be exposed to it before birth is highly controversial. The ambivalence that many people have about alcohol is amply reflected in their attitudes toward drinking by pregnant women. In Germany (Vogt, 1995), Austria (Honigmann, 1963), and Switzerland, they are generally encouraged to drink beer, just as women in France, Spain, Portugal, and Italy are encouraged to drink wine. Popular beliefs based on generations of experience and reinforced by folk proverbs hold that those who drink are more healthful and hardy than those who do not, and that their offspring are also. Beer and wine, in the different parts of the world where each is more popular, are both thought to strengthen or purify the blood, enhance bones and growth, and generally to nourish the fetus (Heath, 1995). Coupled with those attitudes is the assurance that such a drink will also increase and enrich the mother's milk, so that the benefits of her drinking can be shared with an infant long after it is born. Homebrews throughout most of Africa, like chicha and pulque in Latin America, are generally believed to have the same advantages for pregnant women and their babies.

In dramatic contrast, there is widespread concern about drinking on the part of many women in the U.S., and government agencies as well as some private organizations caution that a woman should not drink if there is even the possibility that she may become pregnant. This unofficial prohibition would apply to a significant portion of the population and is sometimes even unofficially enforced by servers who will decline to serve a visibly pregnant woman in public drinking establishments. The justification given for such restriction is that ethanol is sometimes a teratogen, altering the germ-plasm in ways that could harm ova or a developing fetus. Fetal Alcohol Syndrome (FAS) was widely publicized as an increasingly common combination of physical abnormalities and learning disabilities with alarming rates of occurrence. Less publicized is the fact that no instance of FAS has been documented in the medical literature in which the mother was not a long-term heavy drinker (Abel & Hannigman, 1995).

In 1999, there are 16 countries that provide advice on this subject to the general public (International Center for Alcohol Policies, 1999). Although there is no consensus about specific amounts that might be harmful or safe, most of these countries counsel abstinence, at least during the first trimester of pregnancy. The United Kingdom and New Zealand are the only countries among those that do not recommend abstinence during pregnancy.

In marked contrast with national governments, nearly all of those cultures in which a homebrew is a basic component of the diet encourage pregnant women to drink with the expectation that beer will strengthen and nourish the fetus. Soon after the birth, a lactating mother may smear her breasts with homebrew in order to accustom the infant to its taste and smell (Muokolo, 1990), and beer itself may be given as a supplement to mother's milk within the first few days. No matter what the basic ingredient, such homebrews are low in alcohol and rich in nutrients, so there is scientific justification for the folk beliefs that they serve to strengthen the infant and growing child just as they did the fetus.

Among the few rites of passage that are commemorated in all cultures, birth is an important one. It marks the beginning for the neonate, and it also usually marks a crucial transition of status for one or both of the parents. For example, parents are often congratulated on the birth of a child, with drinks as a salutation. In Mexico, the Tarahumara hold a fiesta with music, dancing, and drinking three days after the birth of a male child and four days after the birth of a female (Kennedy, 1978). The Chagga of Tanganyika brew a special "child's beer" to celebrate when the navel of a recently born child heals. Another "third son's" beer is shared with friends and neighbors when a man celebrates the birth of his third son (Gutmann, 1926). Many of the ethnic groups in China consider alcohol so important for ritual purposes that a special batch is prepared soon after a girl's birth, to be used in connection with her eventual marriage (Xiao, 1995). In similar fashion, a wealthy couple in the U.S. may buy and store a considerable amount of fine wine at the birth of a child, expecting that it will be appropriately enhanced in quality and value when subsequently used to celebrate a daughter's marriage, or a son's coming-of-age or graduation from college.

Infancy and childhood are defined differently in different cultures and each is recognized and treated differently for various purposes. With specific reference to beverage alcohol, a few noteworthy illustrations of when people drink with relation to those ages follow. The Han dominant population in China have six separate rites of initiation at various stages of life for a boy, and drinking is an important part of each of them (Xiao, 1995). No matter where he lives, an Orthodox Jewish boy should be ritually circumcised during the eighth day of life, at which time he is given a taste of wine and the men who are present usually enjoy a drinking party (Snyder, 1958a). Among the Azande, a boy's circumcision occurs later (between six and ten years of age), but it, too, is an occasion for celebratory drinking (Evans- Pritchard, 1937).

At an early age, most French children are given "reddened water" (or diluted wine) as food during meals (Anderson, 1968). The drink is made less dilute over time so that, in this way, the child gradually becomes accustomed to drinking wine by learning at home, with the family, and there is no mystique attached to it. The same occurs in Greece (Blum & Blum, 1964), and there is similarly early exposure in China and Mongolia.

In preindustrial England, the same norms applied to both adults and younger persons in many fields, and it was only after 1500 that separate standards for drinking emerged. Among the concomitant changes in drinking patterns were the gradual emergence of drinking as a recreational activity and the introduction of new and more potent beverages, first beer and later cheap spirits (Warner, 1998)

Adolescence, coming-of-age, or young adulthood, similarly, are far from being universally agreed-upon stages or ages, but each tends to be important for certain purposes in various cultures. With respect to drinking occasions, these are some examples that catch one's attention around the world.

When a Jivaro girl is welcomed back to the community after a 4-day retreat on the occasion of her first menstruation, she is honored by being given the foam from a freshly brewed batch of beer (Karsten, 1935). German youths are still often subjected to a bout of heavy drinking by solicitous fathers who consider such an experience important as a transition from adolescence to manhood (Vogt, 1995). The 4-day ceremony that marks puberty for a Cuna age-grade, that cohort of males or females who have passed the previous rite in childhood but who have been waiting for this communal transition ritual, is one such drinking occasion. A wedding party is another. Fifty years ago, the Panamanian government provided rum for the Cuna puberty celebration, although it tried to suppress local production of chicha during the rest of the year (Stout, 1948).

Specific details of courtship and marriage differ enormously from one society to the next, but some kind of ritual observance usually marks so significant a change of status, and alcohol often plays an important part in such observances. Throughout much of sub-Saharan Africa, beer-dances are primary occasions during which young people meet prospective spouses (Haworth & Acuda, 1998). Similarly, beer is generally the first, and often the most abundant, gift that a suitor brings to the parents of his intended bride. It is not uncommon for the prospective groom and the woman's male relatives to engage in a series of lengthy drinking bouts during several months before an agreement is reached. Like many African populations, the Ewenki of China use drink (beer, wine, and/or spirits) as an important part of the ritual gift-giving by a suitor to the

A Jewish family drinks wine as part of the religious ritual of Passover. Some suggest that the introduction to alcohol within sacred contexts serves as a form of immunization because so few Jews develop alcohol-related problems. © *CORBIS/Hulton-Deutsch Collection.*

parents of his prospective bride. However, they add a special twist to such giving: once such a gift is drunk, it is understood that the parents approve of the marriage (Xiao, 1995).

Prenuptial parties, for male friends of the prospective groom and separately for female friends of the prospective bride, may occur for several nights before a Scottish wedding, often with heavy drinking as a series of pubs are visited, with leave-taking and joking to signal publicly the major changes of status. With minor variations, this pattern probably recurs throughout most of Europe and North America. A Jivaro woman is not supposed to drink for a few days during preparation for her marriage, but the wedding ceremony may last even longer, during which great quantities of beer made from manioc or palm fruit are drunk by men, women, and children alike (Washburne, 1961). In Mexico, the Tarahumara culture is generally so puritanical that even a husband and wife may need to drink a little beer in order to be sufficiently at ease to have sexual relations (Bennett & Zingg, 1935), and a wedding is marked by drinking on their part as well as by the guests.

In much of Europe and North America, a wedding is an elaborate opportunity to display the wealth of the bride's family, with lavish food and drink provided following a ceremonial toast to the new couple. Drinking at weddings is an extremely widespread custom, but drinking as an integral part of the wedding ceremony itself is less so. Orthodox Jews do it wherever they may be, obviously including Israel (Weiss, 1995), as do many of the tribal populations in northern India (Mohan & Sharma, 1995). In Poland and Russia, drinking is also part of the wedding, combining praise for both participating families as well as best wishes for the couple (Moskalewicz & Zieliński, 1995; Sidorov, 1995). Among the Lepcha of Nepal, the couple must together drink to empty a huge mug of beer to solemnize their marriage (Gorer, 1938).

Among the many commitments that are implied almost universally by marriage is mutual sexual access with few restrictions that can be imposed by others. As important as such a prospect may be, it is rarely touched on explicitly during the ceremony, although the topic of sexual intercourse is often the subject of crude joking for several hours afterward, especially while friends of the bride and groom are drinking in celebration. Scatological humor in such a context may range from subtle wordplay, such as punning with allusions to sexual organs or sexual acts, to pantomimes of intercourse using the full body and broad gestures. In the Ardennes region of France, the vaguely naughty notion of sex is associated with the equally taboo realm of excretion; neither is discussed in polite company under other circumstances, but among the pranks that are played in the boisterous postwedding party is preparation of a unique drink that symbolizes the charged atmosphere of that situation by literally and figuratively mixing sexual allusions with other bodily functions (Reed-Danahay, 1996). A chamber-pot is used as the drinking vessel, in which chunks of chocolate are mixed with champagne. The appearance is very like that of excrement in urine, for which the container is appropriate. Some guests comment jokingly about the volume of one or the other substance, or the proportion of their combination to the pot. While the newlyweds retire to their bed in a nearby room, guests sing, shout, play musical instruments, and generally maintain a noisy hubbub, in a manner similar to that of a shivaree which traditionally takes place analogously as a postwedding party in both Scotland and Ireland. The liquid is sipped and the chocolate is nibbled by the boldest among them, but major portions are left to comingle and increasingly approximate the real thing.

In cultures that pay attention to the anniversary date of one's birth, it is often celebrated in a small way as an occasion for minor indulgence, including gifts and special food and drink. Those countries that have a relatively high minimum legal drinking age often find that that endows beverage alcohol with a powerful mystique and attractiveness. The celebration of that birthday when one may first legally drink (even if one has been drinking illegally for some time) is often marked by excessive drinking, sometimes at the encouragement of age-mates, as a vestigial rite of passage (Schulenberg, O'Malley, Bachman, Wadsworth, & Johnson, 1996). Others, especially elders, may mark their birthdays with moderate celebratory drinking. In Iceland, it is only the even-numbered birthdays that are celebrated with drinking (Ásmundsson, 1995).

The celebration of a wedding, graduation, or promotion by any member of the family or domestic group may be marked by drinking; the ritual burning of a mortgage that has been fully paid is another. The Tiv of Nigeria have a drinking party to celebrate each man's maturation ceremony and another to confirm the decision that two friends become blood-brothers. (Downes, 1933). Many kinds of initiation rites in China include drinking as an important feature. These include the first shooting by a corps of military troops, the welcoming of visitors whether in public or private, military and political reviews, harvest time, honoring the sky and earth, and showing reverence for everyone's elders, whether alive or dead (Xiao, 1995). Among the Ama-Bomuana of Africa, only adult men who have been initiated—and hence given "beer names"—are allowed to drink (Davies, 1927).

A warrior's first kill was marked by a communal beer fest lasting several days among the Tupinamba (Staden, 1928, p. 1559). In sharp contrast, the Jivaro warrior spends several days away from the village, eating little and drinking beer while restoring his equilibrium after having heatedly killed an enemy. If he was lucky enough to take his victim's head, it may take a week for him to shrink it meticulously to the size of a tennis ball. Such a trophy infuses the victor with extra strength, after which he can rejoin his fellow warriors to celebrate with a beer fest (Karsten, 1935).

Menopause is viewed in many cultures as an exceptionally empowering experience, after which a woman becomes "like a man" in many respects of power and privilege. Being generally allowed to drink on an equal footing with men is one such benefit. The Aztecs of ancient Mexico privileged older people of both sexes, with drink and drunkenness not only permitted but expected, whereas both were largely prohibited (except on a few special occasions) to younger people, except for priests (Taylor, 1979).

Even after death, drinking occasions do not end. It is commonplace that a wake be held before burial, with drinking among friends, neighbors, and relatives of the deceased; Irish, Camba, and Spaniards are just a few examples of those who hold such occasions. The undercurrent of conversation at such an event often includes specific mention that people feel as if, or truly believe that, the deceased is drinking with them. There is often an interruption of drinking for the funeral, but it resumes after the burial. Occasionally drinks are poured directly on the grave, specifically intended for the enjoyment of the deceased. Libations and offerings of alcohol to dead ancestors at other times are often more than figurative or symbolic, being described by the actors as comprising genuine sharing or communion in a sense that they consider quite literal.

OTHER DRINKING OCCASIONS

People's lives are also marked by numerous occasions that are not clearly linked with the life-cycles either of individuals or of social groups but that are often construed as appropriate for drinking. For example, you find an arrowhead, or an ancient coin, or a talisman by the side of a walkway where it's evidently lain for decades. A fellow singer, dancer, or actor who not very enthusiastically went off to an audition returns to tell her roommates that she got a role in a major forthcoming production. A collector offers to pay a good price for that ugly old vase you just inherited from your aunt. A farmer stacks the last forkful of hay, or stick of tobacco, or cartload of rice under shelter as fast-gathering clouds begin to loose a heavy rain. Each of these is likely to be a drinking occasion.

Two Tivs in Nigeria are satisfied with the way in which the tribal council reached a mutually satisfactory resolution to their conflict. A group of Abipone warriors in Paraguay are preparing for battle and want both their wits and their bravery to be at peak. Two days later most of them return to camp victorious and want to celebrate. Each of these is likely to be a drinking occasion.

A couple make the final payment on their mortgage and realize that, after many years, they finally own their own home. Another couple, planning to move to a community they don't know, have just finished selling the home that meant so much to them for years. Having just completed the complex calculations of their annual tax return, a third couple are pleasantly surprised to discover that they owe less than they had expected. Each of these is likely to be a drinking occasion.

While transferring from one flight to another in an unfamiliar airport, a man encounters an old friend he's been thinking about. A neighbor who has long been looking for a used car, a pedicab, or colt, or book, or something else, finds it in good condition at a reasonable price. Someone wins the lottery for a sum that exceeds a normal month's wages. The crop has been planted, the tools have been put away, you're tired, and there's still a half-hour of this beautiful day in which you would not feel guilty about resting a bit. Each of these is likely to be a drinking occasion.

One man's daughter was admitted to the college of her choice. Another is being visited by a healthy young man of good repute who is about to ask for permission to court his daughter. This trip's catch brought premium prices at the fish auction, and the crew are going to end the season and disperse. A new father proudly boasts about the birth of his first son. A doting daughter has assembled friends and relatives to celebrate her parents' 50th wedding anniversary. Each of these is likely to be a drinking occasion.

One person's company just won a crucial contract. Another learns about having been given a promotion and a larger salary increment than expected. A third has laid the last stone, and decided that the wall looks good and sound. A group of army comrades decide to play poker rather than go to watch a film. Each of these is likely to be a drinking occasion.

To be sure, in some contexts, any or all of these events might be an occasion for simply a quiet sense of satisfaction, or for adding another flag to a shrine, lighting a candle, saying a prayer, pouring kaolin or chicken blood over an old wooden figure, or some other gesture of celebration or thanks. For many around the world, however, each such event is interpreted by some as an occasion for drinking, and people do just that.

Among the Baganda of Uganda, it is only the several widows of a recently deceased king who have the honor of drinking the beer in which his entrails have been cleaned (Robbins & Pollnac, 1969). Beer is mixed with saliva and blood for an especially powerful symbolic drink that is shared by two Chagga men when they become blood brothers, accepting long-term commitments of mutual support in many realms of life (Downes, 1933). It is virtually mandatory to drink heavily and to provide abundant drinks for others when Peruvians request a friend or relative to serve as godparent (to a child, a business enterprise, a building, or some other venture that should be so defended), or when a young man is seeking permission to marry a daughter of the household (Doughty, 1971). One ceremonial context in which drunkenness is not only acceptable but expected, is the "farewell ceremony" with which Quiché and other Highland Guatemalan Indians celebrate the completion of a year-long cargo, costly and exacting mandatory service in a political and religious position that rotates among various members of the community (Adams, 1995).

The victory of a favored athlete or team in sports, or of a candidate or a political party in elections, or of a competitor in any exhibition, are all often marked by celebratory drinking. The loss of a job, a pet, a contest, a lawsuit, or some other valued thing is often marked by "compensatory" drinking, in a negative rather than positive mood. Sometimes the symbolism of drink is enough in itself, without anyone's actually imbibing. For example, when a bottle is broken over the bow to christen a ship, or drink is poured over the winning sports team, or a bottle may be opened with a dramatic gesture and simply poured around in a public square to signal approval of victory, whether in war or at the polls. In each of those last three instances, the most commonly used drink is champagne, in the others, it may be any alcoholic beverage. The instances mentioned in this paragraph may have diffused to other regions as part of the growing, worldwide cosmopolitan capitalistic culture, but they are certainly seen with some frequency in much of Europe or North America.

In dealing with Finnish attitudes, opinions, and drinking habits, Mäkelä (1987, pp. 177–178) paid special attention to the suitability of various alcoholic beverages, and found remarkable consensus with respect to attitudes toward the propriety of serving alcohol on various occasions. Alasuutari (1992, p. 2) arrived at the same finding from the opposite direction, noting that drunkenness tends to be associated with freedom of the individual—in reaction to the normally heavy constraints that are imposed by society. "In Finland, in fact, it seems that alcoholic drinking makes almost any situation special."

Social context was closely analyzed by Beck, Summons, and Thombs (1991) in their attempt to understand drinking by U.S. high school students. For them, however, context appears to have had as much to do with subjective emotions as with time and place. They included Social Facilitation (at a party, with friends but not parents), Stress Control (alone, for self medication), School Defiance (at or near school, to defy rules and authority), Peer Acceptance (with a group, to gain approval), and Parental Control (at home, with parents).

Among the Cheyenne, it is reported that not only is a sharp line drawn between drinking occasions and nondrinking occasions, but that one is not welcome at a drinking occasion unless he or she participates (Bing, 1997). For the Navaho, the number of occasions that are considered appropriate for drinking has increased considerably in the past 20 years, but the discrepancy between what is an appropriate one and what is not remains enormous (Henderson, 1997).

In literally hundreds of conversations with people of many occupations, ethnic affiliations, and levels of U.S. society during the past year, the 20 most frequently mentioned drinking occasions (among a total of several hundred) were: party, New Year's Eve, having friends over, dinner, wedding, bull session (aimless discussion among friends), poker, anniversary, birthday, picnic, wake or funeral, business lunch, prewedding party, promotion, winning the lottery, payday, senior dance, fishing or hunting, St. Patrick's Day, or to "cure" a hangover.

The list could go on, almost interminably, if the people with whom the author talked in 23 different countries in the past three years are any indication. In Poland alone, Moskalewicz (1997) was able, by using a mailed questionnaire, to elicit "more than a million" different responses to the simple open-ended question, "When is it all right to drink?" In Finland, respondents were even more specific, not just talking hypothetically but naming those occasions on which they had in fact drunk beverage alcohol during a single week; their total, too, was considerably over a million (Simpura, 1987).

Of course, there are variations. Muslims will readily tell anyone that there is no occasion when it is all right to drink; presumably, a Mormon, Southern Baptist, Seventh Day Adventist, or any other abstainer would agree with that assessment. By contrast, there are alcoholics (and some heavy drinkers who show none of the diagnostic criteria of alcohol abuse or dependence) who will begin with "Anytime!"—and go on to enumerate a dozen or more occasions that are no more special than "morning," "with lunch," "during a work break," "when I get home from work," "when I meet a friend."

It is clear that these illustrative examples will serve better than an encyclopedic inventory to convey the variety of settings, motives, and moods that may be involved in shaping when it is that a person may drink. Each of these could be analyzed and interpreted as reflecting attitudes and values in that context and that time, but perhaps the most dramatic point to be observed is that, when people are asked in an open-ended manner, they tend almost without exception to associate drinking with positive and enjoyable occasions. The risks and dangers that are well known with respect to alcohol are not clearly associated with drinking, which is cast in a predominantly celebratory light.

THE HISTORICAL PANORAMA

If we refocus our attention from the individual, domestic groups, and the community to look at when people drink in a broader perspective, there are some historical issues that deserve attention. Some have talked about the ancient Near East as having been "a beer culture" for centuries before the Christian era, or the "wine culture" of the classical northern Mediterranean nations in the first millennium can be contrasted with the "beer cultures" of so-called "barbarians" further north (McKinlay, 1948).

A common misconception is that drinking patterns are immutable. Long-term historical changes are evident as shown in laws, paintings, political and social movements, and the waxing or waning popularity of specific beverages or usages. Less obvious, but more tightly documented, are some of the changes that occur within a decade or two and are portrayed by ethnographers, as for example among the Camba (Heath, 1971; 1991b), Iroquois (Dailey, 1968), and various Alaska Native communities (Honigmann & Honigmann, 1945). It should be no surprise that there is a lack of uniformity in the directions that such changes may take, including sometimes reversals that take a community from dry to wet and back again within a matter of months; an extreme example is Barrow, Alaska, in the late 1990s (Klausner, Foulks, & Moore, 1979; Parker, 1995).

The Phoenicians introduced wine to North Africa where it spread, as did the emergence of cities with permanent buildings, public works, writing, complex elaborations of the social and occupational structure, and agriculture and commerce in general (Lutz, 1922). Many of the paintings in Egyptian tombs portray the growing and harvesting of grapes. Some show the production of wine and others the royal couple drinking it, often to the accompaniment of music and dancing by female slaves. It is striking that the famous tomb of Tutankhamon ("King Tut" of Egypt around 1340 B.C.) had its own wine-cellar, with the contents labeled in more detail than most would be for today's market (Lesko, 1977). Adjoining the burial chamber was a separate room containing 26 sealed jars, each indicating the vintage year, the location of the vineyard from which the grapes were picked (like today's *appellation contrôlée*), and ownership of that property (analogous to the name of the chateau or company). In addition, the name of the chief winemaker who oversaw the production was listed, a nicety rarely encountered nowadays although knowledgeable people recognize the crucial importance of that role. Throughout pre-Islamic history, the Arabic-speaking world not only produced good and abundant wines, but it was also the birthplace of distillation. The pleasures of both drinking and drunkenness were immortalized in eloquent poetry, and with beautifully crafted and inscribed drinking vessels.

The spread of grapes across Europe closely followed the conquest by Roman legions. Grapes were introduced to the Americas largely to provide wine for Catholic sacramental use, but to Australia on the whim of a gardener-physician. Homebrews are still local and beers tended to have less outreach until international licensing. Spirits, by contrast, have long been an ideal commodity for trade, even on remote frontiers, largely because they represent high value in small volume, are easily divisible, easy to transport and subject to little spoilage, and have the added advantage of being readily consumed. Thus there is the expectation that the user would want more but couldn't produce it, thereby becoming dependent on the trade, even if not dependent on the substance. Although these distinctive values made distilled spirits an important tool of colonialism on almost every continent (Jankowiak & Bradburd, 1996), the initial reception differed from place to place.

The Iroquois of northeastern North America offer a case history of drinking that is strikingly different from most stereotypes regarding Native American experience with alcohol. This should serve as a warning against glib generalizations about historical trends in that connection. Like most American Indian populations, they had not made or used any beverage alcohol prior to their contact with Europeans. But they were early offered spirits in trade for furs and they cautiously accepted them, together with guns, cloth, tools, beads, metal pots, and blankets.

Among the Iroquois, brandy and other drinks were welcomed but, contrary to the stereotype, only in small quantities. They were used in a novel way, by young men for whom a vision-quest was an important rite of passage (Carpenter, 1959). Adolescents would go into the forest, away from settled communities, and take turns striving to dream about the animal-spirit that they thought would thereafter be their constant companion and protector. Friends would pool their resources to assure that each, in turn, would be rewarded with an appropriate vision. Using liquid spirits was easier than the traditional method of combining sleep deprivation with self-imposed hunger and thirst, and apparently produced the same kind of religious experience while friends of the lucky young man watched soberly.

It was not until the early 18th century that the Iroquois seem to have learned about brawling as an outcome of drinking, presumably following the model of white trappers and traders. By 1800, drunkenness had become widespread and problematic, both secular and violent in ways that strained family ties and community relations (Dailey, 1968). A young member of the neighboring Seneca, himself a recovering alcoholic, had a different kind of vision based on what he'd learned about Christianity, and he preached a gospel that blended it with his native religion (Wallace, 1969). The new messianic syncretism included abstinence as an article of faith, and predicted that peace, harmony, and many of the values that had been lost would be regained if people returned to a nature-based nativistic way of life, renouncing their attachment to European commodities and drink, and subscribing to a code very like that of the Christian Sermon on the Mount. That sect is still vital among American Indians throughout the area today; it bears the founder's name as the Handsome Lake Religion. It is noteworthy that this population never got involved in producing beverage alcohol, and even more noteworthy that their drinking occasions went from zero to numerous and back to zero in just a couple of centuries—a relatively short time in historical perspective.

A different combination of changes is taking place, more rapidly, among the Tonga in Zambia. Beer continues to be important to them (Colson & Scudder, 1988), although in very different ways from those described in the 1960s. A succession of changes in the local way of life ranged from massive resettlement to improved transportation, and the arrival of a money economy, all of

A Saami reindeer-breeder's family in the Russian arctic welcomes a Chukchi author with a meal. The dictates of hospitality often require that a visitor be given drink in addition to food. © *CORBIS/Dean Conger.*

which affected drinking patterns in different ways and for various reasons. A national brewery started producing *chibuku*, still an opaque beer but a clearer one with the cachet of being bottled (which also makes it stay fresh longer), and distributed it through new taverns that provide fixed settings for recreation and sometimes even music. Small amounts of lager beer have also become available and are preferred by those few who wish to be seen as more sophisticated or cosmopolitan. Illegal drinks with somewhat higher alcohol content are drunk by a few, but the new drinks are not used in ritual or other traditional ways. Brewing for work-parties has virtually disappeared, as wage labor has replaced reciprocal labor exchanges. Social drinking with no other purpose is now common among both men and women, as is drunkenness. Both the frequency and quantity of drinking have increased; bottled beer is replacing homebrew, and drinking is less integrated with the totality of village life. With the incursion of Christianity, the symbolic and ritual importance of beer is being attenuated. With the switch to beer produced outside of the village, brewsters found their work no longer profitable, and lost both income and status by no longer brewing. Payments that used to recirculate within the village and region now go to outside providers, making beer drinking a drain on the local economy rather than a boost to it as before.

With wages in money, younger men now drink, and with permanent sources on the fringes of the community, some drink longer and more than within the tightly knit traditional neighborhoods. Taverns are, in a sense, novel venues where old rules no longer apply, and heavy drinking is sometimes described as providing brief release from stress, although it sometimes also results in boisterous or even antisocial behavior.

Even these few vignettes demonstrate vividly the extent to which the historical panorama of drinking differs from one sociocultural context to another, and how, in each instance, environmental factors from beyond the local community impinge upon it.

The trend for average per capita consumption of alcohol in the U.S. was slowly but steadily upward from the repeal of prohibition to about 1980. From that time on, consumption has been falling overall, with the rate of spirits consumption falling more than that of wine and wine more than that of beer (Clark & Hilton, 1991). There are different currents within those broad general trends, to be sure. Wine overall enjoyed a sharp but brief rise with the fleeting popularity of wine coolers in the early 1980s, and another surge in the sales of red wine in the mid-1980s when the so-called "French paradox" (demonstrating positive benefits of wine-drinking with relation to coronary heart disease) gained broad publicity. Microbrews rapidly gained popularity and for a time outstripped imports in the beer market, although they still represented less than 10% of all beer sales, with just three producers dominating. Although overall sales of distilled liquors are down since 1980, yet they have not all been affected equally. In the U.S., there has been a gradual shift from "brown goods" (darker colored drinks, such as whiskey and brandy) to "white goods" (lighter colored drinks, such as gin and vodka). Specifically, vodka and tequila have increased not only their shares of the market but overall volume. Scotch whisky (their preferred spelling) lost considerably for a decade, before single-malt Scotch gained new popularity as a luxury drink. An older and newly affluent population appears in many respects to have taken the counsel of some advertisers that, if they are to drink less, they should enjoy drinking "better" (meaning, with more expensive drinks).

Those recent changes in the U.S. are by no means unique. They were mirrored in the experience of several other jurisdictions that were studied in the International Study of Alcohol Control Experiences (Mäkelä, Room, Single, Sulkunen, & Walsh, 1981): California (a single state in the U.S.), Finland, Ireland, Netherlands, Ontario (a province in Canada), Poland, and Switzerland. All of those regions had high consumption in the 19th century, followed by a long tradition of concern about drinking, expressed in popular movements and often with political struggles for temperance. Each also has a larger-than-usual tradition of research on alcohol in recent decades, on the basis of which, members of the project, under the auspices of World Health Organization's Regional Office for Europe, were able to compile and compare detailed data on production, consumption, and trade during the latter half of the 1900s, as well as problems and policies concerning alcohol.

The findings of this project are of special interest because they reflect uniform methods, ongoing discussion, and a serious attempt to arrive at meaningful comparisons and generalizations, unlike the majority of studies which are done independently and are of only limited comparability, Even so, cultural variation was striking. Finland and Poland both showed very low levels of overall consumption, with distilled spirits predominating. Both showed only a few health problems related to prolonged drinking. Drinking was similarly patterned in the Netherlands, but public inebriation was rare, in contrast with California and Ontario where it was conspicuous among an underclass group of repeaters. Switzerland, with the highest level of aggregate consumption, showed few signs of social problems in connection with drinking. By contrast, Ireland, where people drank less, had occasional disruptive behavior in pubs, which is where most of the drinking took place. "In broad terms... [a]s each society has its peculiar drinking habits, the mixture of problems varies accordingly, and, in cross-sectional comparisons, there are few positive relationships between consumption level and the incidence of problems closely connected..." (Mäkelä et al. 1981, p. 62).

When the focus is shifted from types of beverage and associated problems to aggregate per capita consumption of absolute alcohol, some other trends appear. To be specific, average adult consumption in the U.S. peaked between 1810 and 1825 at around seven gallons (26.5 liters). Immediately after the repeal of national prohibition, it was 1.2 gallons. (4.5 liters), rising by 1980 to nearly 2.8 gallons (10.6 liters), and then falling by 1995 to 2.2 gal. (8.3 l.) (Williams, Stinson, Stewart, & Dufor, 1995). Although the numbers are different, the general shape of the curves tracing recent changes in average per capita consumption were similar in France, Italy, and Sweden to what they were in the U.S., rising rapidly from World War II until the 1970s, and declining steadily through the 1990s. By contrast, alcohol consumption in general, and that of each type of beverage individually, continues to increase in Denmark, Finland, Great Britain, Japan, and Luxembourg (Edwards et al., 1994).

The usual warning is in order to remind us that such numbers can be deceptive if we take them literally rather than as markers that may signal historical trends. Even in the U.S. which is the most fully documented country in this respect, self-reported alcohol use adds up to no more than 60% of the alcohol that is sold in a given year, and sometimes only 40% (Room, 1993). It is generally agreed by survey-researchers that heavy users under-report their drinking more and more often than do others, which means that whatever data we may have from such ostensibly scientific sources are themselves suspect (Room, 1990; Martinic, 1998). In spite of those shortcomings of the numbers themselves, however, they may be useful, as long as we are careful to avoid the trap of attributing to them a concreteness that is not justified. For example, the directions of trends can be discerned by comparing surveys or sales records from different time periods, as has been done here, although over-interpreting the numbers for any given year may be risky.

For example, the recent general decline in drinking in the U.S. that all observers have remarked upon is neatly reflected in the proportion of U.S. adults who were drinkers in 1978 (69.6%) and in 1990 (65%), while those who were heavy drinkers (five per day at least weekly) fell from 6.2% to 3.9% (Midanik & Clark, 1994). In a sense, it is irrelevant whether those numbers are precisely accurate or not, if we assume that the distorting factors are either random or similar at different times.

On the international scene, it is remarkable that drinking tends to be increasing in some developing countries (Grant, 1998) at the turn of the 20th century, as it is decreasing in many of the more metropolitan countries (*Productschap voor Gedistillerde Dranken*, 1997). Some of this has to do with the increasing popularity of European and North American alcoholic beverages throughout the rest of the world. An interesting aspect of this is the finding that such changes in drinking patterns tend to be additive rather than substitutive (Mäkelä et al., 1981); that is to say, traditional drinking patterns tend to endure for long periods of time, especially among the poorer members of any society, even after novel drinks and ways of drinking have become fashionable at upper levels.

PROHIBITION AND RESTRICTIONS

One of the most distinctive features about beverage alcohol in cross-cultural perspective is the amount of affect that is invested in it—whether positive or negative. With respect to most realms of behavior, people who choose not to participate are generally indifferent when others do. But those who do not drink are often vocal, persistent, and influential in criticizing those who do, so the history of alcohol has been irregularly punctuated by prohibitions and restrictions, both legal and popular.

There are some societies in which beer or wine is still thought to be a gift of the gods, as was the case in ancient Babylonia, Egypt, Greece, Rome, or Aztec Mexico, and some in which drink is legally banned, such as contemporary Saudi Arabia, Afghanistan, and Pakistan. Other cultures have had differing kinds and amounts of limitation put on drinking over the ages. Much of our discussion throughout this book deals with customs about when, where, and how it is considered inappropriate to drink, even in populations that are generally accepting of drink. More striking as examples of popular ambivalence to alcohol—recognizing risks as well as benefits, and appreciating some effects but fearing others (Room, 1976)—are the various movements that have sprung up irregularly around the world to curtail drinking. Some restrictions are merely situational. An inscription on an amphitheater at Delphi, dated around 5 B.C., banned drinking there and listed the fine (McKinlay, 1951). In recent years, many university and public stadia have reinstituted that ancient pattern. The Abipone are unlike most peoples in that they never drink with food. But beer made from the fruit of the thorny algarroba bush is important to them for frequent but important parties that precede and follow combat among male warriors. Before going into battle, they drink, in the belief that beer makes them both more quick-witted and braver. After a successful battle, they again drink beer to celebrate. Other societies in which drinking with daily meals is routine

are careful not to drink when embarking on dangerous enterprises, but our interest here is more on situations where drinking has been habitual or customary,
and restrictions were imposed to make it less so.

One of the most famous among legal prohibitions of beverage alcohol was
the 14-year "noble experiment" in the United States (1919–34) that supposedly outlawed commerce in beverage alcohol throughout the country (Aaron
& Musto, 1981). However, the law said nothing about drinking, so those who
had stores on hand drank with impunity, as did those who had special exemp-
tions, such as medical or religious. Throughout prohibition, wine was available
"for sacramental purposes," and it is rumored that many individuals pretended
to be clergy just in order to get access to sacramental wine. Physicians were
authorized to prescribe whiskey for various ailments, and some drugstores or
pharmacies were especially licensed to dispense it by prescription only. Ethanol
is still listed in the U.S. pharmacopoeia (U.S. Pharmacopeial Convention, 1995).

But prohibition is rarely so absolute as that in the United States was supposed to be. For example, Iceland banned the sale of strong beer for several
years, during which spirits were easily and legally available. Then it banned
spirits, while making strong beer generally available. Denmark, Sweden, and
Finland all experimented with partial prohibition—that is, dealing with specific
beverages—and each such trial was subsequently abandoned as unsuccessful or
even counterproductive.

Commonplace reasons why such prohibitions fail have to do with easy
availability of beverage alcohol, whether through smuggling, illicit production,
or the corruption of officials who should be enforcing the ban. Illicit production
(moonshining), whether at home or on a large commercial scale, is easier than
most people realize, and need not involve elaborate equipment, much personnel,
or even great technological skill. Bootlegging or smuggling can be big business,
or, on a small-scale, it often provides some minor zest in the lives of people
who view it as a victimless crime, providing a nonthreatening way to defy the
authorities. An Iranian-American who recently returned to her home country
tells of friends there who served homemade wine at dinner in "a small act of
rebellion" (Bahrampour, 1999).

When India gained her independence, prohibition was written into its Constitution as an aim, but the relevant legislation was up to individual states. Most
of them experimented with prohibition, but nearly all have repealed it. Even
after the end of national prohibition in the U.S., various states retained their
own such laws until 1956; some counties, cities, towns, and other jurisdictions
remain officially dry even now.

Prohibition appears to be widely accepted or enforced in those states where
Islamic law prevails, but few other such experiments have been successful. After
the lifting of ethnic prohibition, Alaska Native ("Eskimo") communities and
Native American ("Indian") reservations in the U.S. have enjoyed local option
for a few decades; about half are now dry, but some have alternated between wet
and dry with some frequency. Although the term "prohibition" is rarely used in

that connection, it applies in many countries to various age-groups (International Center for Alcohol Policies, 1998a).

Historically, there have been various attempts to ban beverage alcohol but most have been short-lived. In Canada, most provinces were dry for part of the 1900s, and a state in Mexico had prohibition briefly. Chinese history is punctuated by brief edicts with such bans, but presumably they had little impact beyond the imperial court, and drinking remained a pervasive aspect of life for most commoners. The same was probably true in Russia until the 1900s, when the outreach of the state became effective. In the 1850s fully half of what were then the United States had voted themselves dry, but most such laws did not last long.

Prohibition, or an outright ban on alcohol, is extreme among the many options that have been tried in the hope of curtailing drinking or reducing various kinds of harm that are attributed to it. Among Sweden's novel social experiments for example, was the rationing of beverage alcohol, with provision for local authorities to deny even the rationed allotment to problem drinkers, and with protections against the transfer of rations from nondrinkers to heavy drinkers. Additional restrictions often involve pricing, taxation, sales limitations, health warnings, and controls on advertising, among others.

In the early 1800s, Canada, the U.S. (Blocker, 1989; Musto, 1987), the Netherlands, and the U.K. all had widespread and vocal but short-lived temperance movements (Levine, 1992). In the 1850s, so did Australia, Poland, and Russia. In the 1880s, Sweden had one, and both the Netherlands and the U.S. saw resurgent temperance movements. Some local variations should be noted: opposition to spirits was often combined with tolerance or even approval for beer, and when the aim changed from temperance to prohibition, such escalation sometimes cost those movements what political power they had achieved.

Even France in the 1960s had a political push that favored milk over wine (Prestwich, 1988). An early part of the Soviet Perestroika movement in the 1980s was a large-scale drive to cut drinking. Vineyards were uprooted, production and distribution of beverage alcohol were drastically curtailed, and home distillation and the wholesale drinking of nonbeverage alcohol (cologne, antifreeze, shoe polish, and so forth) created a new set of problems the authorities had not anticipated (Sidorov, 1995).

The idea of curtailing drinking for political purposes was made explicit in Poland, when striking workers agreed to temperance in support of their Solidarity movement in the 1980s (Moskalewicz & Zieliński, 1995). Tanzania, Sri Lanka, Pakistan, and Zambia are a few of the countries in which independence was associated with calls for general sobriety as a defense against abuses that people associated with alcohol under the old order.

A self-styled "new temperance movement" in the U.S. has rephrased the issue from one of morality or religion to one of public health and economics (Heath, 1989; Wagner, 1997). Elaborate studies that purport to represent the costs of drinking often make costs to individual drinkers look like costs to every taxpayer, and ignore or deny that there may be any benefits on the other side of the ledger (Heien & Pittman, 1989).

The World Health Organization, especially the European Regional Office, has been unequivocal on this point for decades. Target 17 in the European Strategy for Health for All by the Year 2000 (World Health Organization, 1993) was an overall reduction of alcohol consumption of 25% in the last two decades of the 20th century. Most European countries have come close to that, but there are some countertrends, especially in developing countries (Edwards et al., 1994; Grant, 1998).

WHY DOES IT MATTER?

It matters much when people drink, because the risks that tend to be associated with alcohol depend almost entirely on the pace of drinking. As research has increasingly focused on problems, it has become clear that the vast majority of people who drink do so without harming themselves or others in any way. Excessive drinking by a small percentage of those who drink is linked with most of the damages to health, property, public safety, and other risks that are, in varying degrees, associated with ethanol. Alcohol-related problems are differently defined in various societies, and at different times in history, but now they tend, in most published discourse, to be many, pervasive, and indiscriminately associated with moderate as well as heavy drinking. Only on rare occasions does a normally moderate drinker drink in a way that results in any such problem.

The reasons why it matters how people identify a drinking occasion are many. In those societies where drinking is at all allowed, it is remarkable that so many people view drinking as acceptable on so many occasions. Beyond that, the fact that alcohol is widely viewed as an integral part of culture is dramatically reflected in the popular assertion that drinking is often what makes an occasion special.

Such common lay usage suggests a problem that inheres in usage of the same term by investigators, who are apt to say that "5 [or 4] drinks per occasion constitute a binge," or "6 drinks per occasion are risky," or "8 drinks per occasion are dangerous."

The slippage occurs most commonly when survey instruments are used that ask about an individual's drinking in various time-units (but never smaller than "a day"). This is the case with several of the most popular questionnaires: the Alcohol Use Inventory, World Health Organization's Alcohol Use Disorders Identification Test, or the Composite International Diagnostic Interview, each of which has been widely translated and is often used to survey how people drink in various countries (for full texts, see Allen & Columbus, 1995).

A peculiar sleight or artifice occurs almost universally when the data that were collected with reference to an entire day are tabulated, statistically manipulated, and subsequently reported as if they refer to a single drinking occasion. The difference may at first seem trivial, but consider a dinner party at which a group of friends each have a couple of drinks while conversing animatedly before dinner, two glasses of wine with the leisurely meal, and a liqueur afterward. Even if they had had no drinks earlier and no drinks later in that day, each of them would be counted as having had a binge. This hardly seems helpful—or even accurate—when it is evident that none was impaired at any time; none neglected anything they meant to do or should have done; and none would even have registered a blood-alcohol concentration (BAC) at the level of "driving while impaired" (DWI) in most jurisdictions. The same would hold with reference to a family for whom homebrew was a major part of the daily diet: in quantitative terms, a binge for each member every day; in qualitative terms, no impairment and no alcohol related problems. To call such drinking risky, or on the threshold of being dangerous is nonsense that does little more than amplify some of the "problems" that are statistically created artifacts (Gusfield, 1996). More to the point, it amplifies such problems in ways that seem to justify increasing restrictions to curtailing moderate drinking without paying any special attention to those few heavy drinkers who, on a recurrent basis, do actually become impaired (often seriously), neglect many of their responsibilities with regularity, and often drive with BACs that exceed the DWI level by 100% or more. If the goal is prohibition—as some clearly wish it to be—then controlling the availability of alcohol is likely to be more effective than most other policies. But if the goal is temperance or moderation—as most say it is—the controls that are most often touted are likely to impact far more on those who are already drinking moderately and temperately, but to have little effect on those who drink to excess. When the aim of public policies is to reduce harm, special attention should be paid to identifying harmful behaviors and addressing them, without restricting behaviors that are not harmful but that bring social, psychological, and physical benefits to many.

Chapter 2

Everything in Its Place:
Where Do People Drink?

Paper pennants and crowded tables signal a major celebration in Pamplona in the Basque Country of north central Spain. On festive occasions, even a city street can be converted into a place to eat and drink. © *Gerry Dawes, 1999.*

As we look around the world, it is evident that people in different cultures tend to have a very different sense of location, space, and what kind of behavior is appropriate where. Drinking is no exception. If we were just considering ethanol as a chemical compound, we would have to recognize that it is remarkably widespread in nature, occurring at the microscopic level endogenous within the digestive tract of the human body—and that of almost every other mammal—usually in amounts too small to affect mood, cognition, or behavior. Similarly, and again naturally, it turns up macroscopically in interstellar space.

But our focus on alcohol as an artifact made and used by people means that we should pay attention to where people drink—or do not drink. Sometimes, they will drink in one place. At other times, such behavior in that same place would be reprehensible, just as it is at any time in yet another place. Sometimes they drink different beverages in different places, and often they do different things in association with drinking, depending on the site that is chosen. In short, drinking is an act that has very different meanings and connotations depending on where it takes place. The ways people feel about drinking or about other people's drinking, and about the changes in behavior that sometimes result from drinking, are all colored by the setting and evaluations of it.

This chapter examines the question of place, context, or setting from a series of different perspectives. Our case study focuses on young men of the Pacific island of Truk, who choose to drink at what might seem to be an awkward distance from their homes and neighbors. As we learn more about what drinking means and does for them, their choice of space makes much more sense, especially as it contrasts with where other segments of the population choose to drink. Next we look at who drinks at home or in living spaces, before broadening our scope to deal with where else people drink within their local communities. Because some choose venues even more removed, it is necessary that we also pay attention to where people drink beyond the community, before turning to our usual question of why it matters to us where anyone should choose to drink—or not to drink.

Case Study: Truk's Weekend Warriors

Truk is a small cluster of the Caroline Islands in Micronesia, where the long tradition of male ferocity and bravery is still acted out, but in ways that are not now aimed at foreigners. Drinking, which was unknown before European contact in the 19th century, has become a focus of affect and fighting among the young men who would earlier have been the warriors. On weekends they are boisterous and assertive in ways that let them prove their masculinity without being a serious threat to anyone outside of their group. The major island of Moen, as studied in the 1970s (Marshall, 1979a), provides a setting that well illustrates how the places where people choose to drink can be important in relation to other aspects of their culture.

Whalers and traders taught people to make fermented coconut toddy and palm wine, and probably, without realizing it, also served as role models for raucous heavy drinking and rowdy drunken comportment. Although the Trukese, already known as fearsome warriors, were late in adopting beverage alcohol, its use spread rapidly, especially among young men. Missionaries preached against drink and drinking but had little impact on those who did not become devout Christians (Marshall & Marshall, 1975).

The Japanese administered the region as a League of Nations mandate, and tried to enforce prohibition among the local people from 1921–59, but they probably were also unwitting role models for the idea that drunkenness provides "time-out" (MacAndrew & Edgerton, 1969), during which personal responsibility is suspended. As a United Nations Trust Territory from 1959, Truk was administrated by the U.S. Navy, until the Federated States of Micronesia became independent.

Marshall found an ambivalent society, in which almost no women drank, some older men occasionally drank in sedate groups in local bars, and most young men spent a significant part of each weekend drinking away from home and posturing in ways that accentuated their independence, fearsomeness, and aggressive qualities, all of which were very little in evidence during the rest of the week.

Their drinking was part of a deliberate effort to stretch—if not break—their society's definition of what was acceptable behavior. It involved quickly getting drunk to the point that they would no longer be held responsible for their actions. What they drank was not elaborate—bottled beer, a homebrewed coconut beer or wine, or an even simpler homebrew based on commercial yeast, sugar, and water fermented for a day or so until it became a beverage called simply "yeast" with a sweetish taste and an alcohol content of about 6–8% by volume. Any of those beverages drunk fast and in sufficient quantities (approximating a quart an hour for 3–5 hours) could produce the state of intoxication that, in terms of local culture, bestowed upon them the highly valued state of temporary insanity. That gave them license to behave in ways that would otherwise be objectionable, but that, in such a state, gave public proof of their unquestionable masculinity, their valor, and their adeptness at the skills of warfare which had long been abandoned in actual practice.

In some senses, it is sad that young men had to resort to drinking "under the tree" (at the bend of the road from town toward the countryside), "on the bridge" (that connects with a small nearby village), or "in the boonies" (in any open space away from the dense cluster of habitations), all in order to demonstrate their manhood through valor. Worse yet, drinking in a rusty taxi as it bumped over the single road that goes around the island seems an ignominious prelude to their crucial exhibition. But when they had drunk enough, the reward they sought was an opportunity to curse the elders, make threatening noises and gestures (which never really hurt the bystanders), and go through the motions that supposedly demonstrated their readiness to fight and triumph over any imagined adversary that may concern them at the moment. A missionary or a friendly anthropologist was not a suitable target, so that young men, no matter how boisterous and assertive they had been, would quit their threats, aggressive postures, throwing of stones, and other gestures when confronted with a person whose status put them beyond the "within-limits clause" (MacAndrew & Edgerton, 1969) of acceptable disinhibition.

In spite of all the bluster, few people were hurt. Stones were most often thrown at buildings where they made satisfying loud noises, but people were hit apparently only by accident. Spectacular exhibitions of kung fu gestures (learned from the movies) rarely landed on anyone. Fistfights occurred only during rare confrontations between groups from different communities, and anyone who made threatening gestures with a machete was usually disarmed before he actually attacked anyone.

No other segment of the population drank so much, or drank to get drunk in the way that young men did. No other group drank to get drunk, and no one else made a show of drunken comportment. The venues that they chose gave them room for their show of aggression and gestures of defiance, well within the view and hearing of young women and others in the community, but far enough away that few bystanders would be hurt. Like their elders, other men of about the same age as the weekend warriors, but who had very different status because they were married or had regular jobs, drank in the tavern. Those who drank in a tavern never drank in the outdoor spots frequented by the demonstratively assertive youth, and those who drank for that kind of exhibitionism stayed away from the taverns. The few women who drank at all did so at home with their spouses. No one drank alone.

No matter how we evaluate the way in which they drank or the ways in which they behaved after drinking, there is no question that the youth of Truk chose unorthodox places for their drinking that would make no sense if we did not also look at that drinking as part of a larger pattern of attitudes and behavior. Those attitudes and that behavior relate to their being a generation without traditional modes of initiation and expression of manhood that they were eager to demonstrate to an audience who wanted to be witnesses—but only at a distance.

LIVING SPACE

At the most fundamental level, we must distinguish between drinking in the open or within some kind of shelter. The construction of even the most rudimentary shade or screen is, in itself, an act that is sometimes loaded with meaning as representing the creation of a crucial boundary between the natural world and the cultural or humanly constructed world. Anywhere in the world, the ritual succah, leafy bower at Succot (a 9-day thanksgiving celebration) among Orthodox Jews, reflects their preoccupation with domesticating space to make it appropriate for ritual activities, of which drinking is an important feature. By contrast, the Andean Quechua choose to be outside when drinking to celebrate the powerful spirits that surround them, and scattering libations in each of the six directions, zenith and nadir as well as the primary compass points (Allen, 1988).

When we speak of living space, we may be referring to a house or a hut, an apartment or condominium, a castle or a dormitory room, a houseboat or a ship's cabin, or simply that portion of a large structure allotted to an individual, couple, or household for a given time. The meaning of home and the details of how architecture relates to living arrangements are far beyond the scope of this discussion, which focuses on where it is generally agreed to be acceptable to drink, or where one is required not to drink.

For many people, drinking is so integral a part of everyday life that they do it without much thinking about it at home every day. Mexican Indians for whom pulque is a basic staple in their diet drink it with every meal, whether that happens to be in the kitchen of their house, in the all-purpose single room of a smaller house, or in the adjoining yard where much of the daily round takes place. For a Kofyar in Africa, it is almost certain that most of the substantial daily intake of homebrew will be out of doors, although clearly within the territory identified with an extended family.

Where people drink is not a simple question of at home, at work, at a public drinking establishment, with friends, or any of five or six other places that may be listed on a questionnaire. A hint of this complexity is seen, for example, in the U.S., where drinking with meals is often done in the dining room, while sitting on a lightweight chair at a high table, whereas drinking as an adjunct to television watching may take place in another room where a large overstuffed chair or couch may not even be near a table. When visitors arrive, it is customary that they be offered a drink soon after they are welcomed and seated in a slightly more formal room with chairs and small low tables ranged in groups or in the kitchen while food is being prepared. If men choose to drink and women not, the backyard or a garage may be a favored drinking spot, unless the house is equipped with a bar specifically for serving drinks, or a den favored as an informal retreat. In pleasant weather, meals may be served—even prepared on a fireplace or grill—outside, and drinks often accompany such a cookout. Variations on these patterns are numerous and frequent, but each social class shares patterns of drinking at home that would be recognized, unremarkable, and even expected by guests from similar backgrounds.

By contrast, Navaho Indians would be unlikely to drink at or even near their home. In Finland and Sweden, men usually choose to stay away from women and children while they drink and avoid the living quarters where anyone might see them. They may, however, enjoy the economy, comfort, and convenience of drinking "at home" by getting together with friends in the sauna, a sweat-bath which is usually in a separate outbuilding near the house. By contrast, Swedish, Tanzanian, Zambian, and Zimbabwean women most often meet in small groups every few days to drink in the kitchen of one of their number. In countries as different as Ireland and Japan, even when drinking is a daily occurrence, it tends to take place in public places intended primarily or exclusively for that purpose.

Vehicles, whether cars, trucks, or wagons, are strangely liminal—private in terms of ownership or access, but of legitimate public concern when moving in ways that might endanger others. The goal of social welfare often gets expressed in terms that restrict drinking—even within a privately owned living space—ostensibly to protect the common good. Many jurisdictions have laws that disallow open drinks within a vehicle, or that mete out extra penalties to drivers who operate their vehicles while impaired by drink (DWI). Some have even established specific levels of blood-alcohol concentration (BAC) as prima facie evidence of impairment. Sweden used to have zero-tolerance in this connection, with mandatory jail sentences for those who were found guilty; like many other European countries, it now uses 0.05% (or 500 mg%) by weight. Many of the United States use 0.1% by volume, and there have been increasing pressures to make 0.08% (800 mg%) the national standard. Because the vast majority of DWI accidents involve repeat offenders with BAC's fully twice as high (National Highway Traffic Safety Administration, 1994), it is not clear whether such lowering of the permissible level would be sufficiently helpful in reducing deaths or injuries to justify the increased burden on police, courts, and moderate drinkers.

Occasions for drinking in living space are plentiful: anniversaries, celebrations, the welcoming of visitors, tasting, a party, quietly relaxing, and many more. Yet it is important that we not lose sight of those who, for whatever reasons, consider beverage alcohol a danger or an abomination and refuse to have it in their homes.

IN THE COMMUNITY

Another major distinction that most people recognize, whether they articulate it or not, is between private space and public space. There are public spaces that are enclosed, just as there are private spaces in the open air, but criteria of rightful access are jealously guarded for both of those kinds of space. It is generally easier and less expensive for anyone to drink at home, whether that be in a house or in the yard or garden, but drinking there often has very different meanings from drinking in a public place, whether enclosed such as a bar or pub or open as at a park or on the street. The appropriateness of a place for drinking is not simply dyadic—acceptable or not—but can shade along a continuum. It may be all right to drink while relaxing in one's kitchen at home, but it may become almost mandatory that one do so when a friend is visiting. It may be

French workers enjoy a break from their labor in the vineyards as they drink a wine pressed from recently-harvested grapes before it is even bottled. © *Stephanie Maze/ NGS Image Collection.*

expected that one drink while sitting at a sidewalk cafe, whereas drinking on a public bench just a few meters away may be viewed with scorn or pity.

As we move outward from the living space of an individual, family, or household, there is a series of increasingly inclusive areas in which norms and views about the propriety of drinking are contested. Fundamental among these are some spaces that are specifically designated for public drinking. The wine shop in ancient Babylon was one such, and we know a great deal about the rules of serving and of decorum because such places were subject to many detailed laws in the Code of Hammurabi, famous as the first written corpus of law in Western history (Harper, 1904). Wine and beer shops were common throughout the Near East (Forbes, 1954), as evidenced in archeological finds; others in well-known Greek and Roman cities were remarkably preserved whether by volcanic eruption or more peacefully by gradual abandonment.

Public drinking places run the gamut in size, location, cleanliness and orderliness, lighting, decor, and almost any other aspect you can imagine. Probably the most public is the single beer-pot in some central African villages, around which men (and sometimes women) drink together while relaxing, talking, and socializing. In southern Africa, the shebeen is often little more than a lean-to or temporary hut for shade in the yard where homebrew is sold by the glass to people who expect little accommodation beyond a hard bench. More lavish ones have fine accommodations and are home to exciting new genres of music.

During the 1600s and 1700s, there was a kind of golden age at English taverns, with poets, playwrights, composers, and authors making them more like social clubs or even second homes (Popham, 1978). The writings of Pepys, Johnson, and Boswell, to name a few, recount vividly some of the hearty good times, hardy drinking, and intellectual ferment that characterized such company. At the same time, lower class alehouses served the working classes (Clark, 1983). Not only was drink available, but such establishments often served also as pawn-shops, the site for common-law marriages or baptisms, employment agencies, and even arenas for boxing, dog- or cock-fighting, and other entertainments (Popham, 1978).

Irish pubs or shebeens in previous centuries were generally patronized mostly by those who had not inherited land or wealth, both of which were in short supply and were reserved to the eldest son. Rural communities were often divided between the devout who dedicated themselves to work and church, and the alternative society with few goals or aspirations, who frequented pubs eager to drink or fight to relieve the monotony of their lives. Within the pubs a hard-drinking and aggressive subculture flourished.

In the late 1800s and early 1900s, saloons in the U.S. took on many of the functions of the earlier British alehouses. With steady streams of immi-grant workers, they provided banking services, a daily newspaper, a fire on the hearth in bad weather, an introduction to politics, and opportunities to talk with others about how to find housing or work in the burgeoning cities or boom-towns. Often selling beer by the bucketful, saloons became the embodiment of what temperance-oriented campaigners thought of as alcohol-related problems: poverty, spouse abuse, child neglect, and waste of earnings on drink. Carrie Nation won fame for herself and invaluable publicity for her cause by not just denouncing saloons but taking a hatchet to them on various occasions. Often frequented by immigrants, most of whom were laborers and a disproportionate number of whom were Catholics (thought by many Protestants to be loyal only to the Pope and not to their new country), saloons were characterized as dens of conspiracy as well as iniquity, vaguely threatening to Americans who were seeing many kinds of competition from the newcomers (Gusfield, 1963). Women were sometimes admitted to social functions at saloons or taverns, but usually only on special days or to special rooms.

A sociologist sang an eloquent paean of praise to what he called "the third place" (Oldenburg, 1997) and has done much to revitalize that tradition in West-ern society. "The third place" is where people can go when they are not at home (first place) or at work (second place), and be in public, but still relatively se-cure. It can be anything from a coffee shop to a barbershop, in small towns a general store or post office, or, for many, a tavern or a bar. Traditionally, each of these is a focal point of at least some community activity, a gathering place where people socialize and converse.

In many communities, the tavern has been a quintessential third place, af-fording the additional advantage of being occasionally patronized by outsiders who bring news of happenings elsewhere, and being large enough to accom-modate gatherings. Much of the planning of the American Revolution took place in taverns (Conroy, 1997), just as the beginnings of labor organization and other political movements occurred in taverns throughout much of Europe. Although drinking—and sometimes eating—take place there, these institutions are far more than drinking or eating establishments. A good bartender or tavernkeeper still often serves to facilitate relationships, broker jobs, cash checks, or locate housing.

Of course, not every place that serves drinks qualifies as a third place in this sense. Socializing and conversing are important components of the ambiance, and disruptive behavior is usually not tolerated by the owner or by the clientele. The ways in which host and regulars cooperate to keep order and to exclude troublesome individuals is an ideal example in microcosm of the phenomenon called informal social control, controls exercised by popular consent, without recourse to law or political power.

Bars, pubs, or saloons tend to be quite substantial, indoors, with furniture sometimes including tables and chairs, other times, only stools; a long bar, perhaps with a footrail, may not even allow for seating. Food is often also available, as are games, music, or other services, sometimes even including commercial sex. Germany and England both had pubs that served as "workingmen's social clubs," offering a cozy fireplace (at a time when few homes were well heated), newspapers (which few workers could afford), opportunities to relax playing darts, cards, dominos, pool, or other games, and to talk (whether about news, work, politics, gossip, or whatever).

Public drinking places are sometimes important as places where one can consume alcohol away from home, but they often have other meanings and functions as well (Sulkunen, Alasuutari, Nätkin, & Kinnunen, 1997). Some public places are intended for drinking, some are even designated, restricted, or licensed for that purpose, and some are used for that even though neighbors or authorities would rather they not be.

In the U.S., the institutions where most public drinking is done are usually commercial establishments that emphasize drink and that pay substantial sums to cater to that trade. They go by various names, such as bar, cafe, pub, tavern, inn, lounge, cocktail lounge, nightclub, or cellar, all of which signal the availability of alcohol, although they also signal the different patterns of drink and activity that one might expect to find in each. For example, a bar is likely to feature beer, with some spirits available, but not a choice of wines (unless it happens to be a wine bar, which can be found in only a few places). Insofar as food is available, it tends to be limited. An inexpensive bar may have small servings, mostly of salty simple snacks such as pretzels, peanuts, or potato chips; a more expensive bar may also provide cheese or various hors d'oeuvres. Pinball machines, pool tables, cards, checkers, and such pastimes are often provided in lower class bars, as is television, especially during games played by professional teams that are known nationally. Higher class bars may specialize in soft music or simply a quiet relaxing ambience. The clientele, largely men, may include a high portion of regulars, who drink there almost every day, and many of whom talk and joke in ways that reflect an almost proprietary interest in the place.

In contrast, a cafe is likely to serve light meals as well, and to have less in the way of recreational facilities. The clientele is more likely to be transient from day to day and not to stay so long when they do come. A pub may be like a bar, but it may also be more welcoming to women and to couples, sometimes with more provision for groups, such as small booths, more tables, games of darts, occasionally a band, and maybe even dancing. A brewpub features locally produced beer, often with imaginative and tasty food as an adjunct. Saloons were commonplace, but were so generally disparaged as dirty and dangerous in the campaign for national prohibition that few institutions nowadays call themselves saloons, except in areas frequented by tourists, where they may try to capitalize on the slightly naughty image of a bygone age. A cocktail lounge tends to be dark, perhaps with a piano player providing unobtrusive background music and a bar well stocked with different kinds of spirits and garnishes for the prompt production of any exotic mixture or cocktail. Correctly or not, many of the couples who go there are thought to be meeting surreptitiously, and high-backed booths sometimes reinforce that image. Food is not likely to be featured and may not even be available. A nightclub is usually larger, often with musicians, singers, dancers, or comedians.

In other parts of the world, the range of alternative public drinking establishments may differ and certainly their locations, lighting, furnishings, ambience, and rules for social engagement all differ markedly (Csikszentmihalyi, 1968). It is also evident that different kinds of drinking places attract different people.

Apart from everyone's drinking with meals and for medicinal purposes at home, the men of Becedas, a Castillian farming town, spend part of evenings and most of Sunday afternoon in any of three bars, where they play cards and talk endlessly. Although there is a steady amount of slow drinking, no one gets drunk, and the consensus is that it would be shameful if anyone did (Brandes, 1979). It is difficult to find a community in Spain in which the pattern described for Becedas does not also pertain, and that is probably equally the case in most of Italy, Portugal, Greece, and the former Yugoslavia.

In the 1970s, a U.S. anthropologist conducted long-term intensive research on community beer gardens in the second largest city in what was then newly independent Rhodesia, now Zimbabwe (Wolcott, 1974). Bulawayo had had its own brewery for half a century, mass-producing traditional-style beer, much of which is sold in public beer gardens in what they call mugs, each containing a gallon (3.8 liters) or a half-gallon (1.9 liters). Each beer garden is a miniature public park, with sheds, benches, tables, trees, and sometimes live or recorded music. Groups of people tend to spend more time in conversation than they do in passing the shared mug and drinking from it. Because the beer is not filtered, solids settle to the bottom. Young people tend to throw them away, whereas many of their elders eagerly eat them as highly nutritional food. Such beer costs less by the mug than European-style beer does per bottle with only a fifth as much content. The beer garden provides an open context in which people living in the city can, when they choose, fit into the roles they choose to act out there, while reserving their choices also to reenact any of the traditional rituals or festivals that meant so much to them back in the rural communities that they had left. In small towns, there may be a single beer garden, whereas cities often have one in each neighborhood. For a long time, the beer garden was one of the few racially integrated venues in South Africa (Wolcott, 1974). Under the so-called "Durban system," they had the added advantage that profits were invested in the same communities (Haworth & Acuda, 1998).

In various countries throughout southern Africa, the shebeen is where a major part of drinking takes place. Although it is an Irish word, shebeen refers to a private house in which drinks are sold; it used to be that the goods were produced right there but increasingly they are from factories. Until the 1960s, shebeens were entirely illegal and many remain so, although few are clandestine. Music, gambling, and sociability are often offered and, like taverns elsewhere, they also serve as places where jobs are available, working conditions and politics are discussed, and a variety of community information is shared among men.

Much of the drinking by Australians takes place at public outlets, and there are some respects in which their bars have become famous. Early in the 20th century when the legal closing time for bars was early, so many drinkers took large quantities rapidly (ostensibly to last them for a while) that "the six o'clock swill" became common parlance for such heavy drinking. Police monitoring of violent incidents showed that most bars had none, whereas a few had many. The supposition was that "bad" bars attracted a potentially violent clientele, and the permissive ambience supported (or at least failed to discourage) aggression among them. Having recognized this subcultural pattern has enabled authorities far more efficiently to avoid, monitor, and contain violence when it does occur.

The degree of security that people enjoy in a bar differs from place to place. Some such establishments are justly noted (or infamous) as sites for easy predatory sexual encounters. Others have earned a reputation as tough bars, and it is noteworthy that aggressive people tend to congregate in just such establishments whereas others gravitate elsewhere, reinforcing stereotypes (Single et al., 1997). It is no surprise that, under authoritarian regimes, public drinking places are often heavily policed, viewed as hotbeds of dissidence, unrest, and sedition.

Laws and regulations that have to do with where one may or may not drink are numerous, and remarkably inconsistent. To take an extreme example, among the various states within the U.S., some specify that public drinking establishments may not be located within so many feet of a church or school; some require that the interior be visible from the street, whereas others specifically forbid that; some require that food be available wherever drinks are served, and others insist that it not be, and a few even hold that drinks may not be served to anyone who doesn't also order food. There are states in which all drinkers must stand at a bar while drinking, and others that insist they be seated; most forbid the entrance of minors, and, until recently, some required that women use

Chileans socialize while eating and drinking in the public, commercial setting of a restaurant in the nation's capital, Santiago. © *CORBIS/Pablo Corral V.*

a separate entrance from men and that they (together with couples) occupy a separate room.

Some drinking establishments set out to serve a particular clientele and others gradually evolve in that direction, sometimes changing as different owners or customers come and go (Popham, 1978). One U.S. bar served for years as a meeting place for boxers and their fans; it was lined with photographs and mementos at a time when that small city was important in that connection. As television changed the sport and business of boxing, those people closely associated with it left for larger cities and fans went elsewhere or stayed at home to drink. The same bar gradually became known as a hangout for Cape Verdeans from the neighborhood, but soon the area became gentrified and affluent yuppies found it a congenial place to "cruise" in the hope of finding a companion for the night (Beck, 1992). Some bars are known as being especially congenial for gay or lesbian drinkers who say they would be less comfortable in an integrated ambience (Read, 1980). A Spanish bullfighters' bar is likely to be crowded not only with those who work in or hang around the trade, but also with photographs, posters, and even assorted ears, tails, or stuffed heads of bulls from famous fights.

Some clubs cater to couples who want considerable privacy and discretion for their illicit meetings in hours when such establishments are legally forbidden to serve drinks (Roebuck & Frese, 1976). In some towns, one bar will be frequented by farmers and another by herders, with their exclusivity quite rigidly adhered to although utterly implicit. People in a bar that's frequented by one soccer team may be cool or even hostile to a player or fan from another. Some drinking establishments become known for prostitution, poker, dominos, billiards, electronic games, raffles, music, or other features, or for distinctive bits of food that they serve. Jazz, blues, and the beginnings of rock and its many variants sometimes flourished in nondescript drinking places, and often continue there.

In Bolivia, politicians are eager to give speeches or to be interviewed in chicha bars, because of the popular belief that one speaks truthfully in such a setting, and journalists obligingly comply by reporting on such events when invited. Until a few years ago, Mexican law did not allow a woman to drink in a cantina, but that has been repealed as part of the gradual lowering of gender barriers in that highly stratified society.

The café that has long played so vital role in middle class and bohemian life in France (Haine, 1996) is replicated in Austria, Poland, the Czech Republic, and in many other countries. It combines light food with drink, a comfortable meeting place for artists of all types: dancers, musicians, painters, writers, and others in that diverse company who are often called intellectuals. The importance of public drinking places is demonstrated, for example, in Canada, where more drinking takes place in bars than anywhere else, and many individuals drink more in bars than elsewhere (Single & Pomeroy, 1999).

By contrast, only 54% of men in the U.S. ever go to a bar or tavern, and only 42% of women. Among those who do go to such a specifically "wet" setting, virtually all drink while there. A higher percentage of both sexes occasionally go to parties, and nearly three-fourths of those who do, sometimes have a drink at the party. The fact that such drinking is commonplace does not mean that the country is awash in alcohol; even among drinkers who go to taverns, the typical number of drinks is about three, as it is for those who attend parties (many people do not do either). Evening meals at restaurants average only 1.5 drinks, and again, that represents only a small portion of the population (Clark & Hilton, 1991). Looking at the same information in a different way, we can see that about 30% of all drinking reported in the U.S. national survey took place at bars and taverns. Another 16% was done at parties, and the same amount "when friends drop in to visit" or "when spending a quiet evening at home." Drinking with an evening meal at a restaurant accounted for another 14%, and 3% was drunk with luncheon at a restaurant. All other contexts together account for the small remainder, so that the majority of our long list of drinking occasions on which people said *hypothetically* that it was all right to drink in actuality account for very little of the drinking that takes place.

It would be an endless task to describe the many kinds of public drinking establishments that exist around the world but this brief listing of a few illustrative examples makes the point about intracultural diversity as well as international differences in patterns. Another important aspect of drinking in the community has to do with drinking that takes place in venues that are not specifically designated as appropriate for the purposes.

For example, in this chapter's case study we saw that young men on a Micronesian island retire to a canoe house or to the bush at some distance from the village while drinking the mildly alcoholic beverage that they themselves prepare. However, they then take pains to assure that the risk-taking behavior that is triggered by drinking and that they consider important in demonstrating their masculinity, will be seen and commented on. They do this by staying close to the village to show their skill and daring.

Bottle-gangs are groups of people, mostly homeless, who join with each other to share the cost of a bottle of beverage alcohol for immediate consumption (Spradley, 1970). Usually the purchase is finely calculated to yield the most ethanol for the price they have available. Some such groups dissolve as soon as the bottle is finished. Others persist for weeks or even months, as different members of the group get money (by begging, from remittances, collecting and selling bottles or cans, and so forth) to resume drinking. The sense of equal sharing and of long-term reciprocity is keen, but they are often scorned by others for their unkempt appearance and occasional trouble with the police. In many jurisdictions, drinking on the sidewalk or on the lawn of a public building is illegal, which results in a disproportionate number of arrests of such people, whereas wealthier drinkers may be enjoying a sidewalk cafe just a few meters away.

Many communities in the U.S. restrict the sale or advertising of drinks in areas that are zoned as residential or within several meters distance from any school, place of worship, licensed childcare facility, or recreation center for young people. In Washington, D.C., the capital city of the U.S., a broad grassy mall often serves as a public park for various kinds of celebrations. For years, it has been a focus of family picnics on July 4th, a holiday commemorating the country's Declaration of Independence. As is customary throughout much of the country, beer was an integral part of many picnic lunches and an accompaniment to many amateur baseball games, until a few years ago when the police decided to ban alcohol there. Many of those who defied the ban (intentionally or unwittingly) had their drinks confiscated, which enraged some libertarians. When the police subsequently made a show of dumping the confiscated beer into a storm-sewer on the street, they violated environmental protection laws, and found themselves answering to other governmental agencies.

The Washington Mall was also the setting for another morality play about the propriety of drinking in public. For several years, one or more breweries had featured prominently among the various corporate sponsors of music, entertainment, decorations, and other adjuncts to the festivities there that celebrated May 5th, a Mexican commemoration of their defeat of French invaders, that has been generally adopted by Hispanics in the U.S. as a day of ethnic pride. The organizing committee recently made it clear that they did not want such further sponsorship, and went on to declare the fiesta dry. Controversy on the subject may not yet be over, because the latest decision has been to accept money from brewers who are willing to underwrite bands, performers, policing, promotion, and other expenses, but the fiesta remains dry, with no beer (or other alcoholic drinks) allowed.

In many other public parks in the U.S. and elsewhere, drinking is not permitted in the open, although all kinds of beverages may be available at licensed dining places scattered through the park, many of which are unusually expensive. As with bottle-gangs, other members of underclass or minority populations, even when they drink less than upper class drinkers, may have more alcohol-related problems with the police or authorities simply because they more often drink in public or are interpreted as disturbing the peace. The empty lots where aboriginal Australians congregate to drink soon become littered in a way that is offensive to "European" townspeople (as many 3rd or 4th generation Australians consider themselves), and condemnation of such drinking is often phrased in esthetic terms rather than in terms of health or safety (Merlan, 1998). The same often happens among Native Americans, accounting in large part for the grossly disproportionate "criminality" that official statistics attribute to this generally pacific and law-abiding segment of the U.S. population (Stewart, 1964). In similar fashion, the move to close many alcohol sales outlets in major cities tends to be focused on people who drink and occasionally urinate in public, impede pedestrian traffic, and are thought to set a bad example for children.

Restaurants often serve beverage alcohol, and, at a certain economic level, people who drink at all are likely to have drinks with luncheon at a restaurant, and even more likely to with dinner—despite the fact that it probably costs at least twice as much as at home. This European and North American pattern appears to be diffusing with the cosmopolitan capitalistic economy.

Distinctive local patterns still survive among public drinking places, however. There are still those in Texas who claim that no beer anywhere else tastes as good and refreshing as that from an icehouse, a barnlike structure that sells nothing but beer on ice, except occasionally some barbecued meat. Many such establishments were in fact commercial repositories for ice in the years before electrical refrigeration became common, and many claim that there is something distinctive about the chill from ice, whether it is "more natural," "more regular," or has some other special quality. The fact that private clubs were exempted from the restrictions of U.S. national prohibition was enjoyed by those who were privileged members and resented by those who were not. In some states, when it was still illegal to sell alcohol by the drink, there were "clubs" where one could join briefly for a dollar, and buy set ups (the rental of a glass, with a shot of soda or water and ice) with which to drink the liquor one had brought from a store (properly hidden in a paper bag, and kept on the floor rather than on the table). Such transparent subterfuges apparently kept to the letter of the law, while discreetly flouting the intent.

As with each of our questions about drinking, it would be inappropriate to neglect the negative. Where in the community should one not drink? A few specific examples, especially applicable to urban nomads, have been mentioned. But the question becomes more complicated when we think about buildings and other areas that are not specifically designated for drinking.

Posing the question to a naive lay respondent, one might get prompt assurance that a church is one such place where a person should never drink. Yet in one of the most sacred acts that take place there periodically, wine is served to each in attendance who chooses to take Christian Communion. In a nearby Jewish temple, wine plays a crucial role in the wedding ceremony. Although the question about people's drinking was posed in terms of space—where—it might more realistically have been in terms of pattern—how—or even motive—why. Once more, we are forcefully reminded that one drink is not equivalent to any other drink, regardless of the fact that they may contain identical quantities of ethanol and other chemical components. Meaning plays a dominant role in any human behavior, which is part of the reason why sheer numerical measures of quantity and frequency of drinking are so frustratingly shallow when we are trying to understand how and why people do what they do.

A colorful illustration has to do with where people drink. Certainly all of the staff in the detoxification and treatment ward of a major Paris hospital had striven valiantly over the years to keep it a "dry" workplace. At considerable personal sacrifice, they had foregone wine with meals, and carefully monitored everything that people brought in, to assure that there be no alcohol to tempt their patients. The director of the hospital had complied with their request that the area be specifically put off bounds to alcohol, so that they could have the added sanction of enforcing regulations rather than simply appealing to the good will of anyone who tried to bring a drink into the ward.

As the staff prepared to celebrate a special anniversary of their work, it became ironically apparent that a cocktail party, such as was customary for such events throughout the institution and that had already progressed in planning, could be problematic in that venue. A last minute call to the director's office elicited a special temporary exemption to the ban, so they were able to bring in unopened bottles, and to drink for a few hours in the staff lounge, a permissive island surrounded by an area of strict prohibition.

In the Western world, the courtroom is one of the least likely places for anyone to drink, and bailiffs are watchful to prevent surreptitious drinking. By contrast, members of the community council who try cases in many African or Latin American communities expect to drink during proceedings, and often the

In northwestern China, Oroquen men drink from birch-bark bowls and eat canned food with chopsticks while at home in their *yurt* or *ger* (a large felt tent). A large portion of the drinking in most cultures takes place in domestic settings. *© CORBIS/Earl Kowall.*

plaintiff and defendant are exhorted to drink after a judgment has been rendered, to signal their joint acceptance of the decision and their commitment to comply.

Most museums are strict in disallowing any sort of food or drink in the galleries most of the time. Nevertheless, on the occasion of a special opening or exhibition, the administration will often serve beverage alcohol and light foods for a reception. At the theater, whether for music, dance, drama, or some other presentation, ushers are usually watchful to be sure that no one in the audience drinks. But during intermissions, strategically placed temporary bars may serve drinks lavishly. Even a library, where concern for the books as fragile artifacts is given as a reason for not allowing food or drink most of the time, will serve both in connection with a reading, a lecture, or an exhibition.

THE GREATER WORLD

When we turn to the question of where people drink in the greater world, beyond their communities, the arbitrary and inconsistent quality of norms becomes, if possible, even more striking.

On most international airline flights, the first thing that is offered to a first- or business class traveler is a drink—regardless of the time of day. There are some exceptions: Air India, for example, does not serve beverage alcohol in the airspace over its home country. In coach or economy class, most airlines restrict each passenger to no more than two drinks, although those in more expensive seating may be offered virtually unlimited drinks. A few critics are asking that no drinks be served on planes, supposedly to curb the increasing incidence of so-called "air-rage," assaultive behavior by angry passengers directed at other passengers or at the crew. Ironically, the dual effect of alcohol as both tranquilizer and stimulant was dramatically illustrated in the experience of a colleague who tells of having been on a plane that turned back from taxiing in order to let the police remove a passenger who was uncontrollably aggressive. The aborted take-off and the unloading of his baggage caused such a delay that the other passengers became restless and outspoken in their complaints, to the point where members of the cabin crew thought it judicious to serve complimentary alcohol drinks in order to quiet them down.

Pressure from international regulatory agencies apparently resulted in the suspension, a few years ago, of what had been a perquisite for Air France pilots that some would have envied and others deplored, namely, wine with meals, in keeping with the French attitude that wine is a "hygienic drink" and a food, unlike alcoholic beverages that harbor some risk.

On trains, although there is usually a specific car where food and drinks can be bought, passengers are usually discouraged from eating or drinking anything that they may have brought aboard. Sea voyages are often noted for the emphasis that is put on drinking, and some international ferries are said to have more to do with drinking than with travel. This becomes especially important where one terminus has exceptionally high duties, taxes, or prices for beverage alcohol (e.g., Finland, Sweden) and the other relatively low (e.g., Latvia, Denmark).

National parks, like community parks, often restrict drinking in open areas, while permitting it in licensed establishments. As the boating population increases and less-experienced people are involved in more crowded areas, there is often increasing demand that drinking be restricted on small craft that may be wholly owned by one or more of the persons aboard. Drawing the line between private space and public risk or concern is a difficult task, especially distasteful for libertarians.

The association between beverage alcohol and sports is a complex one that has resulted in bad feelings when enthusiastic fans of a team sometimes appear to turn into destructive hooligans after a game is over. Demonstrations are not only boisterous but sometimes include the breaking of windows, overturning of automobiles, and similar random damage and disruption, usually restricted to the vicinity of the arena or stadium but sometimes spilling into other areas. English soccer fans are among the most notorious for such behavior, but it is by no means limited to them (Scott & Reicher, 1998). Despite the fact that there has been considerable journalistic viewing-with-alarm, there has been little systematic study of this phenomenon, but sociologists who pay special attention to crowd behaviors in various contexts have generally attributed such mischief more to assertions of group-identity than to the effects of drinking or drunkenness (Smith, Abbey, & Scott, 1993). Nevertheless, in attempts to curtail such outbursts, there have in recent years been increasing restrictions placed on the sale and drinking of beverage alcohol in such settings.

Some sporting events are not intended to be fully dry, but become so about halfway through. Concessionaires who are allowed to sell drink during the first few innings or quarters may be required to discontinue serving at some point so that most people will have metabolized the ethanol in their systems by the time the game is finished. Some college and university administrations in the U.S. have reacted to increasing descriptions of bingeing on the part of students and the deleterious consequences of such behavior by forbidding drink on their property. When the rules are not impartially enforced, with alumni and other older persons conspicuously drinking at tailgate parties (picnics, often served from the lowered rear door of a station wagon), at a stadium, accusations of hypocrisy often result in friction.

So strong is the feeling that drink belongs that Europeans and Americans sometimes even "remember" it in an inappropriate context, where it never appeared in the first place. While being introduced to the world of modern art, many encountered Manet's *Dejeuner su l'Herbe* as a painting in which the lines and angles added to their appreciation of the composition, and the nude female bodies contrast dramatically with the somber dress of the somewhat stiff gentlemen picnicking on the grass by a river. People know vaguely that there was some kind of scandal when that painting first was shown in public, but that is presumed to have had to do with the stilted Victorian mores of the time, or the anomaly of juxtaposing classical nudity with everyday reality within a single frame. The real scandal for today is that much of what many remember about it as a drinking scene is totally false. The man prominently gesturing at the right isn't really making a toast, and there's not a wine bottle in sight, neither in the picnic basket nor on the widespread cloth. Many are a little incredulous when, asked to look closely at the picture; they realize that the event depicted was dry.

If we expand the scope of our question about where people drink, we are confronted with a couple of geographical anomalies that remain unanswered despite sporadic speculation. One of these has to do with large gaps in the spread of beverage alcohol as a part of human culture in centuries past. It is still a great mystery to anthropologists and historians why two large areas of the world did not have indigenous beverage alcohol before the time of contact with Europeans. In most of North America (Canada and the U.S., roughly north of latitude 35), native peoples did not produce alcohol, and the same is true throughout most of Oceania (the islands of the Pacific). Both areas included appropriate climates and abundant plant materials that could easily have been fermented and distilled. It is true that there were other psychoactive substances, not just available but known and used, but that was also the case in much of Africa and Latin America, large areas where native drinks were many, diverse, and of fundamental cultural importance. To be sure, neither barley nor the wine grape, *vita viniferis*, grew in either area, but that could be said of most of the rest of the world where other crops served as well to produce beer and wine as do those that are now the mainstays of commercial production. Agriculture was well advanced, and various kinds of technical knowledge were highly developed by imaginative peoples who had invented remarkable social and cultural institutions and developed fairly elaborate cuisines.

Another geographical mystery that has not yet been adequately addressed by scientific methods has to do with the association of heavy drinking and drunkenness, linked with distilled spirits, with high northern latitudes, what some refer to as "the vodka belt" around the Arctic. It is an easy guess that some part of the answer may lie in the fact that more drinking occurs during seasonal darkness, regardless of clock time (Levine et al., 1994), but the fact that even greater extremes of weather, light, and isolation occur regularly in the Antarctic, where beverage alcohol is readily available at reasonable prices, with almost no heavy drinking and drunkenness (Mahar, 1999), suggests that, as is so often the case, the real reasons may not be so obvious.

WHY DOES IT MATTER?

It is a standing joke about real estate that three factors affect value: location, location, and location. Space on earth is far from fixed, with volcanoes and deltas sometimes appearing to create or expand the land mass, while erosion, flooding, building, and other processes appear to diminish it. But many people live their lives in blissful ignorance of such large-scale issues and are much more concerned about the simple propriety or feasibility of certain behaviors in certain buildings, rooms, or locations. However arbitrary such judgments may be—and their variation from one culture to the next suggest that they are, in fact, determined more by local custom than by more fundamental reasons—they are by no means inconsequential.

People get arrested and jailed for drinking in some places, where it is forbidden. Others may be scolded or chastised for doing so elsewhere, where it's just discouraged. A business person can lose his or her livelihood by serving drinks without a license, or for doing so fully licensed but at the wrong time of day or day of the week. Some people are extremely fussy about the context in which they drink, and some pay dearly to do it in a particular place. Others choose scrupulously to avoid a place where anyone might be drinking, and complain that it offends them to see someone with alcohol, no matter what their age, gender, ethnicity, dress, or general demeanor.

Few of the attitudes or values that people hold about drinking are captured in statistics of the sort that have been gathered so far about where people drink. What we do see are associations between the places people choose and certain other aspects of drinking. For example, those who drink with the family at daily meals are likely to socialize the coming generation with regard to drinking. They do this in a way that is effortless and not self-conscious, treating alcohol as a normal part of living with no mystique and no special power to transform them magically into anything or anyone else. Those who hide their drinking, by contrast, set the stage for inquisitive young people to experiment on their own, expecting something marvelous to come from drinking.

For those who learn that their drinking in public places is offensive to precisely those people they resent, drinking can become a form of social protest, asserting both difference and the fact that the drinkers have rights as well. Those who pay attention to inequitable access to drink in various places learn or are reinforced in their awareness of the political economy (Singer, 1986) and a wide range of other inequities that have greater social and cultural consequences.

Chapter 3

Cast of Characters:
Who Drinks, and Who Doesn't?

Mexican women enjoy shots of mezcal while shopping in the market. Although women do drink in most cultures, there is sometimes a double-standard about where and how often they do so. *Reprinted with the permission of Macmillan General Reference, a wholly owned subsidiary of IDG Books Worlwide, Inc., from* The Food and Life of Oxaca, *by Zarella Martinez. Photography copyright © Laurie Smith.*

In the broadest sense, of course, everyone drinks and has to drink in order to survive. Quenching thirst is one of the basic human needs, and lack of drink is far more quickly fatal than hunger or deprivation of sex or of shelter. But there are many people who do not drink beverage alcohol. In this chapter, we will look at different populations around the world to get some idea about the various meanings and uses that drinking has among them, including some who have collectively chosen not to drink. We will also look at subgroups within populations.

In order that any community or population can be better understood, described, compared, and interpreted, the researcher must go beyond the idiosyncrasies of each individual and the confusing complexity of everyday interactions in order to pinpoint key aspects of the social structure (who is who) and of the social organization (who does what). In outlining the structure, special attention is paid to the network of statuses that more or less maps where people stand in relation to each other. The same person thus can be seen as female, middle-aged, mother, daughter, spouse, sister, aunt, cousin, grandmother, homemaker, brewster, farmer, lender, creditor, senior, junior, coreligionist, political opponent, and an almost infinite host of other things, depending on what person she is relating to and what aspect or aspects of life happen to be salient in a particular context or situation. In dealing with the social organization, it becomes necessary to identify the correlative roles (dynamic aspects of those statuses) as they relate to each other. For example, a mother is expected to be nurturing, supportive, a mentor and a model, whereas a daughter is to be obedient, cooperative, faithful and devoted. A spouse, by contrast, should be sexually and economically sharing, comforting, congenial, and so forth. By looking at both the structure and the organization, the statuses and roles, one can go far toward figuring out how a social system operates, how things get made and done, how teaching and learning happen, how norms and values are perpetuated, and a large part of how people choose to do some things and not others.

With specific reference to drink, some of the subgroups to which investigators have paid most attention are those that people themselves use when talking about categories of people. These tend to be what sociologists call the standard demographic variables: age, gender, marital status, occupation, and for some contexts, education, socioeconomic class, caste, or religion. There are some additional distinctions that different societies consider relevant when grouping individuals or when categorizing them as component parts of the larger system. Not every such distinction is relevant everywhere, but some generalizations do emerge, as do patterned differences. For example, nationality, ethnicity, or cultural affiliation are other kinds of labels that are often significant with respect to how people act and think about drinking.

Many kinds of behavior are prescribed for some persons, forbidden to others, or marked off with a variety of rules signaling who may, should, must, or dare not engage in them. As is true with respect to other aspects of culture, such rules are not always made explicit or clear, but people learn them through a lifelong combination of role models and examples, stories and gossip, as well as prescriptions. In addition, people are constantly being rewarded in small ways for conforming, or punished for violating the norms. Socially acceptable patterns of drinking include just such largely implicit rules about what roles different actors should play.

In this chapter, we will look at several dimensions of identity and how they relate to drinking in selected cultures around the world. The case study deals with Navajo Indians, the largest tribe in the United States, and shows briefly how much reality diverges from the popular stereotypes about who drinks. It will be important also to note how some rules about who may or may not drink have changed over time, and how some continue to be changing even now. Because the complex webs of social organization differ so much from one society to the next, and because networks are so varied and so richly endowed with meanings, our presentation begins with a brief discussion of the ways in which people have tried to find out who drinks, and some comments on the limitations of those data. Beyond that, our substantive discussion of who drinks and who does not is grouped into those categories that social scientists have found to be broadly applicable across cultures and throughout history: age, gender, education and occupation, ethnicity and religion, other social categories. Then we turn to pay special attention to abstainers, that theoretically important group who choose not to drink. In short, this chapter is an attempt to sketch out roughly the cast of characters in the world of drinking occasions.

Case Study: Navajo Indian Drinking

The largest tribe in the United States, the Navajo epitomize many of the problems of Native Americans (American Indians), including poverty, unemployment, and ethnic prejudice. Widely dispersed in the arid southwestern part of the country, they have, like many tribes, voted to keep their reservation dry, ever since national and state prohibitions were repealed and they were given that option in the late 1950s. Nevertheless, many of them continue to drink, just as they did earlier (Heath, 1964).

Because drinking is ideally a social occasion, it most often occurs when traditional ceremonies (combining healing and religious observance) bring large crowds together, or when a rodeo, fair, or other such special occasion does. Drinks tend to be certain brands of fortified wines, whiskey, or malt liquor that would be cheap if there were not the surcharge occasioned by bootlegging (smuggling, and clandestinely selling, which puts the dealer at risk of arrest). Small groups, usually of men but sometimes including a few women, tend to cluster on the fringes of a crowd, or walk some distance away so as not to be conspicuous, and share a bottle or more in unceremonious rounds. The shaman or curer may drink openly from time to time to improve his performance, just as a skilled and popular politician may drink to warm up before giving a speech. A few notorious Indian bars (usually in towns bordering the reservation) are regularly frequented by those few Navajo who drink often in public places, and they get a reputation as noisy, boisterous hangouts.

The few long-term studies that have been conducted show that these highly visible forms of drinking are far from typical, however. Most Navajo drinkers actually are older males, often relatively wealthy and prestigious members of the community. Contrary to expectations, drinking sometimes enhances more than it detracts from ceremonies, inasmuch as some of the elders use drinking occasions as opportunities to instruct young men about the many and complex aspects of that part of their culture. And drinking by the curer may help his memory as he chants long myths, creates elaborate sand-paintings, directs the ceremonial dancing, sings various roles (sometimes in falsetto), and tends to the patient and his or her family, sometimes almost continuously during four days and nights.

When they drink, young Navajos tend to continue until they are drunk. If they become aggressive, their targets are not those among whom they have been drinking but others, often at some distance, with whom strained social relations are a function of role expectations (father-in-law, or brothers, for example, but never mother-in-law). If away from home, a drunk is likely to be arrested as a public nuisance, and a convenient fine is often whatever massive handmade silver jewelry he may be wearing at the time. The elders, by contrast, usually drink quietly, moderately, and with no negative outcomes.

Although their large reservation has a sparse population in terms of persons per square mile, the land is so poor and the economy so underdeveloped that pressures to leave often overcome emotional and familial attachments to the land. As the Navajo have increasingly entered the money economy and the labor market, new opportunities have proliferated, and new stresses also. We are fortunate that a couple of scholars have paid close attention to their drinking not only on the reservation but also in nearby towns, over a considerable length of time—attention to personal experiences, larger contextual factors, and the dynamics of change in the world about them.

It is striking that they found the heaviest drinkers among the Navajo to be not, as many would predict, the poorest, unemployed, low status individuals, but rather the most wealthy, who are secure in their professional, economic, and social status. Not only did that pattern emerge in the major baseline study (Levy & Kunitz, 1974), but it persisted during a quarter of a century during which many other things changed significantly (Kunitz & Levy, 1994).

Another widespread misconception is that those Indians who drink the most would be those most assimilated and acculturated, between two worlds in their orientation, and unsuccessful in their own societies as well as in relations with the dominant surrounding culture. On the contrary, Levy and Kunitz (1974) found among the Navajo that "... the highest intensity of involvement with drinking and the greatest use of alcohol was found among the most traditional and least acculturated group, while the lowest use and involvement was found in the most acculturated off-reservation group." It was and remains vaguely shameful for a woman to drink more than a sip or two, lest she be thought to be a "loose woman" who might be sexually available.

The stereotype that scornful outsiders often bring to Navajo drinking is the idea that alcohol would serve as an escape from their intolerable life situation. What people with such an expectation fail to recognize is that many of the most successful Navajo do not aspire to acculturate or mimic the lifeways of the surrounding population. On the contrary, they are comfortable with many aspects of their life, dressing informally, driving pickup trucks, and living in traditional octagonal hogans, often far from electricity, paved roads, or indoor plumbing.

Far from providing an escape, drinking often serves to help such people stay in touch with the world around them and with the cosmic harmony that is a primary value in their naturalistic view of things. Supported by a core of traditional institutions including clans, and extended families with tight bonds of affection and mutual support, in a system where most sickness can be diagnosed and treated in traditional rites where everyone takes part, they often find the surrounding culture not just unattractive but repulsive. Competition is not valued, and one must be wary of excelling at anything that was not approved by the divine beings who went before. A singer or healer is a shaman, combining some of the best qualities of a priest, physician, and operatic stage manager, who can gain power from altered states of consciousness. He is able not only to help sick people by conducting elaborate rites but can, in their view, even help to restore an imbalance or disharmony that has affected the entire community. In such a situation, drink can be a tool for the common good, as long as it is properly used by those who know best how to use it.

LIMITATIONS OF THE DATA

It is not always easy to know who drinks and who does not. In even the simplest and most open of societies, there are certain realms of behavior where privacy prevails, certain areas where an outside observer is not welcome, and certain times when people do things among themselves while the researcher is asleep or away. In other cultures, the very complexity and diversity may militate against one's being able to sample the full gamut of behaviors, or to identify all the various ways that people of different sex, age, or social position drink, or do anything else, for that matter.

Where the aim of an investigator is not just to make a qualitative description but also to count and measure details in such a way that statistical manipulations of the data will be meaningful and quantitative comparison with other studies can be made, then one is tempted to rely on a survey, selecting a manageably small sample of the population, and trying to elicit accurate information from or about those individuals. The sample may be random, representative, or sometimes even deliberately skewed to include a disproportionate number of respondents in some specific category that appears to be of special interest or importance.

Construction of the instrument, which most laypersons would call a questionnaire, is an elaborate and highly specialized task (Cahalan, Cisin, & Crossley, 1969; Room, 1990). The intent is to provide a uniform stimulus that will elicit responses that are both valid (that is to say, true), and reliable (that is, consistent if the same question were asked another way or at another time). The precise phrasing of each question is important, in the hope of avoiding any misunderstanding or reservations on the part of any of the many respondents. The sequence in which the questions are posed is also important, both for rapport and pacing of the interview. A delicate balance is sought between asking too few questions, which will limit the amount of information collected and the associations that can be demonstrated, or too many questions, which can be expensive and, worse yet, is likely to annoy respondents. People often assume that devising a questionnaire is easy, but trained specialists devote meticulous attention to successive drafts, each of which is pretested on a few people before it is reproduced for use in the field. The peculiar combination of drudgery and excitement that is involved in this kind of research has, to my knowledge, never been written about in other than a dry and idealized way, but it is evident in discussion with any serious practitioner of the craft.

Public opinion polls evolved into social surveys with increasing attention to sampling and to eliciting details about quantity and frequency of drinking. The United States has been in the forefront during much of the 50 years that this has been sporadically done, and researchers in other countries have often adopted many of the same questions, paying little attention to cultural variations that might render them less appropriate in other contexts. A brief and informally written account of this history explains many of the continuing shortcomings of survey research (Clark, 1991); a more detailed and scholarly account has also been written by one of the pioneers in that field (Room, 1991b).

Anthropologists have tended to be critical of such research, largely because the basic premise that a survey "... is the only way to learn what individual respondents do and think" (Clark & Hilton, 1991, p. 1) is patently false in the experience of those who have learned that observation and informal interviewing yield both more and more valid details about both behavior and beliefs (Heath, 1977). It is undeniable, however, that surveys are far more efficient as a means of collecting quantitative data about large populations. Ideally and increasingly, qualitative and quantitative research are being used as complementary rather than conflicting approaches to expanding our understanding of the world of drinking occasions. Much of the rest of this chapter about who drinks is based on national or regional surveys which provide insights that no amount of meticulous observation and description could yield. Another important part of our discussion comes from ethnographic studies that look closely at patterns of behavior in a natural setting and try to interpret meanings and functions in relation to that specific context.

One issue that has concerned epidemiologists who try to count and measure who drinks what, and to correlate those data with consequences has been the basic questions of frequency and quantity, how often and how much people drink (Room, 1991b). Any population shows a range of variation, but grouping individuals into classes or types allows for significant simplification of the data, at some cost to the precision of findings to be sure. At the outset, it seemed important to distinguish drinkers from abstainers, but even that is not so simple as it may appear. There are many people who never choose to have a drink on their own initiative but who will join a toast at New Years, a wedding, or some other special occasion, and respondents are usually called abstainers if they report having had no more than one drink in the past year. For more detailed discussion of the meanings and limitations of this category, see a later section of this chapter.

Even after nondrinkers are excluded, there remains a varied segment of the population who say they drink. Their consumption varies from as little as two drinks a year to as much as 30 drinks a day, requiring that any generalizations, to be meaningful, must relate to smaller and more homogeneous groups. In the United States, when such studies were developed in the 1950s, the apparently simple scheme of separating drinkers into "light," "moderate," and "heavy" groupings on the basis of frequency and quantity during a week or a month seemed adequate for analytical purposes. But now we find that the threshold commonly used for "heavy" is so low that it would include many who drink according to the cautious Dietary Guidelines for Americans (U.S. Department of Agriculture & Department of Health and Human Services, 1995), and it is difficult to learn about risks (or anything else) concerning those who drink more.

In light of the increasing scientific evidence that moderate drinking is often beneficial for health, several governmental agencies have explicitly provided guidelines for "moderate" or "sensible drinking" (International Center for Alcohol Policies, 1997). Usually based on in-depth review of the literature by committees including medical and other specialists, such recommendations have, nevertheless, differed considerably, reflecting the extent to which attitudes impact on even so limited a judgment. To cite the extremes, the recommendation in Netherlands is 20–30 g. of ethanol "a few times a week" for men or women; in the Basque Country of Spain, it is 70 g. per day for men but only 28 for women.

In chapter 1, we already saw how the failure to delimit what is meant by a drinking occasion and the peculiar convention of treating all of any day's drinking as if it took place on a single occasion have resulted in misleading pronouncements about risks and danger associated with drinking. Other researchers have vividly shown how much of the relevant terminology that is considered basic among English-speakers in Europe and North America fails to be understood, even by English-speaking professionals, in other parts of the world (Bennett, Janea, Grant, & Sartorius, 1993; Helzer & Canino, 1992; Room, Janca, Bennet, Schmidt, & Sartorius, 1996). In spite of all such limitations, it is to surveys that we turn for indications of what portion of the male population drink and what portion of females, which beverages are drunk most by different classes, whether drinking increases with age, and similar questions.

GENDER AND AGE

No matter how small, isolated, or relatively homogeneous a society may appear to be on the world stage, there is none that is truly homogeneous. Every population, in its own way, allows, expects, requires, or limits the behavior of individuals on the basis of broad categorization or classification. Among the basic categories that societies attend to, gender and age are universal. Although what they mean and how they affect life chances differ enormously from one culture to another, none ignores either of them.

Gender

One of the most universally recognized ways of classifying people is by sex, or, more accurately, by gender, which is the social and cultural expression of what are often and sometimes erroneously thought to be the recurrent differences between the sexes. Rightly or wrongly, gender plays a major role in shaping the ways the world drinks (Plant, 1997), but not all of those differences relate to biology. The statistics that we have concerning proportions of populations who drink provide a good illustration of the kinds of large-scale information that can effectively be compiled by means of social surveys. As a complement to those numbers, the fine-grained descriptions of events and patterns of behavior that illustrate how those numerical differences are played out in everyday life can be obtained only through observation and open-ended interviewing, which are the core of ethnographic methods.

For example, a 1990 survey showed that 71% of adult males in the U.S. were drinkers and only 59% of women (Hilton, 1991f). In Ireland, the comparable figures are much lower: about 55% of men and 10% of women drink (Plant, 1995). By contrast, 90% of French men drink and 70% of French women do (Nahoum-Grappe, 1995); in Germany, the figures are almost as high at 87% and 68% (Vogt, 1995). A real difference is easily noted when we find that India's drinkers are only 13% of the adult male population and 3% of adult females (Mohan & Sharma, 1995).

Those 1990 figures help us to distinguish a few "wet cultures" in Europe from a "dry" one in Asia and an intermediate one in North America. But they do not much help us to understand what drinking means to anyone, nor what roles it may play in everyday life or with respect to celebrations. Although they clearly show that more men than women drink in those countries, there is no hint about whether they drink in the same or very different ways, on similar or different occasions, for like or unlike reasons.

It may be that survey data such as these give early hints of historic changes. For example, in 1970, 75% of U.S. adult males were drinkers and only 56% of females (Hilton, 1991f). If the numbers are accurate, fewer men were drinking 20 years later, and more women. Does this mean that the drinking behavior of the genders is converging? That may well be happening, not just in the U.S. but also in several European countries.

In almost every society where attention has been paid to drinking, women as well as men are known to drink. It came as a surprise to some that, when researchers carefully analyzed data on alcohol use from the 139 societies that were then well documented (Keller, 1965), they found only four that did not allow both sexes to drink, and only one that accepted drunkenness on the part of men but not women. That degree of permissiveness is greater than many would expect, but it does not contradict the general observation that, typically, males drink more and more often than females.

As is often the case, even so broad a proposition is not without exception. In recent years, a couple of interesting cases have come to light in which women drink more than men. In a multitribal study among Native Americans in the western U.S., Weibel-Orlando (1986) reported that "... rural Sioux women drink more frequently than do the rural Sioux men" (p. 178) [and] "... rural Sioux women actually consume more alcohol per session than do the rural Sioux or Five Tribes men" (pp. 179–180). In Malaysia, another interethnic study found that "Most participants [of both sexes] reported using alcohol for special occasions only.... An exception to this were the 7 female Malay users of alcohol with daily consumption of wine in quantity being the common pattern. Daily use was also more common among Chinese females (21%) than among Chinese males (5%)" (Armstrong, 1985, p. 1804). The samples were small in each of these cases, and the subjects were recent migrants, but those variables do not lessen the fact that they contradict, perhaps importantly, what had been thought to be a universal pattern.

From a strictly biological standpoint, it probably matters that a given amount of alcohol generally has a greater impact on females, partly because they tend to be smaller, partly because they tend to have more fat (and thus less water in their systems to dilute alcohol), and partly because they generally have less of a specific enzyme that helps to metabolize alcohol in the digestive tract.

More sociological explanations have been many and varied (Neve, Lemmens, & Drop, 1997). Usually burdened with repetitive and requisite tasks of tending to children, cooking, hauling water and firewood, women generally have less free time than do men in which they need not worry about drinking as possibly being an interference. In terms of access or availability of alcohol, it is generally women who are better placed than men, especially in developing countries, inasmuch as they are usually the producers of homebrew and are often among the major distributors of commercial beverages when they become popular.

It is often said that females are more at risk or have more to lose than men, when honor, shame, parenting, and other values are involved, especially where there is a markedly double-standard for the genders within a population. Anyone who has paid attention to issues of sex or gender must be struck by the frequency and degree to which social and cultural conventions diverge from the logic of biology, and a widespread double-standard with respect to drinking probably has roots in power relationships as do most other double-standards (Wilsnack & Wilsnack, 1997). For example, drinking by men may be more acceptable because men normally enjoy more time-out than their female counterparts, but that leaves unresolved the question of why women enjoy less time-out. Similarly, it is often said that men "have less to lose" in the event that drinking should result in impairment, but the question of what might be lost, how valuable it is, and who can better afford to lose it remains unstated.

Some sort of double-standard for men and for women is fairly common, with respect to morality in general as well as with respect to drinking. The details differ from one culture to another, but an historical glimpse at the English case is suggestive of a pattern that is now widespread in Europe and North America. Until the 1700s, both men and women in England enjoyed considerable freedom in terms of where and when they might drink, but a sharp decline in real wages at that time effectively sanctioned redistribution of household income in favor of men. Drinking away from home flourished as a male-dominated activity, and, at the same time, classical sources describing Roman female temperance were given new emphasis. As commercial brewing became more widespread and profitable, beer with hops began to eclipse ale, and men took over what had been a major women's realm of economic activity. The alewife and brewster quickly became images of scorn whereas they had earlier been seen as nurturing and companionable. The home began to take on the imagery of a sanctuary of sobriety, managed by the temperate housewife (Warner, 1997).

Not only do men drink more than women in almost every culture, but there are many in which drinking itself is interpreted as an heroically manly act. The New Zealand "kiwi bloke" sees drinking as a badge of masculinity (Park, 1995). The *machismo* (or exaggerated assertive masculinity) of heavy drinkers throughout Latin America is associated with boisterous and often dangerous displays of daring (Gutman, 1996). In Germany (Vogt, 1995) and Sweden (Nyberg & Allebeck, 1995), women and children are not supposed to be around when drinking takes place. The Japanese are another population who feel strongly that, although drinking with meals is acceptable with people of both sexes and all ages present, drinking by men for sociability is a very different kind of activity to which neither women nor children should be exposed (Yamamuro, 1958). Young hooligans, from Truk to the U.S. to the U.K., combine drinking

An African-American couple transforms their move into a new home with the addition of a celebratory drink. In general, African-Americans appear to drink less than, for example, white or Hispanic populations in the U.S. © *Index Stock Imagery/Chuck St. John.*

with bravado as a way of supposedly demonstrating that they are on the way to becoming men.

The fact that men gather to drink together far more often than do women does not mean that there are no occasions when women exclude men from a session that involves considerable drinking. Striking examples of this latter pattern are some of the Dionysian rites in ancient Greece, which included not only drunkenness but prostitution on the part of women as gestures of worship (Dodds, 1956). Throughout much of the 20th century, housewives in Sweden have enjoyed the institution of "kitchen party," whereby groups of friends and neighbors visit to talk and drink in each other's kitchens by turns (Nyberg & Allebeck, 1995). Much the same thing is evolving in recent years among middle-class urban women in New Zealand (Park, 1995), and in Zambia (Haworth, 1995). Among the Sikaiana of Polynesia, women tend also to drink in same-sex parties, when they can get coconut-sap toddy from the men who make it. They prefer to avoid the sexual advances and the occasional fighting that take place at mixed drinking parties that may last for days. They also avoid becoming drunk, in order to continue overseeing children, food preparation, and other tasks (Donnor, 1994).

Most cultures allow men sometimes to drink to intoxication, and some encourage it occasionally. Although most allow it for women, only a few positively sanction it for women once in a while; among them are the Cuna of Panama (Stout, 1948), and the Quechua (Allen, 1988) and Aymara (Carter, 1977) of the Peruvian and Bolivian Andes.

Among the Paraguayan Abipone, not only was it not allowed that women drink but they were also expected to monitor the men's drinking and to gather up the weapons if there were any hint that someone was becoming aggressive. The line between a jovial drunken celebration and a free-for-all may not have been very clear to an outsider, inasmuch as most of what they did while drinking was to sing and brag about their bravery and skill in warfare (Dobrizhoffer, 1822).

The fact that women have often been the principal or sole manufacturers of beverage alcohol is well known, but its implications have not been fully explored. Homebrewing often allows a woman to use her domestic skills, together with surplus agricultural produce, to yield a value-added marketable product. In many jurisdictions throughout history, both brewing and selling were monopolized by women, often with the active support of the government. Licensing, where it was meaningful, was often reserved for widows or for unwed mothers. Where licensing does not matter, married women often reserved the profits from such ventures for special household needs, or for the education of their children (Maula, 1997). In England from 1300 to 1600, an exceptionally well documented society, an historical study of the subject may hopefully serve as a model for others (Bennett, 1996).

An interesting sidelight to the widespread role of women in making and serving alcohol (whether as brewster, alewife, shebeen queen, waitress, or in another capacity) is the demonstration that easy access to drink does not necessarily mean that one will drink more. Many of the restrictive policies that are currently being recommended and implemented have their basis in the assumption that control of availability is crucial to lessening all kinds of drinking problems, an assumption which the overwhelming body of evidence that we have from historical and cross-cultural studies does little to confirm (Heath, 1988b, 1995).

Gender is an important basis on which any population differs with respect to norms about drinking and associated behaviors but it is far from being the only one.

Age

In every known culture, people are treated differently in large part because of their age. Life expectancies vary, so that a 50-year-old may be middle-aged in one setting and old in another. Responsibilities vary so that an 8-year-old may be charged with the care of a younger sibling, hauling water, gathering firewood, and other tasks in one society, while an 18-year-old may be still virtually free of responsibilities in another. Various culturally-labelled stages in the individual life cycle have very different meanings, especially with respect to drinking, as we have seen in chapter 1. Here are a few of the other ways in which age impinges on the world of drink.

The age at which people may begin to drink is not always clearly specified, but alcohol use certainly varies over the course of a normal lifetime, and in all but a few societies people often hold strong opinions about the propriety of one's drinking at various ages. Hippocrates of Cos, the Greek father of Western medicine in the 4th century B.C., had no doubt that infants ought to drink in order to gain strength, but held that they should be "given their wine diluted and not at all cold" (quoted in Grivetti, 1996). In somewhat surprising contrast, his contemporary, the philosopher Plato, held that "boys under eighteen should not taste wine at all...," although he praised it as "the cure for crabbedness in old age" (Plato, Laws 2.666.A-B).

It is common that infants are given homebrew, whether beer, pulque, chicha, or some similar fermented beverage as food, not only from birth but often earlier, as expectant mothers are encouraged to nourish their unborn children by drinking more than usual. It is also common that a symbolic taste of a stronger beverage containing alcohol may be given to a child early in its life. One of the instances well known in Europe and the Americas is wine touched to the lips of a Jewish boy in connection with the circumcision ritual on his eighth day.

Popular sayings in many cultures encourage nursing mothers to drink, both to stimulate and to enrich their lactation. When they do, that of course introduces a heavier concentration of ethanol into the small body of the suckling than the woman has in her larger body. Far from worrying about any harm that may be done, adults in those cultures are more likely to approve, citing the idea that "wine builds strong bones," or "cleanses (or strengthens) the blood," or that homebrews in general, and especially those made by them, are exceptionally healthful and nutritious.

In modern France (Nahoum-Grappe, 1995), Italy (Cottino, 1995; Lolli et al., 1958), Spain (Gamella, 1995), Portugal, or Greece, it is not unusual for parents to put a little wine in the waterglass of a child, to lend symbolic color and to encourage participation in the rituals of toasting or drinking with meals that are so normal as to be routine. Similarly, throughout China, adults often dip chopsticks into a drink and let children lick them. In such a context, young people learn that drinking is nothing special and that one's behavior should not be affected by it. Learning to drink in that way invariably implies learning simultaneously how not to drink. The French child's glass gets gradually darker over time, until it may be virtually unadulterated wine before adolescence (Anderson, 1968). There is no mystique, then, about drinking, and no unrealistic expectation that it will make anyone more good looking, more powerful, or more sexy. Those few adults who drink too much and say or do inappropriate things are chided, talked about, or even ridiculed, so that drunkenness and impairment come to be viewed as unpleasant rather than attractive.

But it is rare that young children are encouraged to drink—or even given access to—distilled spirits, other than occasional symbolic tasting of an elder's drink. One exception to that widespread pattern is the Dusun of Borneo (Rutter, 1929), who drink both rice beer and palm-gin at almost every social occasion and who consider both drinks to be powerful medicines for virtually every childhood malady. Drunkenness is not any more uncommon among Dusun children, than it is among their elders of both sexes.

Most non-Western cultures pay little attention to a minimum age below which one should not consume beverage alcohol, but at least 48 countries have specific laws that set such a threshold (International Center for Alcohol Policies, 1998a). In 1998, the highest such age was 21 (Malaysia, South Korea, and Ukraine, as well as most states within the U.S.). Iceland and Japan set 20, and others lower, many with a variety of exceptions allowed under special conditions (at home, with parental consent, accompanied by an older guardian or spouse, and so forth). In the U.K., a child over five may drink at home with parental consent; some jurisdictions distinguish between beer and wine (generally permitted at a lower age) and spirits. Often the minimum legal age, although popularly believed to relate to consumption, actually relates to purchase and possession, behaviors that are far simpler to police and enforce. Such is the case in the U.S. To have so high a minimum age is especially ironic in a country where 18 marks legal adulthood for voting, concluding contracts, marrying without parental permission, serving in the military, and other important purposes. Some critics have pointed out that prohibition-by-age lends a special aura to drink that makes it especially attractive precisely because it is reserved for elders and associated with glamour and power.

The idea that children need to be somehow protected from alcohol is alien in China, France, and Italy, to name only a few major countries. Among the few surveys of drinking patterns that asked about children's use of alcohol, it was found in Cameroon to be "... an important element in the traditional life ..." one which "... corresponds with general drinking patterns" (Yguel et al., 1990, p. 122). In a similar manner, it is not at all unusual for young children to drink in Honduras (Vittetoe, 1995) or in Chile (Medina, 1995), just as it was not in the U.K. or U.S. until the mid-1700s. Early Egyptian papyri counsel a good mother to send her child off to school with enough beer and bread; cafeterias in many French schools offer wine in coin-operated machines, just as kvas (a weak beer made from bread) is available to anyone from machines on urban street corners in Russia. Distilled beverages are similarly sold by machines in Japan with no regard to the age of buyers, although these are currently being phased out.

Children are welcome in any grocery store in Spain or France, where wine and other drinks are sold with no concern for age. In many small towns throughout Spain, the only place where one can get ice cream, a favored treat in summer, is at the bar. The author was recently surprised to see a sign in the window of a bar indicating that minors under 16 were not allowed. Having never before encountered such a notice in more than 20 years of annual sojourns in Spain, he went in for a drink and eventually got around to asking about the sign. The owner gestured to an electronic game-machine in the corner and explained, "It's that damned machine. Sure, it makes money, but not only is it noisy, we have to look out for the kids. Those games are addictive, you know." No bar without such a machine made any effort to exclude children of any age, and some Spanish bars, like pubs in Great Britain (Jackson & Smyth, 1976) are much like community centers, with whole families spending long evenings there enjoying games, music, talk, and socializing among friends and neighbors.

The age-grade of adolescence, intermediate between childhood and adulthood, is often marked at the onset by puberty but, even with so dramatic a start, it is not recognized as a meaningful category in many societies. Those who do pay attention to such a class of person often expect them to apply themselves to learning the skills and graces that will be important when they later assume adult roles, with marriage and greater responsibilities. In some other societies, however, it is a privileged prolongation of childhood with responsibilities deferred and considerable freedom in terms of a youthful subculture that is allowed to include some slightly asocial or antisocial aspects. For example, Winnebago Indians afford a young man the luxury of being a "hell-raiser" (Hill, 1974) for several years with heavy episodic drinking and harmless pranks expected. Such behavior helps these young men "get it out of their system" before each settles down as a "family man." Truk's weekend warriors (cf. chapter 2 case study, Marshall, 1979a) and their neighbors (Nason, 1975) who combine drinking with assertive youthful risk-taking, reflect a similar pattern, as do South Boston "townies" looking for adventure and fights downtown (Burns, 1980). Episodic heavy drinking is often associated with aggressive and other excessive behavior on the part of adolescents where it is tolerated. In addition to being tolerated, it may even be approved. Societies, often deliberately, appear to provide for such drinking and release of tensions.

It is ironic that so much of the scientific literature about drinking in this age-group deals with college students, if only because they comprise so unrepresentative a sample of their respective populations. Although we have a disproportionate amount of data on drinking by students, we are similarly almost lacking data on other youths who are not in school or college and who constitute the vast majority of their age-mates. Reliance on students is by no means restricted to those few countries that have extremely high rates of postsecondary schooling and where most of the studies of drinking are published. Such diverse and scattered countries as Israel, Kuwait, Malaysia, Singapore, Zambia, and Zimbabwe also have disproportionate information about students, and a marked lack of information about the general populations (Grant, 1998). One need not know much about scientific methods to recognize how much cheaper and more convenient it is for professors to survey or experiment on that group than it would be to seek out their age-mates, or others in that community or any other.

The same age cohort, of both sexes, may drink heavily almost every night in urban Spain without causing any trouble other than a little noise in the vicinity of the bars where they congregate (Gamella, 1995). The high rate of accidental deaths among U.S. teenagers is often attributed to drinking, whereas it might with similar justification be attributed to youthful risk-taking or poor handling of automobiles; inexperienced and often untrained youths are licensed to drive, sometimes at the unusually low age of 16.

This has prompted some authorities to raise the possibility of developing a kind of drinking-license (a permit, based on some education and training about how to drink and what to expect) that might qualify some of those who are legally underage to drink on campus, whereas unlicensed drinkers would still be subject to penalties (Gose, 1996). Concern over young drinkers has become especially acute with reference to college students in the U.S. in recent years. Among the many reasons for this is the fact that they are a young population (roughly 18–22), many of whom are away from home for the first time and newly freed from other scheduling constraints, amid a group of age-mates who often value socializing. They constitute an educational elite (statistically, if not always intellectually), ostensibly slated to be the leaders of tomorrow, and yet, a few each year fall victim to a toxic overload (sometimes resulting in death) as a result of drinking too much too fast as part of a fraternity initiation or other prank. In addition, episodic heavy drinking clearly interferes with studies, sleep, and social relationships for a significant number of college students at different kinds and sizes of schools and in different areas (Wechsler, Davenport, Dowdall, Moeykens, & Castillo, 1994; Wechsler, Dowdall, Davenport, & Rimm, 1995). Not only do many of the drinkers suffer deleterious outcomes from such drinking, but others who live near them may be bothered by "secondary binge effects" (Wechsler, Moeykens, Davenport, Castillo, & Hansen, 1995).

In an irony that signals the concern that many people have about protecting young people from alcohol, there are instances in which the legal drinking age is higher than majority (the legal age for signing contracts, voting, holding office, getting any kind of license, or other adult rights and privileges). Although it is rarely phrased in such terms, this prohibition-by-age is often acutely resented by young people. It also appears often to be flouted by those who wish to sample the forbidden fruit, imbuing drinking with a mystique that is especially attractive to risk-takers and other vulnerable youths. Such a ban also virtually assures that underage drinking, being stigmatized from the outset as deviant behavior, will result in outcomes that are problematic for those who publicly indulge. It often also results in intemperate drinking by the inexperienced, who are likely to hide their drinking from their elders. The crucial fear that alcohol is a gateway to drug use appears unjustified (Golub & Johnson, 1998), just as does the presumption that early drinking leads to problems later in life (Prescott & Kendler, 1999).

Much of recent episodic heavy drinking among young people that has at-tracted negative attention appears to have such roots, occurring where young people are supposedly most protected from drink. Tragically, the lack of su-pervision by beginning drinkers out to enjoy novel experiences, often results in harm to property, or injury to individuals, sometimes even in death. The concern that granting young people permission to drink would result in worse outcomes—the opposite of what we would expect on the basis of cross-cultural evidence—perpetuates the paradox of so-called protection which often turns out to be far more harmful.

Restriction by age is rarely so clearly spelled out as it is in those countries that have a minimum legal drinking age. Few ethnographers have tried to be very specific when differentiating "children" (often described as not drinking) from "youths" or "young people," with the implication that, unless otherwise specified, anyone may drink.

Alcohol use varies over the course of a normal lifetime, with a general tendency to increase from puberty until marriage and then to decline gradually. In the U.S., the high age at which it is usually legal to drink (21), results in a foreshortening of one's drinking career, with males below 26 being far heavier drinkers than any other group (Fillmore, 1988). For young men in Finland (Ala-suutari, 1992), drunkenness is valued as a proof of the freedom of the individual, in protest against the older generation in general, but especially against the sup-posedly oppressive religiosity of the church, with both emphasizing self-control, denial of individual desires, and acceptance of social constraints. There is some indication that drinking was reserved for the elderly in Aztec Mexico (Madsen & Madsen, 1969), in striking contrast with the fear of many North Americans that drinking is especially risky for them.

The Chamula of southern Mexico (Pozas, 1962) are like many populations in their strict adherence to the rule that individuals within a group drink only in sequence according to age. By contrast, there are other groups, including the nearby Mestizos described by Kearney (1970), who insist that everyone present drink simultaneously, and who are offended if anyone declines. Among most of the peoples in Nigeria, it is common courtesy that the oldest present are the first to drink, with others taking turns in sequence by seniority (Oshodin, 1995). The Tupinamba of Brazil (Staden, 1928) are another group who, no matter how often they have a drinking party, are careful that individuals are served—and drink—in strict sequence by descending age. The Chagga reserve the largest dried calabashes as vessels for the drinking of beer by the oldest and highest status males; gradually smaller calabashes mark relative age and status among other members of a drinking party. Similarly, the top foam of the homebrewed beer is a delicacy reserved to the senior person in any such group.

Although young and marginal men are most often seen drinking among the Navajo, that has more to do with their drinking patterns (in bars, at rodeos, on the fringes of curing ceremonies, or on the street in towns bordering the reservation) than it does with quantity and frequency. Close attention to actual alcohol consumption by a cross-section of that Native American population has clearly shown for a long time that older well established men actually drink more and more often but do so in less conspicuous ways (Levy & Kunitz, 1974; Kunitz & Levy, 1994).

The transition from adolescence to adulthood is often marked by a ritual, sometimes by marriage, initiation into warfare or hunting. Or it may go unmarked. When it is marked, there is often clear specification in the literature that part of the altered status is permission to drink.

We have seen a peculiar exception to that (U.S.) in which even official adulthood does not convey the legal right to drink, but usually it comes much earlier. Quite apart from minimum legal drinking age, the customary age for drinking is the same or lower. Among the Meo of Laos, "Every adult must drink at specific times according to age, sex, and social role" (Westermeyer, 1971). Among the rites of passage that pertain to drinking in various societies, we can cite marriage as an extremely common one and the birth of a child as another (see chapter 1 for other examples). In fact, it is not at all uncommon to find that adolescents drink more than their elders. Contrary to the stereotype that many people believe about drinking as a progressive habit, it is commonplace to find the phenomenon generally called "maturing out," whereby both the frequency and quantity of drinking declines, often markedly, in middle age from what it had been earlier. This runs against what many members of Alcoholics Anonymous believe, but it is well documented in terms of surveys, with a few exceptions that will be mentioned.

EDUCATION, OCCUPATION, CASTE, AND CLASS

In non-Western societies there is often little differentiation among people in terms of education, occupation, caste, or class, and yet, in those societies where any one of these does matter, it tends to loom large in the life and the life chances of the individual and his or her family. What is nominally a concern about education often proves in reality to be more a concern about formal schooling. Occupation and caste are virtually synonymous in India and yet quite distinct elsewhere. Class can relate to one or a combination of factors: to hereditary status, to prestige, to family income, or to a host of other variables that are not always clearly specified. In looking at these several categories, it is clear that every society is made up of smaller societies, and many cultures have spawned distinctive subcultures. That these difference sometimes find expression in the world of drink and drinking occasions should come as no surprise, although some of the specific ways in which the differences are expressed may be of interest.

Most social surveys mistakenly use the label "education" to refer to number of years, grades, or forms of formal schooling, with no recognition that education is a lifelong process that occurs in many other contexts as well. To be sure, schooling does loom large in shaping the opportunities available to individuals in most developed countries, and increasingly that is the case in developing societies as well. It tends also to show some correlation with patterns of drinking.

Quantification lends itself to the identification and labeling of trends or associations. We all know that not every correlation implies causality, so one must look more closely at the minutiae of actual behavior if one is to understand the meanings and implications of some such numbers. Illustrative of the findings of survey research on the topic at hand is the fact that, among those with some secondary schooling or less, 73% of Canadian adults are drinkers, and among those who completed secondary schooling, 87% are. In that same population, 88% of "managers/professionals" drink, and 86% of "blue-collars" (Cheung & Erickson, 1995). In Egypt, a predominantly Islamic country, the wealthier and more highly educated members of the population drink more often and drink more in terms of quantity (Ashour, 1995). It might be tempting to interpret those findings as indicating that drinking increases with education, and that it also increases with wealth and prestige. In many European countries, those both appear to be the case. But in Ireland, much of Asia, most of Latin America, and on most Indian reservations in North America, the opposite is true.

It matters, for example, that most of the drinkers in Egypt happen to be Coptic Christians. It also matters that, in a pattern that is reminiscent of feudal times in eastern Europe, plantation owners in Malaysia still provide part of the pay to east Indian workers in moonshine, and encourage even more drinking as a way of recapturing their wages and keeping them in virtual debt-servitude (Arokiasamy, 1995). In much the same way, mine-owners in eastern Africa pay part of the wage in drink to their employees who are away from home for several months and living in isolated mining-camps (Mitchell, 1956).

In a broad sense, traditional and homebrewed drinks tend to be favored by those with less schooling, and commercial, international, or cosmopolitan drinks by those with more. So much is that the case that a more prestigious drink (usually much more expensive) may be chosen in a public place by someone who does not have the educational or other status that would normally be associated with a specific drink, but who is aspiring to or attempting to demonstrate that higher status. Since schooling often figures prominently in the assignment of social class or status, that same shift from homebrew to bottled beer is often a marker of transition (or aspiration) from lower to middle class in Africa and Latin America, and spirits are often a marker of transition (or aspiration) from middle to upper. The enormous success that has been enjoyed by European and American beers in developing countries may be partially due to their value as objects of prestige that are generally affordable, and widespread efforts to counterfeit European and American spirits may partly result from their use as badges of status.

There have been a number of studies that indicate different drinking patterns among members of different occupations. Few such studies provide much more than information on quantity and frequency of drinking, although some also link those data to rates of various kinds of drinking problems. In many developing countries and cultures, occupational differentiation is minimal, so that such categorization has little meaning. However, in complex industrial and urban settings, one's occupation can play an important role in self-identification, social stratification, hours and amount of free time, work expectations on the job, and so forth.

To illustrate how such classification can relate to drinking patterns, it is commonplace that popular stereotypes arise, some accurate in the sense of reflecting norms, but none invariably true. Actors, painters, musicians, and other bohemians are generally thought to drink more than farmers or shopkeepers. Priests, teachers, and physicians are (often incorrectly) thought to drink less than most people. Some bartenders and waiters find that frequent sipping while on the job can be a hazard. Although they themselves tend not to drink much, cocktail waitresses appreciate beverage alcohol in a variety of ways and often manipulate the symbolism of drinks in ways that elicit larger tips from their customers (Spradley & Mann, 1975). It should be no surprise that laborers in breweries (although not brewers) drink more than most people; until recently, many breweries offered ample opportunities for anyone in the plant to drink freely. Distilleries and wineries generally do not give such a perquisite to their employees.

Social workers and librarians are generally abstemious, at least in comparison with artists and writers, some of whom drink so much that there is serious consideration by scholars of a possible connection between drinking and creativity. There is an entire journal devoted exclusively to studies of alcohol and drugs in literature (*Dionysos: The Journal of Literature and Addiction*). It is often a subject of popular humor that all of the U.S. novelists who have won the Nobel Prize for Literature also happened to be notoriously heavy drinkers. The bohemian lifestyle that is so closely linked with many modern artists in urban milieus includes a focus on drinking as both relaxation and socialization. In India, traditionally, different castes have represented different occupations. In Australia, pearl divers are often given a drink whenever they successfully surface with a promising oyster shell, and many alcoholics, rightly or wrongly, attribute their later dependence on alcohol to that informal system of reward (Brady, 1998).

It is not uncommon, cross-culturally, to limit the drinking of an individual whose role makes him or her responsible for the fate of many. In the days of the Old Testament, this is probably why the high priest was not supposed to drink (Lev. 10:9). In more recent times, there are legislative efforts in some countries to protect the public from risk in various ways. One such is requiring that bus drivers, train engineers, airplane pilots, and others on whose skill and keen judgment the lives of many people depend, not drink for a specific number of hours before they begin their work.

In medieval Europe, monks were often portrayed by artists as benign drunks, and criminals as aggressive ones; although it is difficult to estimate how accurate those stereotypes may have been, everyone seems to agree that both groups

Christian nuns in Belgium enjoy drinking as part of a regular meal. Some drinking practices, including abstention, are associated with people of a particular culture or occupation. © CORBIS/Hulton-Deutsch Collection.

included a disproportionate number of heavy drinkers. Miners and factory workers also have reputations as heavy drinkers in many cultures (Taussig, 1980). In Bolivia, rum and coca are both consumed and offered as a daily gift to the malevolent spirits who are thought to guard the riches in a mine (Nash, 1972).

In the centuries before large-scale mechanization became so integral a part of industry, drinking on the job was commonplace and posed few problems. With the increasing pace and risk of work in modern factories, however, there has tended to be a separation between work and drinking for most blue-collar workers. A huge U.S. automobile manufacturing plant is remarkable for the extent to which the subculture of the employees includes and supports drinking on the job (Ames & Janes, 1987). Professional gamblers, some journalists, and people involved in the field of publishing talk about themselves as often having to drink as part of getting along well with people who are important to their doing their job. Much union business is transacted while longshoremen drink (Mars, 1987). Throughout history, the armed forces of several nations have had reputations as heavy drinkers when they are off-duty, and sometimes heavy drinking appears to have been a deliberate preparation for ensuing combat.

The popular stereotype of the drunken sailor looks very different when critically examined. Long sea voyages in earlier centuries were difficult because fresh water so quickly spoils when kept in casks. To make the putrid water palatable, an English admiral had it mixed half-and-half with rum; the resulting drink was called grog, in honor of "Old Grogram," his nickname because he favored uniforms made of that blend of silk and wool. Starting around 1740, a portion (or "tot") was doled out, under strict supervision, daily to each sailor. Subsequently, lime juice was often added; it had the dual value of improving the flavor of the drink and staving off scurvy, which was a chronic problem among sailors with their limited diet. Hence, British sailors came to be known as "limeys." The custom of serving grog on English naval ships survived until 1970 (July 31 was "Black Tot Day"), when it was discontinued in the interest of safety and efficiency (Pack, 1982).

The U.S. Navy's regulations on drink have differed markedly, an interesting microcosm of changing attitudes and policies over two centuries in a highly controlled institution. In 1794, there was a daily ration of a 1/2 pint of distilled spirits or one quart of beer; the beer option was dropped three years later. By 1831, sailors were given another choice. Anyone could forego his daily drink and be paid an extra six cents. In 1842, the ration was reduced to one gill (1/4 pint), and commissioned officers, midshipmen, and enlisted men under 21 were excluded. The commutation rate dropped to three cents a day in 1847 but went up to four in the next year. In 1862, the spirits ration was discontinued and spirits were banned from all naval vessels (except as medical stores). Pay in lieu of drink rose to five cents a day. In 1893, wardroom and steerage offices were allowed to form a "wine mess" whereby wines they had bought could be served with meals. A total ban on alcoholic beverages aboard came in 1914, and it was extended to include all military posts in 1917. By 1918, a 5-mile dry zone was required around U.S. bases. In 1985, the Navy decided to comply with state laws ashore, but still banned drinks aboard. Medical stores are still excepted from the ban, and an occasional shot of whiskey is prescribed "to lessen shock or reduce tension."

Sailors in other capacities often go without drink for long periods of time, cautious about the dangers of a situation in which they are always on call, battling the elements and doing hazardous work. But when they come ashore, many choose to drink and to do so in excessive ways. Cowboys after a cattle drive, lumberjacks returning from the forest, workers ashore from oil rigs, and others who spend considerable blocks of time away from mixed company often follow the pattern of episodic heavy consumption when they have long-deferred pay, alternating with long periods of abstention.

Diviners, priests, and shamans among the Ixil and Quiché Indians sometimes speak of heavy drinking as a burden required by their jobs (Adams, 1995; Colby & Colby, 1981). In Chile bakers often complain that too much free time during the day causes them to drink too much (Medina, 1995). Chefs' apprentices often find that they should have left more wine for cooking and taken less for drinking. A "big man" in Papua New Guinea is thankful that his position as nonhereditary regional leader does not require that he sample each of the cases of beer that he must distribute at periodic feasts where members of widely dispersed communities trade all kinds of goods and keep the peace (Marshall, 1982).

In some contexts, specific beverages are associated with specific social groups. Mass-produced commercial beers appear to be favored by younger males in the U.S., and brandies by older and wealthier males. Sweet and colorful mixed drinks are favored by females, whereas single-malt scotches appeal to men. Among the Azande, homebrews made from millet, maize, or banana are thought to be good for any man, woman or child; however, when any one of those drinks is distilled, the resulting liquor is the prerogative of only a few men who have high status as local chiefs or nobles.

The fact that caste is more important than religion for certain realms of life is vividly illustrated in the western Indian village where two castes use different intoxicants. Members of the prestigious Brahmin caste customarily drink bhang, a tea made from cannabis leaves, whereas the lower-caste warrior Rajputs drink daru, a liquor distilled locally. Both groups are devout Hindus; each prides itself on the favored drink, and each abhors as sacrilege what the other caste drinks (Carstairs, 1954). In another instance, a man was expelled from his caste simply because his son drank some wine (Patnaik, 1960).

Within the discipline of sociology, there is heated discussion about whether class has more to do with wealth, status, occupation, education, self-concept, or some combination of those factors. Ironically, most of what is written about drinking patterns and class does not reflect such conceptual subtleties, but relies on simple indices of either household income or self-identification.

In the U.S. for example, consumption of beer is greater among the lower class and of wine and spirits among the upper class (Hilton, 1991d). The same tends to hold in most of Europe. For reasons that are not at all clear, low income drinkers in North America tend to drink in larger groups and for longer periods of time than do high income drinkers (Single & Storm, 1985). In France, the middle class drink the least, and they also have reduced their drinking most rapidly in recent years (de Certau et al., 1998).

Some fortified wines, notably muscatel and cheap sherry, are favored by bottle-gangs and dependent drinkers who have found that they provide the most ethanol for a given price. In some regions, spiced rums, ginger brandy, or flavored spirits (blended into pseudo-wines derived from neither grapes nor any fruit) provide that advantage. In China, until the 1980s, most "wines" were syrup-flavored spirits with water added. Poorer blacks in urban neighborhoods seem to prefer malt liquor (only about 6% alcohol, but popularly believed to be stronger), which is often sold in 40-ounce bottles. By contrast, liqueurs, ports, and expensive sherry tend to be reserved for elaborate dinners or receptions among social elites. The recent popularity in the U.S. of "crafted" beers—beers made with hops and with modern technology, but in relatively small batches—

has resulted in the emergence of a new constituency of beer drinkers, wealthier and better educated than stereotypical beer drinkers of the past.

ETHNICITY, RELIGION, AND OTHER CATEGORIES

Ethnicity

It has been a long tradition to write about "ethnicity" in relation to alcohol, and it could indeed be a significant variable in many respects. For example, it may be meaningful that the prevalence of drinking is higher among Whites than Blacks, especially among women (65% as compared with 54%); the difference is even greater between Hispanic and Non-Hispanic women (Hilton, 1991f). But the potential significance may be eclipsed by a basic methodological shortcoming. In other contexts, this author has already complained about the "muddling of models" that has made social categorization in terms of ethnicity so confused and confusing an approach in alcohol studies that it is of extremely limited analytic value (Heath, 1975, 1991c).

This shortcoming is not just a terminological nicety; it takes on special importance when, for example, the most long-term prospective study on the natural history of alcoholism concluded, after following the same population for 40 years, that "ethnicity proved to be the single most predictive factor"—even though investigators had expected otherwise (Vaillant, 1983; Vaillant & Milofsky, 1982). Their criterion of ethnicity was simply national origin of paternal grandparents. Another major study in the U.S. also found ethnicity to be more important than personality or family structural variables in predicting problem drinking, but they assigned ethnicity on the basis of national origin of maternal grandparents (Greeley, McCready, & Thiesen, 1980), just the opposite.

Linguistic and cultural distinctions occur even in modern nation-states. Spain has its Catalans, Basques, and Galicians, Belgium its Walloons and Flemish, and so forth. The U.S. census categorizes people as "White, Black, Hispanic, Asian/Pacific Islander, American Indian/Alaska Native, or Other," but various kinds of health statistics are reported in terms of different categories. Obviously, such groupings do not conform with self-identification or group affiliation in many instances, nor do they clearly or consistently relate to biological inheritance, gene pools, the channels through which people most often learn norms and values, or even the labels that are popularly attached to various groups.

Ethnicity does not have to do with forms but with relationships (Gutmann, 1999). Most social boundaries tend to be remarkably permeable, and the mobility of individuals between or among social groups is a widespread phenomenon, a reality experienced by many, not just a vague theoretic possibility.

In spite of all the shortcomings mentioned above, ethnicity cannot be ignored in some contexts. For example, the loud and ostentatious drinking of Chinese in Malaysia is often cited as one basis for ethnic prejudice (Arokiasamy, 1995). The firewater myth (Leland, 1976) and associated stereotype of "the drunken Indian," however inaccurate they may be in some respects, are firmly imbedded in the views of many in the U.S. (Westermeyer, 1974), just as is the stereotype of "the drunken aborigine" in Australia, even though a much smaller portion of them drink than do their "European" compatriots (Saggers & Gray, 1998).

To many who are unfamiliar with the fallacious imposition of the six census categories on the U.S. population, it is surprising that there are not more and greater differences in drinking patterns among so-called "ethnic" subpopulations within the U.S. Among those that other investigators have deemed worth mentioning are that Hispanic men tend to continue (or to resume) heavy drinking later in life (Caetano, 1991), whereas Blacks and Whites tend to ease off at around 30. Fewer Black young people drink, and they tend to drink less (Herd, 1991). Fewer women other than white, drink in groups, and those who do, drink less (Hilton, 1991d).

Although the national survey had too small a sample (even when oversampling for Blacks and Hispanics) to allow differentiation by country-of-origin, education, income, and other variables, other surveys that have focused on each of these categories have shown that any presumption of homogeneity within such inappropriate, ostensibly ethnic, categories is unfounded, and major variation was found within each along the demographic axes that have proven useful in dealing with other populations (Caetano, 1991; Herd, 1991). Although African-Americans drink less than their White counterparts, the percentage of heavier drinkers among them is higher, and heavy drinking continues to a later age (Hilton, 1991e).

In Australia, heavy alcohol use has long been a part of cultural self-identity, forming a central part of "mateship," friendship stressing egalitarian convivial relations (Hall & Hunter, 1995). Ironically, Australians are not heavy drinkers, in international perspective (*Productschap*, etc., 1997). The inherent weakness of "the firewater myth" is that, according to Graves (1971), "... the vast majority of Navaho [sic] drunkenness, at least in Denver, can be accounted for *without recourse to the fact that the subjects are Indians*" (p. 307; italics in original), so that the problem lies not so much with Indians as with "the wider society within which Indians are trying to survive."

China now recognizes 56 "nationalities" (analogous to ethnic minorities in most countries), and 80 languages, although nearly 90% are Mandarin-speaking Han people (Shen & Wang, 1998); drinking appears to play important roles in terms of hospitality, sociability, and medicine for all of them (Xiao, 1995). The stereotype of Irish drinking and drunkenness is still often applied to Irish-Americans, although they actually have a much higher rate of abstention than most other segments of the U.S. population (Stivers, 1976).

Religion

Another basis on which people categorize themselves and each other is religion. In many traditional societies, membership or adherence to a religion was often coterminous with membership in the ethnic group. The modern spread of missionaries has changed that, and we find that religion tends to be one of the most striking demographic variables when it is compared with drinking patterns.

It is well known that Islam tends to favor prohibition, but the ideal of combining Qu'ranic injunctions with temporal law has been realized in only a few countries. (I will discuss Muslim abstinence in slightly more detail in a later section of this chapter that deals with many kinds of abstinence.) For various reasons, some Muslims drink, and it turns out that, in Egypt they drink very much as do their Christian compatriots (Ashour, 1995); in Cameroon, they drink more than native religionists (Yguel et al., 1990); in Israel, Islamic youths drink nearly as much as Jews in the same schools (Weiss, 1995).

Jews have long attracted special attention with respect to alcohol because the weekly ritual of Sabbath means that every individual is exposed to whatever risks may inhere in drinking (and they are often supposed, by laypersons, to be high), and yet remarkably few Jews, no matter where in the world or when in history, have shown any evidence of loss of control, drunkenness, alcohol abuse, dependence, or alcoholism (Bales, 1946). In fact, there is a widespread saying in Yiddish that "*Schikker ist ein Goy*" (to be drunk is a gentile thing). The Sabbath is greeted by hymns and a prayer (Kiddush), after which everyone present is supposed to drink wine before sitting down to a meal. The end of the Sabbath is again marked by prayer and wine. It is also common for senior Jews to enjoy some distilled spirits after each major meal. In those senses, we have a population with no abstainers but also one with virtually no problem drinkers.

Interpretations of the special "immunity" of Jews to alcoholism or alcohol-related problems have tended to focus on sociocultural factors. The philosopher Immanuel Kant (1978/1798) offered the early sociological observation that, like women of his time, Jews confronted such widespread prejudice that they were obliged to be especially circumspect in their behavior. Unable to afford the risk of offending anyone, they made it a point to avoid inebriation and the loss of control that was believed inevitably to go with it. In more recent years, the focus of attention has shifted to a more social-learning theory, a combination of religious practices and cultural attitudes (Snyder, 1958a, 1958b). The use of wine each week to inaugurate and to conclude the sabbath makes for universal exposure to the substance, but in a sacred, ritual context.

The ways in which Jews are introduced to alcohol and think about it are intimately linked with social support, family, friends, and religion. A boy child is given a few drops of wine as part of the ceremony marking his circumcision, and drinking is formally integrated into sacred contexts, which are also familial, at home thereafter. Alcohol is treated as a good thing in moderation, but it would be wrong to use it in excess. In a country such as the U.S., where some suppose that any child who has a taste of any alcoholic beverage is likely to become addicted to it, and eventually to hard drugs, universal Jewish drinking with impunity is noteworthy. Although the action of drinking may be similar, the meanings are vastly different, so are the expectations, and so are the effects. As simple as this may appear to be, it is a fundamental reality about drinking that many people, including academics and medical personnel, seem not to comprehend (MacAndrew & Edgerton, 1969; Marlatt & Rohsenow, 1980). As Jews in many areas abandon or diminish their participation in orthodox rituals, it is noteworthy that the frequency of drunkenness and drinking problems increases (although it still remains relatively low, in comparison with most societies).

A curious variant on the question of who drinks occurs in the Batuque religious cult in northern Brazil (Leacock, 1964). Although practitioners are fiercely Roman Catholic in some contexts, they proudly practice Afro-American Umbanda in others, part of which includes frenetic dancing and drinking while they are "possessed" by various friendly spirits. They are familiar with the spirits and individuals tend to be visited by the same spirit from time to time, often manifesting a distinctive manner of speaking, dressing, and drinking while possessed. They are careful to differentiate between the persons, who are said not to drink, and the possessing spirits, many of whom do drink rum in fairly large quantities. A remarkable feature of such incidents is that a parishioner who recovers from possession does not show signs of having drunk as much as he or she appeared to during the state of possession. Leacock suggests that rum in this instance may serve as various hallucinogenic drugs do for neighboring Indian populations, to facilitate the mental dissociation that is interpreted as possession.

Drinking rum is also an important part of elaborate ceremonies that combine ancient Mayan traditions with Roman Catholicism in southern Mexico (Eber, 1995; Pozas, 1962), or Inca traditions, again with Catholicism, in Ecuador (Maynard, Frøland, & Rasmussen, 1965) or in Peru (Allen, 1988; Mangin, 1957). The combined burden on finances and health that is imposed by having to serve in such a role for a year at a time every few years has prompted some Indians to opt out of the ritual *cargo* system (Cancian, 1965) in the only way that is not thought miserly by others, that is, by converting to Protestantism (Willems, 1980). It would be unfair to suggest that such converts have no other reasons, but many are frank about what a relief it is no longer to feel the obligation to spend or drink so much on religious festivals.

Although most Muslims believe that their religion disallows drinking, others find it no hindrance. Although some Buddhists insist that Buddha forbade the use of alcohol other coreligionists drink heartily, openly, and often (Xiao, 1995).

Other Social Categories

Recently, some governmental agencies have begun to refer to drinking and drug use among various "special populations," and data are being compiled about such categories as youth, elderly, the handicapped or disadvantaged, lesbians or gays, and other groupings which are not likely to yield significant comparisons. Without belaboring the philosophy of science, it is evident that, although such categories are by no means meaningless, they do not correlate closely with a wide range of other socially or culturally significant variables.

It has been commonplace throughout history that colonizers use alcohol in the early stages as a tool of colonization, a scarce economic good with which they interest and engage native peoples, and later as a substitute for cash which can keep those peoples in an underclass subservient to those who control the supply (Jankowiak & Bradburd, 1996). Eventually, as those who have been colonized gain some wealth and autonomy, it is common to reverse the earlier stance and to prohibit drink to that same population as happened in North and South America (Mancall, 1995), and much of Africa (Ambler, 1987; Pan, 1975), and Oceania (Casswell, 1985; Saggers & Gray, 1998).

There are relatively "wet" and "dry" cultures, in which the differences include not only large versus small average per capita annual consumption of ethanol (Smith & Hanham, 1982), but also associated differences in terms of values concerning freedom to drink, the appropriateness of drinking in various contexts, and other behavioral norms (Room, 1992). Breton, Russian, Han, Camba, Kofyar, and many other cultures are "wet" in these terms, as are all of those countries along the northern periphery of the Mediterranean (Portugal, Spain, France, Italy, former Yugoslavia, and Greece) among others. On the "dry" side of what is obviously a continuum rather than a bipolar dichotomy are Bedouin, Cantonese, or Hopi cultures, and countries as diverse as India, Israel, and Saudi Arabia.

Another way of classifying large populations is in terms of the predominant beverage, so that investigators sometimes talk about "beer cultures," "wine cultures," and "spirits cultures" (Smith & Hanham, 1982). In those terms, some of the world's many beer cultures are Quechua, Tarahumara, Tonga, and Tiriki. Much of Germany, Austria, Australia, and England can also be said to fall into that category. France, Italy, Portugal, Chile, and Agentina are prototypically wine cultures. Gaelic, Eskimo, and Camba are unquestionably spirits cultures, as are Japan, Russia, and the several Scandinavian countries.

Such groupings do not imply uniformity in drinking patterns, nor do they exclude regional variants. For example, parts of Switzerland and Germany favor wine, whereas other parts favor beer. A prevalence of spirits does not preclude anyone's also drinking beer or wine, and many individuals obviously drink all three, depending on the context.

Among the other categories that are relevant in a cross-cultural survey of drinking as behavior is one that is not demographic in nature but that relates specifically to drinking. Those who drink alone, solitary drinkers, turn up in discussions of drinking problems, risk, and dependence, more often discovered in clinical settings than in surveys. It is an odd proof of how universally drinking is thought of as a social activity that these exceptions are almost invariably cited in negative terms. In many societies, drinking alone is virtually inconceivable; in most, it is viewed as deviant, dangerous, and a little sad. It is true that many of those whose heavy drinking has resulted in a combination of problems, some of which are personal but many of which impinge on others, have found their social networks shrinking as friends and relatives retreat or are cut off

(Bacon, 1973). It is also true that solitary drinking has often been listed as one of the diagnostic criteria for alcoholism, alcohol abuse, or alcohol dependence (American Psychiatric Association, 1980; World Health Organization, 1997).

As major segments of the world's population are aging, however, it may be timely to reassess our view of solitary drinking. Instead of its signaling that the drinker has rejected sociability and is seeking solace in alcohol, it is often the case that sociability is not easily available, or that one is choosing an interlude of solitude, neither of which should interfere with the enjoyment of a drink or prompt one to drink more. Increasingly, people are living alone, eating alone, and drinking alone, none of which implies an antisocial outlook or a wish to flout society's mores. It is probably long overdue that hasty or blanket stereotypic judgments about the inappropriateness of solitary drinking be set aside and each case be individually evaluated in terms of the situation and motivation of the drinker.

ABSTAINERS

Although most of this book is about when, where, what, how, and why people drink, it is also important that we pay attention to that sizable segment of the world's population who do not drink. All around the world, there are many people who choose not to drink. As is the case with almost every other aspect of the world of drink, this is a complicated issue.

Someone who lives in Iran, Saudi Arabia, or the state of Utah might well wonder "Who are all those drinkers?" when confronted with statistics about the threat that alcohol poses to public health and social welfare around the world. In the same way, a French, Italian, or New York citizen, for whom drinking is a normal part of everyday living, might wonder "Who are all those abstainers?"

Like most questions about categories of people, there is no easy answer. To begin with, to be counted in the category of abstainer does not necessarily mean that beverage alcohol has never touched one's lips. Among those who systematically conduct social surveys in the United States, someone who drinks no more than 1 drink a year is labeled an abstainer (Room, 1991b): that is currently close to 36% of the adult population (Hanson, 1995a). A single annual celebratory drink is allowed within that definition, if not expected, even for a person who insists that he or she doesn't drink or would "never touch the stuff."

In Poland, survey researchers found that it was necessary to use a distinctive definition for abstainer, one who does not drink vodka (Moskalewicz & Zieliński, 1995). The reason was that, almost without exception, everyone who said at the outset that he or she did not drink or did not drink at all revealed subsequently that they did, in fact, habitually drink beer, wine, or both, but considered only vodka to be "real drinking." Although the wording might vary, there are numerous instances (generally not well discussed in the published literature), in which researchers in the U.K., U.S., Canada, or Australia have had similar responses, with distilled spirits (liquor, hard liquor, or "the hard stuff") being construed as the only really alcoholic beverage, whereas beer and wine were thought not to contain alcohol, or at least not enough to be worth mentioning. That leaves unaddressed the question of whether the drinker who has two, three, or four drinks a year is more like the drinker who has 12 to 20 drinks each day than to the abstainer. It is inherent in the process of categorization that pigeonholing is always questionable, especially at the extremes along the borders of the categories. Another problem arises when people categorized as abstainers are contrasted with people in other categories, as often occurs with respect to health, life expectancy, employment, and other variables. Whereas the stereotyped abstainer had had fewer than a dozen drinks over his entire life, another abstainer may be a recovering alcoholic who drank that many every day for many years before quitting.

Fortunately, most lay people do not have to wrestle with the questionable logic or consequences of such distinctions. At the same time, one might wish that responsible scientists who are striving to demonstrate significant correlations between drinking and other events would be even more careful about their classifications and the characteristics that they use to distinguish among them. For general purposes, it might seem sufficient just to call an abstainer someone who does not drink. But even that runs up against peculiar exceptions on the international scene. For example, Chilean authorities identify only 20% of their adult population as abstemious (or abstainers). Their definition is considerably more liberal than that in the U.S., although less so than that in Poland. The category includes not only those who never drink, but also those who drink "no more than five times a year, in small quantities, and without drunkenness" (Medina, 1995, p. 34). That Denmark is home to a much wetter or more permissive culture can be inferred from the fact that a recent survey there listed as abstainers those who "had no more than a single drink per week" (Andersen, Grønbaek, Becker, Thorsen, & Sørenson, 1998).

Clearly, there is no international or cross-cultural consensus on what constitutes an abstainer. Even if an objective measure were to be chosen, for example, with an abstainer defined as someone whose drinking falls in the lowest percentile of the population (which would be extremely difficult to determine anyway), such an approach would still be problematic, especially in light of cross-cultural differences in tolerance or expectation of alcohol consumption. It could even put us in an endless chicken-or-egg quandary, as when Partanen (1990, p. 70) pointed out that "Per capita figures of alcohol consumption do not make sense unless the proportion of abstainers is taken into account." In some societies, the proportion of abstainers reaches a majority: more than half in Zambia (Haworth & Acduda, 1998), 63% among Mexican women (Natera, 1995), and 51% among Chinese women (Xiao, 1995).

Probably the most fruitful way to begin looking at abstainers is briefly to list the variety of reasons people give for having made that choice. The majority around the world presumably would cite religious motives or convictions, whether they be Buddhist, Muslim, Hindu, Jain, Christian, or other. It is note-

Two elderly Lepcha brothers in the Sikkim region of India share locally-brewed whiskey. Often older people drink less than they did at an earlier age. © *CORBIS/ Nazima Kowall.*

worthy that so many religions include at least implied doctrinal opposition to drinks and drinking, most of which are adhered to by a majority of believers or practitioners.

Another large group who choose not to drink are recovering alcoholics or former problem drinkers who believe that abstaining is the only way that they can continue to enjoy the improvements in their lives that came with abandoning drinking patterns that had been problematic for them. For many, it is an article of faith that they have a disease (Jellinek, 1960) that cannot be cured, and that they remain at risk for the rest of their lives. Some even go so far as to decline to refer to themselves as "recovered" and insist that, because dependence and abuse are ongoing processes with relapses frequent, they are still "recovering" (even after 30 years without a drink). There is ample evidence that such a deterministic or fatalistic view does not apply to everyone, and large numbers of former excessive or problem drinkers are now moderate or social drinkers without problems (Hester, 1995; Sobell, Sobell, Toneatto, & Leo, 1993). Nevertheless, the lifelong rejection of alcohol that has consistently been advocated by members of Alcoholics Anonymous has many subscribers in countries around the world (Mäkelä et al., 1996; McCrady & Miller, 1993).

Other categories of abstainers are relatively small and diverse; there has been little systematic study of the subject. Some people say they simply do not like the smell, or taste, of alcohol. Since ethanol is virtually odorless and tasteless, we can assume that they are referring to the taste and/or smell of some specific beverage(s) to which they were once exposed. That does not diminish in the least the validity of their reasoning and, unconscious or subconscious motives notwithstanding, it seems wholly appropriate to accept that they have chosen not to drink for the reason that they give. It would be interesting to find out whether there are commonalties with respect to the beverages that those people rejected or the circumstances in which they arrived at their decision to abstain.

Others say that they do not like the feel of drinks—the bitterness of beer, or the sharp burning sensation that accompanies the first drink of distilled spirits for many people. Another reason is that some people do not like how beverage alcohol makes them feel. Queasiness is one reaction; gastric disturbance with even a minuscule dose is another way that people suffer. Some are uncomfortable with the slightest sense of dizziness, facial flushing, loss of coordination, sensory diminution, or other effects, any of which can beset a naive drinker after only minimal consumption. For a long time, facial flushing was thought to be a protective factor for many Oriental persons against excessive drinking; there is a relatively widespread genetic propensity for sweating, flushing, palpitation of the heart, and general discomfort to result from just a drink or two among Japanese, Korean, Taiwanese, and some other populations. But recent studies with larger samples have demonstrated that there is almost no correlation between frequency and severity of flushing on the one hand and alcohol consumption on the other.

Some fear that drinking any alcohol may make them alcoholic. For some, this stems from the sad realization that one or more grandparents, parents, cousins, siblings, aunts, or uncles had a history of drinking problems. Misunderstandings about vague recent reports on a genetic predisposition to alcohol abuse and dependence have prompted many young people simply to avoid the risk by avoiding the substance. Others fear that a single drink might make them lose control, or put them at the mercy of anyone who might want to exploit them in some way. Some women abstain because they fear that drinking might damage their fetus or nursing infant.

It is dangerous to drink alcohol in conjunction with certain medications, prompting some others to abstain. Many specific medical problems are aggravated by drinking, such as hypertension, cardiac arrhythmia, and hepatitis, to name a few.

Many abstainers decline to give a reason because they feel that such a choice is private and no one else's business. Among those who choose not to drink, however, a few cross-cultural patterns deserve some more attention because they account for so large a portion of those who abstain.

Merely to cite religious reasons for abstention provides little explanation of why a great many people choose not to drink. Some further exploration of the worldviews of large cohorts of abstainers shows that the rationales they give are far from uniform. Officially, one might assume that it was a ban direct from Allah that dissuades most Muslims from drinking. To be sure, most Muslims do not drink because they believe that to do so was prohibited in their holy book, the Qu'ran (or Koran). A few Muslims do drink, justifying that by noting that the Qu'ranic injunction which is not a law, is specifically with reference to dates and grapes as sources of "strong drink," leaving alcohol that might be derived from grain or other sources as quite acceptable. Others stress that the injunction is phrased as a question rather than a command ("Why would you …?" rather than "Thou shalt not …"), thereby allowing greater discretion and freedom of choice (Badri, 1976). Others choose selectively to focus on another verse of the Qu'ran in which it is said that strong drink brings good to the lives of men (Midgley, 1971). Or they stress that the warning against drink was explicitly intended to prevent a devout person from being distracted during prayers, and that moderate drinking would never be such an interference. Another author, who pays close attention to the specific wordings of various Islamic injunctions (Lemu, 1992), also emphasizes the extreme popularity of drinking among Arabs before the coming of Islam, and that Islam itself took a gradual approach toward prohibition. Perhaps part of the reason that some Muslims drink is that the injunctions are not phrased in absolute terms, nor are they against drinking as such. Rather, the warning is against the deleterious effects of drunkenness, such as interfering with one's consciousness of god, being boastful or shameless, or destroying the family. Interpretations vary markedly even in scholarly exegeses.

At any rate, the prohibition that is commonly thought to characterize the entire far-flung Islamic world is neither ancient nor is it uniformly accepted by contemporary Muslims (Badri, 1976). To be sure, we know little in detail about Muslim drinking patterns, but there are a few studies that deal with attitudes and practices among students, and some others that address the numbers and facilities available for treatment. In Cameroon, a survey of drinking patterns yielded the surprising finding that "… those who drink most are Muslims" (Yguel et al., 1990, p. 121). Perhaps the most salient points that can be made from a social science perspective now are that most of the same Arabic-speaking populations were lavish in their praise of both drink and drunkenness in pre-Islamic times, and that, as incomplete as this prohibition may be, it tends to be more generally respected than most secular efforts at imposing the same restrictions. Such an interesting phenomenon occurs when sacred and secular law coincide or are indistinguishable, as in Pakistan, Saudi Arabia, Afghanistan, Kuwait, or the Islamic Republic of Iran.

Hinduism, like Islam, is far more diverse than most outsiders realize. As a religion that allows for many different beliefs, it includes some groups who consider alcohol an abomination and others who cherish particular kinds of drunkenness as valuable religious experiences. We have already seen how members of one caste in a village in India (Carstairs, 1954) routinely drink a locally distilled liquor and deplore any use of cannabis, whereas those of a higher caste in the same village enjoy cannabis tea and point to the drinking of daru liquor as proof of the lower intrinsic worth of their neighbors. In one tribal variant of Hinduism, orgiastic drunkenness is important (Pertold, 1931). Mahmood (1997) cites an interesting case in which one of the "Scheduled Tribes" (a linguistically and culturally distinct population accorded special privileges under India's constitution) drink heavily, contrary to the Hindu religion. They are erroneously called Hindus (as are 83% of the country's population), because census-takers were aware that they treat nature in a religious manner, although they worship no Hindu deities.

Nor is Buddhism so ascetic and uniform as is often thought. Beverage alcohol often plays important roles in hospitality, curing, relaxation, and dietary habits of Buddhists, including deeply religious persons. Drunkenness is often cited by poets and artists as an important adjunct to one's fullest appreciation of nature and a source of creativity. To be sure, Buddha's fifth commandment was against drinking, although it appears not to be adhered to with any regularity; as in Islam, interpretations vary in voluminous exegeses. The earlier Vedic hymns in India condemned drinking as leading to quarrels (Prakash, 1961), although the same people developed an elaborate pharmacopoeia of alcohol-based beverages to deal with various ailments.

Within Christianity, there are a number of Protestant churches or sects that are similarly abstinent as an article of faith. Sometimes called fundamentalists, ascetic Protestants, pentacostals, or evangelicals, these include, among others, many denominations of Baptists, Methodists, Seventh Day Adventists, Jehovah's Witnesses, and Church of Christ of the Latter Day Saints (Mormons). Jesus's first miracle was transforming water into wine to satisfy the large audience at a wedding, and there is no indication of his ever having said anything against drink or drinking (Seller, 1984). At the famous last supper, with his disciples on the night before he was crucified, he chose wine to represent his blood in the ceremony that has come to be known as the Eucharist (or Communion), making wine the principal sacrament in Christianity. Nevertheless, there are many passages in the Christian holy book, the Bible, which are now interpreted as referring to beverage alcohol as poison, with the implication that its use violates the sanctity of an individual's body, which is itself a kind of holy temple. Some have gone to great lengths in attempts to prove that every positive reference to wine that occurs in the Bible should have been translated as "grape juice." Part of the peculiarly Protestant rejection of alcohol may have grown out of John Wesley's early preaching against the social ills of his time which he attributed largely to alcohol abuse, such as poverty, spouse abuse, neglect of children, and so forth.

Another way in which Protestant Christianity relates to abstinence has to do with missionary activity around the world. There are many Protestant missionaries who provide medical services to diverse populations around the world, others who promote literacy and education in a broad sense (sometimes with an emphasis on linguistic analysis), but the majority are evangelical in both thinking and actions. For them, abstention from alcohol is a matter of faith and of basic values. Personal enjoyment and material satisfaction are thought to be dangerous, if not downright sinful. In many communities where drinking has traditionally played an important role for many people, missionaries have been vocal and adamant about denouncing alcohol as evil. Converts have had to renounce drinking; and abstention has itself become a primary symbol of one's status as a Protestant.

It is striking that, in recent decades, native populations are responding to the ascetic teachings of such missionaries in novel ways. In cultures where problem drinking is commonplace, or where lavish expenditures on alcohol play an important role in social or political relations, some individuals find it convenient to affiliate with Protestant churches as a way of publicly demonstrating that they wish to opt out from those onerous commitments to drink. This is not to say that religious faith is absent or irrelevant in such cases, but only to point out the functional value of such conversion, as it has often been articulated not just by observers who are well grounded in the social sciences, but also by many of the actors themselves and by friends and family. Latin America is one part of the world where this pattern is becoming relatively common, especially in rural communities where frequent festivals featuring heavy drinking, sponsored in turn by various members of the community, have traditionally been important for prestige (Barlett, 1980; Cancian, 1965).

Fully half of U.S. adults drink less than once a month, and only 49% of men and 25% of women drink at least once a week (Clark & Hilton, 1991). Daily drinking is reported by just 12% of men and 4% of women. Information about quantity is similar to that on frequency in demonstrating that many are very light drinkers: 30% of men and 42% of women drink 15 or fewer drinks per month (Clark & Hilton, 1991). Although some critics complain about the ubiquity of alcohol in U.S. culture, it is far from being wet in international or cross-cultural perspective. In fact, the U.S. is not near the top of the list of countries in terms of per capita consumption, although it is above the median (*Productschap voor Gedistilleerde Dranken*, 1997). One of the things that makes the U.S. unusual among industrial nations is the relatively high portion of the population who do not drink at all. About 30% of U.S. adults were abstainers in the 1930s and perhaps 35% are at the beginning of the 21st century (Clark & Hilton, 1991). Estimates in other countries include: about 20% in Norway and Sweden, 15–20%

in Canada, 15% in Finland, 13% in France, 5% in Great Britain, 6% in Austria, and 5–10% in both Belgium and Germany (Armyr, Elmer, & Herz, 1982).

When we add the 15% of U.S. adults who claim to have only one drink per month to the one-third who are abstainers, it is evident that nearly half of Americans hardly drink at all—meaning, of course, that the other half do most of the drinking (Clark & Hilton, 1991). Incidentally, it is not because a great many of those who are abstinent today drank heavily earlier; only about 6% of abstainers were formerly heavy drinkers.

Gender is more important a variable than income or wealth when we are considering those who do not drink. Few countries and almost no non-Western societies have numerical data about abstainers, but among those jurisdictions that do, the genders differ markedly. For example, in Denmark, only about 2.1% of males and about 6.1% of females say that they drink no more than once a year (Schiøler, 1995); in Ireland, the numbers are 24.5% for males and 36.3% for females (Plant, 1995). In Sweden, only 10% of adult males identify themselves as abstainers, whereas 25% of women do (Nyberg & Allebeck, 1995). In Northern Ireland, by contrast, 33% of men abstain and fully 50% of women. In Britain as a whole, the figures are only 7% and 12% respectively (Plant, 1995). Rates of abstention appear to be increasing in most European countries in recent years, as they are decreasing in most other parts of the world (Smart, 1997).

In many societies where most people drink much of the time, abstaining is a deviant form of behavior, and people who do not drink are distrusted or regarded with suspicion. Even in modern France, an abstainer is generally scorned because, as a "water drinker;" he or she is presumed to be dour, a kill-joy, and even likely to be critical of any enjoyment that others may have (de Certau et al., 1998). In Chile, an abstainer is generally distrusted; the assumption is that the only reason one might not drink is in order to be able to take advantage of others when they have had too much (Medina, 1995).

In most of the world, where drinking is customary, it is considered a slight if one declines to accept the offer of a drink. The implication, whether intended or not, is that one presumably considers himself socially superior to sharing such informal communion, a gravely offensive view. Just as drinking together can help to blur the social and cultural distance between people, any refusal to do so may erect an impenetrable barrier.

Not only does the United States have a high proportion of people who choose not to drink, but about 10% of adults feel strongly that no one else should drink either (Clark & Hilton, 1991). Although most who hold such prohibitionistic views probably do so for religious reasons, there are some who do so from a feeling of deep moral conviction quite apart from any sacred motives.

Such a temperance-oriented mentality has gained ascendancy in various parts of the world at various times, as will be discussed in chapter 6, when we look at why some people drink and why others choose not to.

WHY DOES IT MATTER?

In addressing the question of who drinks and who does not, we lay bare much of the dynamic aspect of how alcohol fits, or sometimes fails to fit within a culture. Our emphasis on drinking as behavior means that the actors are crucial, having chosen drinking from a broad repertory of alternatives and fitting it within their crowded regimens. Even those who have chosen not to drink are by no means indifferent about it; some of them have strong feelings and often are called on to muster their values about alcohol.

Because drinking is a socially learned behavior, it matters greatly who does and does not, and role models can have enormous impact (whether intentionally or not) in socializing younger people about how to act before, during, and after drinking. Sometimes who drinks is a vivid portrayal of power or prestige. Sometimes bonds of identification or affect are intensified or attenuated on the basis of who drinks and with whom.

Delineating the cast of characters for drinking in a given population is also a task that throws into sharp relief some methodological approaches that are used in scientific studies of alcohol. In this chapter, more than most others, we have seen how surveys yielding quantitative data can be combined with observations yielding qualitative data to help us better understand just who drinks.

Social scientists have been remarkably cavalier in terms of identifying units that they compare as ethnic groups, sometimes treating religion (e.g., Jewish) as if it were analogous with sect (as in Mormon), national ancestry (such as Chinese-American), linguistic group (for example, Sioux Indian), type of religion (ascetic Protestant), or supposed race (Black or Gypsy). Mixing such categories is not only logically inconsistent in that such differentiation is not based on any uniform criterion, but it also often does violence to the ways in which individuals tend to identify themselves (and, hence, choose to share values and norms).

Another of the principal limitations of even such detailed data as can be compiled through surveys is the important fact that numbers, as valid as they may appear, can really be misleading when one tries to relate drinking behavior to its outcomes. For many years there has been a vocal and strong temperance movement, couched in scientific terms, that has as its explicit objective curtailing drinking by everyone everywhere. In the name of public health, several national and international campaigns aimed at reducing overall drinking, on the assumption that the wide range of alcohol-related problems occur in direct proportion to the average per capita consumption of ethanol in any population. Proponents favor a broad range of restrictive measures, usually including but not limited to higher taxes on beverage alcohol, shorter hours of sale, increases in the minimum legal age, fewer sales outlets, warning labels, and restrictions or bans on advertising. Many such restrictions have been adopted by various jurisdictions, and per capita consumption has decreased in most of the capitalistic world.

This "control of availability" theory is usually said to be based on the writings of a French statistician (Ledermann, 1956), who asserted that the per capita consumption of alcohol within any population is distributed along a log-normal curve. That was the case, he theorized, because so many people drink very little and very few drink a great deal, with the lower limit being zero and the upper limit, set by an estimate of physiological tolerance, at one liter of absolute alcohol per day. The number of assumptions that are built into his distribution-of-consumption graphs must give us pause, especially homogeneity within the population, norms and values of individuals irrelevant, and so forth. But this model was appealing to some because it suggested that any change, by any one individual anywhere along the curve, would change the overall shape of the curve. If that were so, reducing average consumption would reduce virtually everyone's consumption.

That idea in turn became the basis for a cautious sociological hypothesis that "... changes in the overall consumption of alcoholic beverages have a bearing on the health of the people in any society. Alcohol control measures can be used to limit consumption: thus control of alcohol availability becomes a public health issue" (Bruun et al., 1975, p. 90). Although just what "bearing" such changes might have was not explicitly stated, others promptly cited these two sources (and to this day still do) as the cornerstone of their theory. Stated as if it were an axiom: more drinking means more problems, and less drinking means fewer problems. The practical implication of such a stance has consistently been that alcohol should be made less readily available to everyone, because that would lower the average alcohol consumption, which would, in turn, diminish problems (Edwards et al., 1994; Moore & Gerstein, 1981). In contrast, empirical evidence from around the world has generally shown fewer problems in those cultures and countries where consumption was relatively high, and disproportionately more problems where consumption was relatively low (Heath, 1988b, 1998b). It also appears that higher prices, taxes, shorter hours of sale, or other restrictions are more likely to discourage moderate drinkers than they are to curtail consumption by heavy drinkers (Skog, 1983), and drinking patterns (Grant & Litvak, 1998) are treated as if they were irrelevant.

The agenda for a new temperance movement was set, with what many assumed to be solid scientific grounding (Room, 1984b). However commonsensical the distribution-of-consumption approach may sound, it has not fared well when challenged on methodological grounds (de Lint, 1988), on theoretical grounds (Heath, 1988a; Parker & Harman, 1978), or on empirical grounds (Heath, 1988b, 1995; Peele, 1987). Nevertheless, the distribution-of-consumption approach continues to dominate discussions of alcohol policy at all levels, presumably because it holds the promise of quick and easy solutions to what have long been serious public concerns (Edwards et al., 1994; Moore & Gerstein, 1981).

Proponents are careful to make the point that, in their view, education holds little promise of effecting changes with respect to drinking, again contrary to what we have learned from cross-cultural and international studies. While it is true that only disappointing results have come from the brief mention that is made of alcohol in most school programs, attention must once again be paid to the difference between schooling and education. Whatever students are taught about alcohol in school tends to come awkwardly fitted into a series of discussions on cleanliness, nutrition, and general health, introduced by someone who knows and cares little about the subject and who may even be uncomfortable talking about it. In many countries, the teaching materials emphasize the harm that may befall a drinker, making points and using illustrations that the students themselves know from observation, if not from experience, are exaggerated if not patently false, worst-case scenarios presented as if they were typical. At least in the U.S., where most states require that something about alcohol be taught in schools, such teaching is often unproductive, or even counterproductive, by confirming to young people that their elders misrepresent drinking, presumably so as not to share the pleasures of it (Hanson, 1995b).

Education, in the broader sense, is a longer but more convincing and more lasting process. It can and does shape attitudes and values so that young people can weigh alternatives and make appropriate choices, on the basis of clear and convincing evidence that is congruent with common experience. Such a program is already available, although little used (Hanson, 1996). With reference to the subject at hand, it would involve frankly dealing with what alcohol is, what it does and does not do within the human body, and how it works there. It would include a recognition of the potential of many kinds of harm but also admit to the potential of many kinds of benefit. It would involve not just one teacher briefly in the classroom, but many people in workaday contexts over a long period. The matter of excess and its differences from moderation would be stressed, with favorable as well as unfavorable examples being cited. The fact that certain behaviors are inappropriate, whether one has been drinking or not, would be a major emphasis, and part of good behavior would be recognizing and respecting the rights of those who may choose not to drink by neither pressing them to do so nor offending them with one's own drinking. A practical aspect would be providing ready alternatives, so that someone who might wish to drink moderately, or just to experiment with drinking, could do so without feeling the need to drink to excess in order to fit in or because of supposed peer pressure.

Other cultures have done all of this for generations, unself-consciously and without even thinking of it as education. It is feasible, even in a culture where different norms prevail. For those who are concerned that such a process is too slow, one might ask that they seriously evaluate the achievements of school-based alcohol education, which has been integral to the curriculum for nearly a century in many jurisdictions. For those who are concerned that not everyone would be convinced, one might ask how many remain unconvinced by didactic efforts that contradict the experience of friends and family.

This is not a counsel that all youth should be taught to drink. It is a recognition that, where drinking is a part of culture that may well impinge upon their lives, the better part of wisdom is to let them know early about drinking, and to equip them to make intelligent choices in that connection.

Ironically, with all the attention that has been paid to who drinks, no one has thought to examine knowledge (or ignorance) about alcohol as a variable among individuals. If the aim is truly the reduction of harm (and not merely the curtailment of consumption), the focus of attention should be on educating those most likely to cause or to incur harm, and not on taking drinks away from the majority whose behavior tends already to be aversive to harm.

Chapter 4

There's More than One Way: How Do People Drink?

Japanese geishas converse with and entertain their customers. Given that drinking is generally known to follow a distinct rhythm, particularly in group contexts, another function of the geishas is to regulate the pace of this rhythm. © *CORBIS/Michael S. Yamashita.*

In looking at how people drink, we bring together several of the strands about when, where, who, and what, to look more globally at the ways in which beverage alcohol fits as an integral part of most of the world's cultures, as it has throughout much of history. Every realm of human behavior impinges upon others, and every other realm of behavior is some how relevant to it in different ways. By examining the how of drinking among various cultures, we should be able to see economic factors linked with esthetics, politics as a reflection of values, attitudes shaping laws, and laws, in turn, impacting back on economics.

It was once said

> Alcohol is to social science what dye is to microscopy ... what this dye does is to show up certain kinds of fundamental features of the structures of the cell, and I propose that we can probably use alcohol the same way to penetrate the structure of social life (Duster, 1983, p. 326).

In a simpler but analogous way, I like to encourage students by assuring them that alcohol provides a window upon culture. Look through it closely enough and linkages between the class system and cuisine can be seen, or religious beliefs and practices as they are played out in everyday life, or how language shapes our views of space and motion, and a host of other aspects of that intricate and interwoven system of patterns that we call culture.

Our case study deals with France, a prototypical "wet" country with a "wine culture" known throughout the world (Sadoun et al., 1965). But many of the images we have of France are blurred and faded by age with stereotypes that no longer hold in a rapidly changing world. An update of French drinking shows how even good research, well disseminated to an interested readership, can shift from representing contemporary ethnography and sociology to being historical source material in the span of a single generation.

The section on etiquette in this chapter deals not with fastidious niceties but, in a more general sense, with what is right and what is wrong when people do decide to drink. Another on paraphernalia is less a cabinet of collectors' curiosities than it is a reflection on human ingenuity in harnessing a wide range of materials to enhance the quality of drinking as a part of life. Rhythm has to do with the temporal aspect, pace as part of drinking behavior, and how it affects the experiences and emotions of the individual actors. The section on excess addresses extreme use, or some would say abuse, of alcohol in ways that show how quantity affects quality. It is only in this context that the themes of drunkenness and dependence can become important because the ways in which most people drink, most of the time, do not result in drunkenness, much less, dependence (or, as some would say, addiction). A glance at activities that are linked with drinking shows how drinking for the sake of drinking, or with the sole aim of becoming intoxicated, is viewed as deviant behavior in most societies, and a range of other behaviors are often imaginative, creative, and enjoyable accompaniments. The chapter closes, as usual, with a few comments on why it matters how people drink.

Case Study: France, Then and Now

The French have long been cited as exceptional and interesting in relation to drinking, largely because they have about the highest per capita alcohol consumption in the statistically documented world. What most public health spokespersons deliberately overlook in talking about French drinking is that, like the Camba, they simultaneously have a low rate of most of the so-called alcohol-related problems that so many critics wrongly insist occur in direct proportion to consumption.

Drinking is an integral part of French culture, not only for its economic importance but as an important part of everyday life. Wine is a major product and export, with French wines consistently judged to include some of the best in the world. The volume of exports is greater than that from any other country. For some older Frenchmen, without wine there is no meal, and distilled alcohol is literally *eau-de-vie* (water of life). However, much of what is written about French drinking nowadays is at least 20 years outdated at a time of rapid change. Furthermore, France is usually treated in stereotypic terms as if it were culturally homogeneous which is far from true. No one a generation ago would have thought of France as a country in which one president would lead a campaign to drink more milk, and another would sign into law strict regulations against different kinds of advertising, and in favor of other advertising that include health warnings, and other regulations restricting the sale or use of beverage alcohol.

The traditional view of French drinking (Sadoun et al., 1965) was probably accurate for the time, when the population was largely rural and farming predominated, before the arrival of large-scale mechanization. The peasant who drank two to three liters of wine throughout every day, but who would be alarmed or ashamed to have it affect anything that he did or said, is still easy to find, especially in bars where a *coup-de-rouge* (a hit of red [wine]) is still a normal breakfast for workingmen. But overall wine drinking is down by nearly 30% in the past 20 years, with higher quality wines gaining in popularity (Nahoum-Grappe, 1995). At the same time, much more beer is sold than before, and women are drinking more, more often, and more publicly. As has always been the case, the choice between red and white wines varies from community to community, with fermented cider being especially popular along the north coast. Bretons are proudly Celtic and often point to this as one of the features that clearly distinguishes them from "the French." (Without getting into an anthropological polemic at this point, it does seem appropriate again to underscore that a culture is rarely the same as a nation-state even though much that is written, especially about drinking, uses the terms interchangeably.) Although brandy is popular throughout France, people proudly distinguish between that produced in the region of Armagnac and that from Cognac, a distinction that is internationally accepted as important and not just a local foible. The French people were proud enough of their 1998 World Cup soccer victories, which were won by a team conspicuously diverse in ethnic terms, so that they now boast officially of just such diversity—a major change in outlook. Just as there is no single unitary culture in France, neither should we expect that any culture will be restricted to a single country. We see continuity between French Basques and Spanish Basques, and Catalans in France share more with Catalans across the border than with their French neighbors in other directions.

The author's interest and limited familiarity with French culture prompted him to devote some time in 1998 to an ethnographic reconnaissance in an effort to update his understanding of the roles of drink, especially in the south. As he had known before, pride in regional products is strong, and one major theme is popular reliance on wine made by themselves or by neighbors for refreshment and with workaday meals. Eating has become far less ceremonial than it was, with few families taking more than one meal a day together. It is commonplace for adults as well as children to rely heavily on ready-made foods and to eat them while walking on the street without wine. There is a wealthy stratum for whom eating is still an important social and aesthetic experience, and wine accompanies virtually their every meal, but it is often a smaller quantity—more expensive vintages from a specific region, unlike the abundant cheap local *vin de table* (generic table wine) their parents drank. Beer, the favored beverage among women and young people, is as often foreign as it is French, and it, like ice cream, appears far more often at sidewalk cafes than does wine. Parents still teach their children from an early age to drink, putting a spoonful of wine sometimes into a glass of water so that the youngsters can join in festive toasting or drinking on those occasions when they dine together. But adolescents increasingly eat and drink more often with their agemates than they do at home, and the warnings and denunciations of drunkenness that were an integral part of socialization have often been supplanted by youthful encouragement and admiration of intoxication as a gesture of liberation or supposed empowerment.

Regional variation is significant, with mountainous locations consuming up to double the proportion of spirits in relation to wine or beer. Coffee has become so expensive that it is often treated as a dessert more than as a beverage; bottled water is making its appearance everywhere, with coin-operated dispensers at gas stations where local wines used to be sold.

In some areas, veneration of the grape has culminated in the establishment of exclusive special societies (often dubbed "knighthoods") that stage elaborately costumed ceremonies purporting to portray some of the history and traditions of wine in that region. Regalia, medals, ranks, initiations, and other trappings combine in an ambitious attempt to imply continuity over the centuries. Many will be surprised to learn, however, that the famous wine culture of modern France does not build on an ancient tradition, but is only about 150 years old. Before that, wines were rarely available except to the wealthy, although limited connoisseurship had been known earlier.

French wines are not only famous throughout the world, but some set the international standard for excellence. France has long been one of the major exporters of wine, as well as being among the top domestic consumers. People there often take special pride in the local products, and are apt also to denigrate the wines from other regions. The elaborate system of *appellations contrôlées* (which identifies the locations of vineyards down to specific local boundaries sometimes even within a given property) is meant to assure provenance, just as distinguishing different *crus* (harvests) within a given year's vintage provides further grading in terms of the sequence of successive pickings.

For some wines, it is known among fans what percentage of different varieties of grapes are used, and some producers take great pains to publicize those details. Where the law allows, labels usually carry the alcohol content, and in the U.S. it is required that sulfites be mentioned if they are present in certain amounts. The fact that there have been occasional scandals about the adulteration of French wines with the addition of cheaper Algerian ones is construed by many as proving the authorities' concern for accuracy in labeling rather than the duplicity of bottlers.

During the last two decades of the 20th century, as the French people drank less wine than in earlier years, they also turned to more expensive ones. Some common, if inaccurate, new stereotypes provide a rough gauge of quality on the basis of containers. Wine in a corked bottle is generally believed to be better than that in a screw-topped bottle. A screw-cap, in turn, is presumed to be used for better wine than one encounters under a crown-cap or a plastic lid. Then there is thought to be a quantum drop in quality as one moves from glass to plastic containers, and wine sold in waxed paper containers is generally regarded as *plonc*, suitable only for alcoholics. Wine that is sold in bulk (*en vrac*) from the keg to whatever container a customer brings, can run the gamut, depending on the source.

Until just a few years ago, a French person with any schooling at all was likely to quote or paraphrase Louis Pasteur, the distinguished 19th century chemist and developer of pasteurization, to the effect that wine is "the most hygienic of beverages," and to make rhapsodic allusions to "a meal without wine [a]s a day without sunshine." To be sure, a sizable portion of the population and even entire communities were engaged in some aspect of the wine trade—raising grapes, processing wine, or trading in it, whether for domestic consumption or for an eager world market.

The grape harvest must be carefully timed in terms of ripeness, as it relates to size, degree of sugar and moisture in the fruit, and weather. Harvesting machines are coming into use at some large vineyards, but handpicking is still favored. A skilled picker can gather about a ton of grapes a day without damaging the vines. Hearty meals are provided for all, and wine flows in abundance. Friends and neighbors visit after the hectic pace of harvesting is over, to sample and discuss the new wines, often comparing them in detail with earlier vintages. Tasting is a serious business with an elaborate vocabulary all its own. Careful attention is paid to color, fragrance, fruitiness, body, strength, and subtle hints of different flavors.

Bottles of different shapes and colors are used for different wines. Although a routine meal at home may involve drinking wine (and sometimes water) from just one or two standard glasses, an elaborate meal may involve six or more different wines, each carefully chosen to complement the food with which it is to be drunk. Discriminating wine drinkers often insist that each wine should be in a glass specifically designed to maximize one's appreciation of the beverage. Shapes vary in the degree to which they concentrate aroma, or the place where liquid first will be tasted along the tongue, and so forth. A specific tasting cup of polished metal (*tastevin*) often includes several convex mirror-like indentations on the bottom to reflect the light in many directions.

In the view of native ethnographers in modern urban France, "a meal becomes not only inconsistent but unthinkable" (de Certau et al., 1998, p. 85) in the absence of bread or wine. Neither is replaceable, and each is intimately linked with other parts of the preparation and consumption of all cuisine.

Although wine is thus a cornerstone of French gastronomy, it must never be thought of as just a food or as nothing more than an adjunct to food. Drinking wine is often decidedly an esthetic experience for the French, providing a delightful context for socializing with friends, reminiscing about enjoyable times past, speculating about the future, and savoring the wine all the time. The famous café society of the *Belle Époque* (bridging the 19th and 20th centuries) is alive and well in major French cities, with lesser versions of its genteel leisure, vaguely bohemian opportunities, and social leveling across the classes in almost any provincial city.

Young people in France, as elsewhere, are less concerned about large meals and more often eat away from home than was the case in past generations. They often spend large portions of the evening and night in the company of friends and age-mates at bars, cafés, and pizza parlors where they are more likely to drink beer than wine. They often speak of wine as if it were a stodgy drink, for older people, too formal for their tastes.

Champagne has circled the world as the paramount symbol of festivity at certain social and economic levels, just as brandy and certain French liqueurs are universally sought by drinkers who care more for taste than for effect. Although much remains the same about drinking in France and the imagery of French drinks, there is also much that has changed. Many of the stereotypes that were fairly accurate in the 1950s are seriously inaccurate today, and the convenient use of France as the prototypical "wet culture," with reference to those archaic patterns, adds little to our understanding of contemporary drinking occasions.

ETIQUETTE AND PARAPHERNALIA

There is a sense in which this whole book can be construed as dealing with rules or norms about drinking, but this section will focus on those situations where almost everyone agrees that the time, place, participants, and substance are right, but still there are specific gestures, or sequences, or verbal formulas that are also appropriate.

Etiquette

Etiquette often deals with what some would consider dispensable microlevel niceties, but those very details tend for others to be acts without which drinking would be less pleasant or proper than they think it should be. Some of these are what a social scientist would call rituals, not necessarily sacred, but highly stylized and repetitive, without being a functional requirement of getting the job done. In drinking, as in few other realms of behavior, toasting is another part of etiquette that often looms large in the minds of those who do it and expect that others will join them.

The etiquette of beer-drinking is enormously variable, even within a single society. Bartenders and publicans in the U.S. or U.K. may be meticulous about the proportion of foam or head to substance when drawing beer from a keg to a glass or a mug, and some are careful not to spill a drop, whereas others deliberately overfill each individual vessel to demonstrate their generosity in an aura of superabundance.

Within the drinking group, it is common in English-speaking countries around the world to have shouting or rounds, whereby each member invites all others to drink at his expense, which they return in succession (Heath, 1995). Unless someone offers a specific toast, English-speakers generally are free within a group to drink whenever they wish, although there is an implicit understanding that one should discreetly be aware of others and not drink much faster or slower than they. Close observation over extended periods of time reveals that people drinking in groups tend to adjust their pace to keep up with the fastest in the group, although that person may drink more slowly in that context than normally alone (Single & Storm, 1985). By contrast, in Spain and Latin America, it is generally expected that members of a group will drink only in unison, when some member of the group lifts a glass or makes a verbal cue inviting others to join in a drink. In some groups, but not all, people wait to take their cue from the senior or superordinate member.

Among the Mongols, declining a drink is interpreted as a refusal to engage them on equal and mutually respectful terms (Williams, 1998). Much the same occurs among males in Mexico (Gutmann, 1999) or, for that matter, throughout most of Latin America. In such a situation, no excuse short of a doctor's warning about a weak liver will be accepted. Coaxing and cajoling can be rebuffed for up to three offers, but to decline a fourth invitation is to risk serious and long-lasting alienation. The Mongols go beyond that in not counting the first drink as symbolically adequate assurance of acceptance; one is expected to drink at least four rounds just to observe the minimum standard of politeness. The Mongol host controls the serving, but constantly challenges his guests to drink more (Williams, 1998). Much of the socializing that they savor derives from the good-natured joking that involves pressure to drink more, and hesitance to take too much too fast. Singing a folk song is one of the few ways in which one may graciously decline a drink, but drunkenness is so often an outcome that a host is expected to provide a place so that guests can sleep off such a bout rather than venturing out into the cold.

The Chagga of Tanganyika do much of their drinking in an extremely formal ritual, with specific gestures and phrases used by the male host and female server, and equally standardized responses from each male guest (Gutmann, 1926). Far from being restricting, however, such formulaic behavior is construed as common courtesy, and such rituals are widely appreciated as providing sociability. In much the same way, the case study in chapter 6 outlines briefly the extremely formal way in which drinking must be done by those who take part in a Camba drinking party (Heath, 1958), although they may spend half of the total time of that party passed out on the ground. One-on-one toasting, the use of a single glass and a single bottle no matter how many people are in attendance, and the formulaic gestures and salutations all together deserve to be called ritual, in social scientific terms.

Among most of the peoples of China, toasting is an integral part of every large meal, and elaborately stylized drinking is important at every level of society when guests are welcomed to one's home, or when they depart (Xiao, 1995). In addition, it is important that the bride and groom exchange toasts with each guest at their wedding individually. Among toasting customs, one of the most consistent is that of overseas Chinese who lift their glasses and shout "YAAAAAAA ... M" just as loudly and as long as one can hold one's breath, ending with an equally loud "SENG" coming explosively with the last of one's breath. *Yaam seng* translates roughly "bottoms up," but the distinctive volume and lengthening of the toast is a highly esteemed skill that individuals cultivate, providing an occasion for good-natured competition, supposedly demonstrating the depth of one's feeling, and generally lightening the mood of whatever the situation (Arokiasamy, 1995).

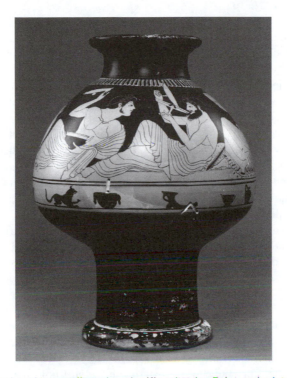

This ceramic red-psykter, attributed to the Kleophrades Painter, depicts a scene from a *symposion* and silhouettes of various kinds of drinking vessels. The original symposium in ancient Greece was a party at which older men coached young men in the arts of logic, conversation, love, and drinking. © *The Art Museum, Princeton University. Museum purchase, gift of Peter Jay Sharp, Class of 1952, through the Peter Jay Sharp Foundation; Lloyd E. Cotsen, Class of 1950; John B. Elliott, Class of 1951; and Jonathan P. Rosen, though the Joseph Rosen Foundation. Photo credit: Clem Fiori.*

Toasting is so much an art form in the Republic of Georgia that skilled toastmasters have celebrity status and are engaged to preside over banquets where their role is to improvise imaginatively within the constraints of a strict sequential pattern (Mars & Altman, 1987), often embellishing with verse, hyperbole, and other rhetorical forms. In the course of a long meal, they may preside over 50 or more toasts in which all who are present are expected to join, with due attention being paid, by turns, to the host, community, region, nation, each guest (individually, in sequence by status) and his or her community and nation, other distinguished people present, and eventually to all who are present. Each toast is supposed to be inventive, apt, interesting, and worthy of the person to whom it is dedicated.

A young Tiriki man offers beer to a woman he finds attractive; if she accepts, and then spits some of the beer into his mouth, they consider themselves engaged to be married (Sangree, 1962). The man must then try to ingratiate himself with her father and brothers, always bringing lavish gifts of beer on his visits, until he wins acceptance. Every step in the elaborate process of courtship and marriage is marked by gifts of beer, and the prewedding bachelor party is marked by heavy beer drinking by the prospective groom and all of his friends at his expense.

When someone in the U.S. says something a little surprising but that one wants to agree with emphatically, it is not uncommon for another person to say, "I'll drink to that!" Or if a wish or goal is voiced with exceptional strength or vividness, someone may say, "Let's drink to that!" This is not to imply that people routinely drink a toast to affirm such agreement, and if there is no drink present, such a statement may be taken as nothing more than a conversational device signaling endorsement. Of course, when such a statement is made and beverage alcohol is readily at hand, there may be actual toasting, and the device can become utilitarian to speed up drinking.

In many parts of the world (certainly including but not restricted to Spain, France, Scotland, Israel, Mexico, and the U.S.), the simplest and most common toast is a wish of health, for one or for all present. Elaborations can be almost infinite, in praise of a person or an institution, wishing a happy outcome for a joint venture, complimenting someone for a job well done, or simply giving voice to some of one's fondest wishes. It often entails the raising of the drinking vessel and everyone's looking at the object of the toast. Historically, two main protagonists would often make their glasses touch, or even spill some drink from each into the other—presumably as a demonstration that there was no poison in either. Sticklers for etiquette in western Europe still hold that the individual being toasted should not drink when others are saluting him or her, but this custom is fast disappearing. In certain circles, people put a premium on the wit, poetry, imagination, or eloquence with which a toast is made, but again this creative kind of wordplay has lost importance in recent years. In general, perhaps, rare and expensive drinks tend more often to be drunk with toasts, whereas everyday ones tend not to be.

There are few writings that deal specifically with etiquette and drink, although many ethnographic accounts contain brief mentions of specific details. For example, we have already seen how the sequence of drinking in some situations is strictly by seniority, whereas in others it is important that everyone drink at the same time. With wines, it is expected that the host in any European context will take an initial sip—sometimes after sniffing the cork, scrutinizing the color, and swirling the wine in his glass—before nodding to the waitperson that others at the table should be served. The sequencing of drinks, and the pairing of particular beverages with particular parts of the meal, are as much a matter of etiquette as they are of gastronomy. If one is served an exceptional drink, it is often expected that a guest will remark upon it.

One need not deal with complex urban societies when taking about the etiquette of drink, however. It is just as important to a Quechua (Allen, 1988) or Aymara (LaBarre, 1948) Indian in the Andes to *ch'allar*, that is, to spill or flick a tiny portion to the gods before taking a drink, as it is that the drink be offered and accepted with specific prescribed phrases. Among the Kofyar

(Netting, 1964) and neighboring groups who drink beer from a common pot, they are meticulous about each man's bringing his own elaborately crafted straw; the idea of sharing a straw would be unthinkable. By contrast, a South African who did not readily share his mug of beer with others (Wolcott, 1974) would be considered selfish and impolite.

Another aspect of drinking etiquette is the expectation of reciprocity. With shouting or rounds in Australia (Hall & Hunter, 1995), New Zealand (Park, 1995), U.K. (Mass Observation, 1943), or in a U.S. tavern (LeMasters, 1975), the reciprocity may be almost immediate. In other contexts, the reciprocity may be deferred, expected in the indefinite future as a return for the favor of a drink at present. Among Papago Indians who have moved to the city in southwestern U.S. (Waddell, 1975), such an arrangement involves not just the debt of a drink but a larger ongoing relationship that may extend to help in many other realms. The Papago often congregate in a few specific bars, which may get to be known as "Indian bars," to meet with fellow countrymen, to learn about the availability of jobs or reasonable housing, and to plan or reminisce among friends. As members of a group who are sometimes subject to ethnic discrimination, they tend to have only short-term and low-paying jobs. An interesting adaptation to such underclass status is the "social credit" that an individual can accrue by buying drinks for others on those occasions when he does have a small surplus, confident in the expectation that others will do the same when he is out of funds sometime in the future. Along with the implication of long-term reciprocity in drinks, there is also an implied commitment of general mutual support. In this way, a circle of acquaintances can become friendly and helpful on the basis of exchanging a few drinks, even if the drinks are months apart. A similar kind of social credit is reported among aboriginal Australians, with generalized mutual help growing out of episodic shared drinking experiences (Collman, 1979).

Tasting is in itself a remarkable ceremony that has drink as its focus. Few foods or other things are ever made the focus of such attention and detailed comment, evaluation, and appreciation in this way. As described in some detail later in this chapter, tasting is a very special style of drinking, for very special purposes. Those who work at it aim not just to be able to say which among the samples they prefer, but also why. The combination of secrecy and evaluation puts each participant in a position that some view as competitive; discussion is expected not to be repetitive but imaginative and apt. To the eye of someone who has no clear idea of what is being done, such a session might well appear to be a recondite and slightly absurd ritual, but its purpose is of earnest concern to those who do take part. An elaborate vocabulary—some would call it a language—is constantly evolving about tasting. At expositions and other competitions, well known judges award medals, rankings and commendations that enhance both the prestige of the makers and the market for the product. Among friends and neighbors, it may be just a pleasant pastime that helps them decide what drink to have next week.

If the bartender or server recognizes a customer from an earlier occasion, and remembers what that person drank, it is a courtesy to greet him or her as a regular, and casually ask, "the usual?" (Spradley & Mann, 1975). Many customers are highly flattered by such behavior and give disproportionately generous gratuities for such recognition. Similarly, it would be considered impolite for a bartender not to listen with apparent patience, and preferably even some commiseration, to a customer's tale of woe, no matter how involved or absurd it may seem (Cavan, 1966).

In South African shebeens (Bailey & Seftel, 1994; Hellman, 1934), the "shebeen queen" is not only the owner and vendor of drinks, but she is also a confidant of customers, an impresario of local talent for entertainment, a lively conversationalist, and always able to manage the crowd. A similar combination of skills or talents distinguish the proprietor of an outstanding (as contrasted with a run-of-the-mill) cantina (Stross, 1967) or *pulquería* (pulque bar) in Mexico, *chichería* (chicha bar) in Peru (Doughty, 1971), or *guarería* (rum bar) in Costa Rica. For that matter, British pubs with such an ambience tend to be preferred by many (Hunt & Satterlee, 1986); there are few drinkers in public places who truly wish to be left alone (Single & Storm, 1985).

A few generalizations may be in order, despite the variation that we see on this topic. When a beverage is thought of as a food, there tends to be less ceremony and etiquette involved in drinking. Time, place, sequencing, and gestures are all less important than is the case with drinking that is compartmentalized as somehow different (even when the eating of various foods is an adjunct to such drinking). And in urban or other cosmopolitan settings within developing countries, drinking patterns are sometimes modeled on colonial antecedents, or on what the local people see (or imagine) of Europeans, often using costly imported drinks or local counterparts and counterfeits (Isaac, 1998).

Paraphernalia

We have already found that to look at how people drink is superficially a simple matter, but to do it in a way that will increase our understanding of the elaborate and emotionally charged realm of human behavior demands that attention be paid to many aspects. For example, it is noteworthy that there has been so much technological elaboration around the simple matter of containers and implements that are associated with drink. Although ethanol occurs naturally from time to time, in many contexts, part of the way in which humankind has made it their own is by domesticating it, putting a cultural imprint on drink and drinking. In simplest terms, this may have to do with little more than the containers in which it is prepared, stored, or served, but elaborations beyond that are almost infinite. To a striking degree, any or all of these may also be the subject of considerable affect or emotion, with strong feelings for and against the propriety of any given artifact for any given drink. Associated tools or appurtenances range from corkscrews to drinking straws, from shakers to strainers, again elaborated to a remarkable degree in different cultures over time, and some are loaded with symbolic value. How people relate to things is an important part of how they relate to the world around them and to each other, so that paraphernalia deserves our attention as an integral part of the world of drink.

For the preparation of a homebrew, a container as simple as a hollowed log can serve, as is evidenced by the contemporary Lacandon Maya making balché, a root-flavored honey beer (McGee, 1990). We have already seen that residue in a ceramic pot is the earliest archeological trace we have of winemaking in Mesopotamia (Badler, 1996). Black South Africans were found to suffer less from iron overload after having switched from homebrew, which had been traditionally made in iron kettles, to commercially produced beers (MacPhail et al., 1979). The preoccupation with cleanliness and sanitation in many modern breweries, wineries, and distilleries is often a surprise to visitors.

The storing of beverage alcohol after it is produced can be no problem at all, if we are dealing with a homebrew that will spoil if it is not drunk within a couple of days. Or it can be a major concern of the makers of commercial beer, which is made in huge quantities, with storage necessary at various stages of production. Storage is even more a concern with wine or spirits; some are also produced in enormous batches that require multiple tanks for holding large quantities, and some are laid down to age for years, or even decades, requiring very different kinds of storage, a number of which markedly enhance the drink.

As in ancient times, goatskins tanned and sewn inside-out still serve as unbreakable and reusable vessels for storing and shipping wines, chichas, and pulque in various regions of the world. Ceramic pots are more durable, often hold larger quantities, and some are preserved after centuries, with their seals intact, after lying in shipwrecks or tombs. In much of the world, clay pots continue to be the usual receptacles for storage, just as they are the usual vessels for preparation, when brewing or winemaking is still a domestic enterprise. Wooden staves can be made into kegs and barrels that are larger and sturdier than ceramic, and, depending on the quality of the wood that is used, they can impart enhancing flavors to their contents. Barrels differ greatly in size and shape; some European winecellars are graced with elaborately carved kegs as large as a small house. Others contain row upon row of smaller barrels, sometimes stacked on each other, by the thousands in cavernous subterranean warehouses chosen for their constant temperature and humidity.

Just as there are physical limits to how large a clay pot it is feasible to fill with liquid, there are also limits to what can be done with wood in that connection. With mass production, breweries and wineries turned to metal holding tanks, many of which have subsequently been lined with glass, fiberglass, or plastic.

Even after having been pasteurized and stored in a clean and tightly sealed bottle or can, beer tends to lose its fresh taste after a few months. Brown glass tends to be a better preservative than green or clear glass because it lets in less sunlight, which shortens the shelf life of beer. The different colors and shapes of wine bottles appear to have less importance in terms of preservation, although they are sometimes symbolically important in identifying types or varieties of wines from different regions. The same is true with respect to containers for distilled beverages.

The sizes of containers also vary dramatically, sometimes for convenience and sometimes for display. Seals, stoppers, taps, and corks themselves are also the subject of considerable concern. High quality corks are made from the bark of a particular kind of oak tree; it has the advantage of keeping anything from entering the bottle while allowing the wine to breathe, giving off minute quantities of gases that subtly affect the aging process. Cheaper corks may be pressed from scraps or made of other materials. Experimental plastic caps were not well received in the 1970s, so only cheaper wines continue to use them. Plastic bottles, metal crown caps, or twist-caps, and plastic hoods were similarly generally rejected by wine drinkers, although they are used for the least expensive products. Tools for corking, uncorking, and recorking range from the simplest utilitarian object to elaborately designed and ornamented gadgets that bear little relation to their basic requirements. Some enthusiasts are so concerned about preserving the freshness of wine, even after a bottle has been opened, that they inject inert gas to refill the bottle.

As we move from storage to serving, there may be an intermediate step of mixing; certainly, it was important in ancient Greek and Roman times, when most wines were mixed with other wines or with water. Often ceramics decorated by the finest painters of the time, or magnificently sculpted if in metal, some mixing vessels are truly exquisite works of art which today grace major museums around the world. Because they have turned up so consistently in the graves of wealthy and distinguished leaders in Iron and Bronze Age northern Europe, archeologists assume that control over wine was one of the bases of their status. These wealthy individuals are thought to have portioned wine out among their subordinates and followers in much the way that leaders in many non-Western societies are still expected to share their wealth and prove their aptitude by demonstrating generosity (Dietler, 1990, 1996). Mixing and serving bowls for wine were at least equal in both their degree of artistic embellishment and in their numbers throughout much of ancient China, Japan, and the Near East, where similar interpretations are probably warranted (Joffe, 1998).

Large and elaborate bowls, buckets, and pitchers are still made of a wide range of materials, including the finest crystal and metals, and often they are lavishly ornamented. Even a simple neighborhood bar or pub may include elaborate handles on the pumps that give the publican or bartender a remarkable degree of control over the flow of beer or ale from keg to glass. And the act of drawing a drink is spoken of by devotees as combining remarkable skill and grace to get just the right amount of foam (but not a drop more), an appropriate fullness (but not a drop less), and so forth. Non-Western peoples have no monopoly on ritual with respect to drink.

Other utensils to which some people attach great importance (but which are obviously not indispensable, as we look cross-culturally) include, for example, special caps such as are attached to spirits bottles to measure each pouring, with the intention that the quantity be standard and uniform, as well as special cans, jars, and strainers for mixing certain kinds of drinks. A special measuring glass may be used, again ostensibly to standardize the size of a drink—although it is symbolically important to some servers or customers that what is actually poured into a drink exceed that measured amount. All such niceties seem to fit with the interpretation of much of public drinking as conspicuous consumption; drinking in a public place is usually much more costly than doing so elsewhere.

In a *chichería* in the Andes, a *pulquería* in Mexico, or a shebeen in South Africa, the storage receptacle may still be a large unadorned ceramic pot, and the serving container a plain clay or plastic cup, half of a dried gourd, or tree-calabash. It is with respect to the individual drinking container that we find the greatest elaboration and variation. In the 1700s in the U.S. and U.K., leather tankards would sometimes popularly be used for beer or ale, with finely made silver or pewter ones for wealthier drinkers. Ceramic tankards, often with metal hinged lids, were popular in northern Europe. Glass tankards 100 years later, were largely replaced by glass tumblers (generally of much smaller volume) early in the 1900s. A yard-of-ale in England was a glass container, shaped vaguely like a coachman's horn, approximately a yard long (about 90 cm.), and holding about three pints (or 1.7 liters). Commonly in the 17th century, and still occasionally in competitive drinking, the drinker is expected to drain it in a single draught. In Germany and Austria, some mugs hold almost as much as that, although the usual is not more than half as large. In beerhalls throughout southern Africa, plastic buckets containing two to four liters are the standard serving, sometimes shared but perhaps more often drunk slowly by a single client.

With mass production in factories of glassware, one might expect to find much greater uniformity, but quite the opposite has happened. Part of the mystique, or perhaps it is the ludic or play aspect of drinking, seems to be expressed precisely in the material realm, with an elaboration of paraphernalia during the 1900s that is truly remarkable. Wherever it began, a large portion of it has diffused to cities around the world as part of the cosmopolitan international drinking culture that, for certain social strata, has come to overlay traditional patterns almost everywhere. Many mixed drinks with different additives are named and served in special containers. Although there are general-purpose wine glasses, there are also specially shaped ones for many different kinds of wine. Beautifully carved wine cups of semiprecious stone, inscribed with rapturous paeans to drink and drunkenness are proofs of the popularity of alcohol among Arabic peoples before Islam, and among eastern Asians before Buddhism.

Whereas some of the material culture that is associated with drinking occasions has hardly changed over the course of centuries, some other paraphernalia changes rapidly. The pull-tabs that provide easy access to beer in metal cans evolved so rapidly in design that historical archeologists familiar with the typology can often use them to date excavated strata to within a couple of years. The degree to which human ingenuity has been invested in the making and use of beverage alcohol should never be underestimated.

Drinking etiquette often involves specific, sometimes even elaborate, gestures and other patterns of behavior as illustrated by this French Polynesian couple drinking from a nutshell. © *Jodi Cobb/NGS Image Collection.*

RHYTHM AND EXCESS

Although our choice of terminology may be unorthodox, this section deals with issues that are familiar in alcohol studies. By rhythm is meant the pace of drinking, not just during the act of ingestion but also the rate over time that can result in the labeling of someone as a light, moderate, or heavy drinker. By excess, we refer to that kind of drinking that is truly psychoactive, the effects and meanings of intoxication or drunkenness, when the amount of alcohol that someone drinks seems to influence the course of other behavior.

Rhythm

Many of us might never think to use the term in reference to our everyday lives, but there is usually a rhythm to at least major parts of what we do. The daily round of sleeping, eating, working, and doing other things is one example. Another is the pace or rate at which we do any of those things. In drinking, too, one can discern different kinds of rhythms. In the short term, this may focus just on what one does while drinking. Over time, it may have to do with when one chooses to drink, or how much at one time and how much at another. With attention to longer periods, it is often possible to see fads and fashions, not only in the behavior of an individual, but collectively in the behavior of a group. Some of these may even turn out to be trends, changes in the market, or historical shifts in taste, popularity, and customs.

Let us first consider the question of rhythm while people are drinking. Long-term intensive observation has revealed that, at least in the midwestern U.S., the pace of drinking in a bar is generally inverse to the tempo of the music that is playing simultaneously (Bach & Schaefer, 1979). Other studies in bars show that members of a group tend, over the period of a half-hour of so, to coordinate their sipping so that, while not doing it simultaneously, they do it at roughly the same rate. The adjustment of pace tends to be upward, approximating that of the fastest drinker. Through all of this, the participants in such a group appear to be totally oblivious of any such strain toward conformity, and even deny it when directly asked after the behavior has already been observed at length (Single & Storm, 1985).

Drinking with meals raises a whole new set of issues. The pace of drinking tends to be much slower than when one is only drinking with snacks (which are often salty, specifically to make one more thirsty). The presence of food in the digestive system means that some of the alcohol is absorbed there rather than going directly into the circulatory system. It also means that the stomach and gut are less vacant and so can accommodate less liquid. Quite apart from those mechanical aspects of drinking with meals is the matter of pace; drinking is interspersed with eating, and presumably often with conversation. In addition, there is not likely to be much attention paid to the possibility that the drinking could be risky if carried to extremes; that rarely happens to people who drink while eating.

As we shift our focus to the rhythm of drinking over time, we find, for example, that the Bantu peoples of Africa had long been heavy drinkers of homebrewed beer, with everyone drinking it throughout the day, both as a refreshing beverage and as an important food in their overall diet (Steinkraus, 1979). That kind of drinking, slowly paced, and of a low-alcohol beer, was more nutritious than intoxicating, and it was unimaginable to them that beer might be associated with any kinds of problems. The eventual introduction of European beverages among them, however, was associated with considerable social disruption (Hutchinson, 1961). These included bottled beer with less food value and more alcohol, spirits with no food value and high alcohol content, and strong wine, which they were given periodically throughout the day as part of their wage while working for Europeans (Onselen, 1976). Other populations throughout much of Africa and Latin America had similar experiences.

Many towns in Spain well illustrate the Mediterranean pattern of steady drinking of alcohol throughout much of the day, resulting in high consumption, but with no drunkenness and virtually no alcohol-related problems. Beer, wine, brandy, and anise liqueur are the mainstays, with grape-based moonshine (aguardiente) a frequent addition. Both red and white wine accompany the midday and evening meals, averaging a liter a day for adults of both sexes. Certain foods are cooked in wine or brandy, and an afterdinner digestive or a nightcap of distilled spirits before going to bed are parts of the daily routine. This pattern is very much like that found in most of France during most of this century (Nahoum-Grappe, 1995) and in Italy (Cottino, 1995).

Strikingly different is the Nordic pattern in which people may have nothing to drink for most of a week or two, but then drink large quantities of spirits in a short time, resulting in extreme drunkenness for a day or two in succession (Suuorinen, 1973). Such episodic heavy drinking, alternating with longer periods of abstinence, was generally called a binge.

In survey research, it is commonplace to ask respondents how often they have had a drink during various periods (within a day, a week, a month, a year, or ever - sometimes retrospectively for "the last" such, or sometimes for "an average" such period) (Room, 1990). On the basis of such information, individuals are then grouped or classified as light, moderate, or heavy drinkers— sometimes with greater elaboration to include both quantity and frequency in a single label.

Few countries and no non-Western cultures have such detailed information available, but a few data from recent U.S. surveys illustrate the kinds of state- ments that can be made on the basis of those questions. For example, we are told that 71% of U.S. men drink and 59% of women (Hilton, 1991d). However, if we ask how many drink in a month, the percentage of men falls, and that of women falls more drastically. If we go on to ask about a week, the percentage of men falls again, and that of women even more sharply (Hilton, 1991d). These general patterns may appear even more dramatic when one considers how very little and how very seldom most people in the U.S. drink. A recent detailed study yielded the following remarkable conclusions (Greenfield & Rogers, 1999). They found that men report drinking fully 76% of the country's total reported consumption, with young adults (aged 18–29) consuming 45% of the alcohol, although they are only 27% of the population. The population pyramid based on consumption rather than age is also remarkable: the top 20% of drinkers apparently account for about 88% of the alcohol; the top 5% account for about 40%, and the top 2.5% drink 26% of the total. According to this analysis, based on self-reported data, most of the drinking in the U.S. is done by a relatively small population of heavy drinkers. Conversely, the great majority of U.S. drinkers appear to have very little and to drink very seldom in comparison.

This is so strikingly the case that we encounter a curious paradox with respect to what has been defined as moderate drinking in the dietary guidelines for Americans (U.S. Department of Agriculture & Department of Health and Human Services, 1995, p. 40), namely, "no more than one drink per day for women and no more than two drinks per day for men." The irony is that a man who drank those two per day would be having 14 per week, which, although moderate as defined by the official guidelines, is "heavy" in the usage of most survey researchers (Room, 1990).

The vast majority of Camba individuals are episodic heavy drinkers; the remaining few (mostly fundamentalist Protestants) are abstainers (Heath, 1958); the same is true of the Sikaiana (Donnor, 1994). The Kofyar (Netting, 1964) and many other peoples who drink homebrew regularly in large quantities and who would appear to be extremely heavy drinkers, even in cross-cultural perspective, although they do not suffer any kind of impairment such as is generally thought to be associated with such alcohol consumption.

Excess

On the subject of excess, there has been less discussion in this book than is usual on the subject of drink for the simple reason that the ways in which most people drink most of the time, are not marked by excess. Of course, that word itself is problematic, being inherently relative. For the confirmed abstainer, two drinks in a year would be excessive, whereas there are distinguished physicians (Doll, 1998) as well as public health agencies in various governments that recommend two drinks (or more) daily as moderate and likely to be of benefit to the coronary health of many middle-aged persons (International Center for Alcohol Policies, 1997). There is widespread agreement among many scientists and researchers nowadays that the threshold to risky drinking—that which puts an individual at increased risk for harm, whether from an accident, from long-term damage to any of a number of internal organs, or from damaged social relationships at work or school, with friends or family, with police or others—is lower than many laypersons believe. Some put that number at five drinks (of .5 oz. of ethanol each) daily; others at six; still others at eight or ten, but there is remarkable consensus that more than that is "heavy" or "excessive" drinking. (The reader must keep in mind that all statements about "benefits" or about "risks" or "harms" that may be associated with drinking certain amounts are necessarily generalizations based on statistical trends within population studies. As such, they have no predictive value for any individual and can tell us nothing more precise than probabilities about the actual future of any drinker.)

Recognizing that such heavy drinking can be dangerous, we must also be aware of the significant difference between occasional or acute episodes and chronic or repetitive drinking in such a manner. The healthy human body is well equipped, for reasons that are not at all clear, to process ethanol in a way that quite readily converts it into water and carbon dioxide, which are then routinely excreted through breath, sweat, urine, or evaporation. The rate at which that process operates differs somewhat from one person to the next, depending partly on weight, body build, the presence or absence of food in the digestive tract, endogenous amounts of particular enzymes, and the condition of the liver, but a healthy person can usually metabolize a "standard drink" (International Center for Alcohol Policies, etc., 1998b; Turner, 1990) in about an hour, and does so at a constant rate. As one drinks faster than that, some alcohol remains in the system (as measured by BAC, blood-alcohol concentration, or BAL, blood-alcohol level), and some cumulative effects may be discerned. Slurring of speech and difficulty in walking tend to occur at around 0.3% BAC (or 300 mg%), affording a not unreasonable rough-and-ready basis for estimating that someone is "visibly" drunk, and, for most purposes, a measure of "excess." What those terms mean, and how they relate to other aspects of the world of drink, will be explored, with some illustrative examples.

A "standard drink" is a convenient measure, sometimes used to regulate commercial sales, and sometimes used by researchers to count and compare beverages that contain differing amounts of alcohol. For example, a typical "drink" (in the U.S. in 2000) contains about 12.5 g. of absolute alcohol (i.e., ethanol) regardless of whether it is a 1-oz. shot of 84-proof liquor or spirits; a 12-oz. can, bottle, or glass of beer (at 4%); a 4-oz. glass of wine (at 12%); or a 2.5-oz. glass of cordial (at 20%). Unfortunately, in the real world, drinks are not nearly so standardized, with spirits at different proofs, servings of different sizes, and beers and wines with different alcoholic contents. In addition, standard drink sizes differ in various countries: for example, 8 g. of ethanol in the U.K., and 19.75 g. in Japan (International Center for Alcohol Policies, 1998b; Turner, 1990). Such variations, coupled with the fact that few individuals can accurately assess the size or strength of a drink, raise serious questions about self-reported estimates of drinking that are the basis of so many of the statistical reports available on alcohol consumption and its relation to other variables.

Most who write about alcohol focus their attention on the minority for whom drinking is not a pleasant or enjoyable part of everyday life but is rather a special venture, and who drink in ways that can be dangerous to themselves or to others. Although the ways in which they do that may equally be patterned by culture, they tend to be disapproved and often strongly rejected by the majority, although not necessarily by the smaller subgroup with whom the drinker more closely identifies. Almost every society has some notion of excess, and, although the nature of such behavior may vary greatly by some quantitative measures, the categorization of excess generally has very negative connotations. Whereas a single drink on New Years Eve may be excessive for a devout abstainer, falling asleep drunk may not be for a Camba. But drinking even a glassful while carrying a patron saint's statue in a religious procession would be excessive for a Camba. Our discussions of when, where, how, and what have included some comments about the limits of propriety—not just contexts in which people consider it all right to drink but also some in which they view drinking as either requisite or inappropriate. Now we look at other limits of propriety in terms of drinking that may be viewed as excessive.

Even if we use gross physical impairment as a relatively simple and cross-culturally recognizable criterion of excessive drinking, we must keep in mind that it is only relatively simple as a criterion, because individuals differ so markedly in the degree to which they are affected by ethanol. The same dose does not produce the same BAC in different individuals, and the same BAC does not have the same effect on different individuals. But we can talk meaningfully about typical or normal effects, extremes, and ranges of variation. Our hypothetical healthy person of around 50–70 kg, with no previous major drinking problems, might reach a BAC of about .10% (or 100 mg%) after having 4–5 drinks in an hour on an empty stomach. Faster or continued drinking would be needed to reach the .30% (or 300 mg%) earlier characterized as probably showing visible drunkenness. At .40% (or 400 mg%), an inexperienced drinker is likely to lose consciousness. At .50% (or 500 mg%), the portions of the brain that control breathing and heart-functioning are likely to be so depressed that those vital functions stop, resulting in death.

Alcohol is unusual in that the limit of behavioral tolerance so closely approaches a lethal dose. Thus, every year one reads about some death from alcohol poisoning, basically from an overdose. When it happens, it is usually to a first-time drinker who was experimenting or who was goaded by others to drink too much too fast. Individuals, however, vary so markedly in both rates of metabolism and tolerance to ethanol, that there have been a few clinical cases recorded where patients were ambulatory with a BAC of .80% (or 800 mg%), at one extreme. Alcohol, like salt, water, chromium, or many other substances that are necessary for human health, happens also to be a poison, but, as any medical practitioner is well aware, the poison is in the dose rather than in the substance.

The familiar word "intoxication" is rooted in the idea of poison. It is a familiar pattern in many societies, nevertheless, that a number of individuals become intoxicated with some regularity, and many of them are eager to repeat the experience. That is what, in this book, is meant by "excess" in relation to drinking occasions, and it does not at all imply that such drinking would be viewed as excessive in terms of the norms of every culture.

Part of our interest in this subject should be the range of variation that we do find cross-culturally. There is a significant difference between drinking and becoming drunk or intoxicated. Many people drink with considerable regularity without ever being drunk, and yet there are others who cannot imagine drinking without drunkenness as an outcome. For that matter, it is not a simple matter to say what being drunk means. In English, as in many languages, there is a scale (however imprecise) that ranges from such low level stages as tipsy, tight, high, relaxed, or feeling good to such high level stages as blotto, smashed, out of it, or dead drunk, with literally dozens of other terms also in common usage. Compilers of slang-dictionaries have repeatedly noted that this is one of the semantically richest aspects of life, elaborated far more than most. These latter terms imply that impairment is recognized as one important aspect of drunkenness, and certainly that is the principal justification for most of the laws and rules that oppose or aim to restrict drunkenness.

Such distinctions should not be construed as peculiar to English however. In Danish, there is a word similar to "coziness" that describes an ideal state to be achieved from "just enough" drinking; this state carries no risk and is relaxing and welcome when achieved (Schiøler, 1995). Perhaps analogous is *ivresse* in French, having to do with gaiety, spontaneity, and zest, the very antithesis of impairment (Felice, 1936; Nahoum-Grappe, 1995), a kind of alcohol-induced rapture that is much esteemed by the French, most of whom heartily deplore clumsy or unseemly drunken comportment.

The Ainu of Japan are among those who consider drunkenness to be a normal state on special occasions, even though they only drink beverage alcohol in religious contexts. For them, a libation is the only way to communicate with the gods, and one must drink part of the libation to assure that the prayer will be listened to. The special kind of altered consciousness that comes from having drunk heavily is thought to provide the ideal relationship with supernatural beings.

Among the Sikaiana of Polynesia, heavy drinking "creates a timeless stream of involvement that is opposed to the segmented and scheduled relations of modernity" (Donnor, 1994, p. 245). Fermented coconut sap (toddy) is the drink of choice, taken only in a strictly formalized way. There is only one cup, and the host apportions drinks equally to everyone by turns. Parties may take place anywhere in the open within a village, and all are welcome to participate. People who are normally shy and diffident drink "to intensify happiness" and often sing, dance, and laugh together. Intentionally or not, drinking also serves to intensify unhappiness in some, so that confrontations over land disputes, complaints against nonreciprocity, boasts, sexual advances, and crying can be among the negative outcomes of such a party, with occasional fighting and property destruction by people who would never be assertive otherwise. A classic instance of what MacAndrew and Edgerton (1969) described as the "time-out" quality of drinking, disruptive or destructive behavior is supposedly dismissed as an inconsequential effect of drunkenness. Not only does such drinking revive their sense of ethnic identity but it also "reaffirms the individual's participation in communal relations" (Donnor, 1994, p. 257). And this all takes place in the context of drinking parties that continue day and night with some individuals passing out or falling asleep from time to time while the others continue to party. Somewhat similar parties around-the-clock with participants drinking to the point of oblivion (dissimilar in the sense that no untoward behavior occurs) typify the Camba (Heath, 1958), for whom sociability also appears to be a major motivation (see the case study in chapter 6).

Those who cherish the exquisite beauty and sheer excitement of human sensibilities may wonder why anyone would deliberately choose to dull their senses. But there are those who live surrounded more by pain and ugliness than by beauty. Some have simply never learned to appreciate the normal feedback of daily living and seek heightened enjoyment in drink. The zest of defying authority, demonstrating independence, or doing something that would otherwise be censured are often mentioned as reasons why other people deliberately set out to make themselves drunk. Drunkenness can provide a brief holiday from responsibility or escape from an unpleasant situation without regard for the fact that both will likely still be there when the individual sobers up.

Occasional drunkenness is acceptable for adult males in Australia, as long as they are not violent. In the Azores, it can be humorous on rare occasions, although it is shameful as a habit. Canadians generally reject it, except occasionally among young males. Chileans, by contrast, almost expect it as an occasional recreation among men, although it is viewed as shameful for a woman. In Chile, the Ministry of Public Health rates as a moderate drinker someone who drinks

A Moscow club sports Soviet-era memorabilia, creating a nostalgic atmosphere in a period in which many Russians are critical of the changes wrought by the introduction of capitalism. Setting—exotic, nostalgic, or other—is often an important component in drinking occasions. © *Yuri Gripas.*

no more than 0.75 liters of wine a day, and who is drunk nor more than 12 times a year, deriving up to 20% of one's total caloric intake from alcohol (Medina, 1995, pp. 33–34).

Although by no means universal, it is common among populations that are economically poor, politically powerless, and subject to racial or ethnic discrimination, to find an unspoken all-or-none premise with respect to drink. That is, individuals and groups often do without any drinking for long periods of time but, when an opportunity presents itself, they drink as much as they can. Far from being a perverse or absurd pattern of behavior, this is often realistic and adaptive, modeled on the way in which they also deal with food and other limited resources.

Jesuit missionaries among various Indian tribes of northeastern North America in the 1600s were sharp enough observers of local customs to recognize that the Indian style of drinking until supplies were exhausted did not necessarily represent gluttony or dissolution so much as it reflected the long-standing tradition of consuming everything available on those rare occasions when any food was in abundance (Dailey, 1968).

Melanesian drinking parties have two very different paces or rhythms, depending on whether the host has specified that the drinking is to be "American cup" or "Indian cup." Evidently on the basis of movies about the old West, they think that the style of most cowboys was to sip their drinks, whereas Indians were portrayed as taking their drinks in a single gulp. A risk inherent in the Indian cup is that a drinker may become intoxicated too soon, and disgrace himself by vomiting or acting in an otherwise inappropriate way that would evoke ridicule from his drinking companions (Nason, 1975).

The pattern of shouting or rounds in bars or pubs at first appears to be an eminently egalitarian custom. But it is sometimes burdensome, as when one would rather economize by buying only a couple of drinks for himself, or when another would rather leave the group but feels that he cannot afford to lose the return on his earlier investment, or to incur the scorn of some from whom he had accepted drinks without reciprocating. For many people, shouting means that they drink more, and they drink longer, than they would otherwise. In this way, the norm for the group may mean excess for some individuals.

In Nordic countries, it is expected that adult males will frequently join groups of friends and drink to the point of drunkenness with some frequency, but it is also expected that they will do so in a place away from home and children. Partanen (1991) speaks of such "heroic drinking" as that "from which all instrumentality and self-reflection are absent," noting that it is a pattern that recurs cross-culturally but with similar values: male, communal, and amoral.

Episodic heavy drinking on the part of college students in the U.S. is being viewed with alarm, although overall drinking by that age-group, as by all other segments of the population, has dramatically declined for at least 10 years. A relatively high rate of traffic fatalities, occasional deaths by overdose, and other dangers and inconveniences among those young people highlight a subcultural set of attitudes that are in conflict with the official norm, whereby they are not yet old enough to drink. They often cite the need for relief from stress as their reason for drinking; the frequency of vandalism suggests that often there is also a component of rebelliousness involved.

In some contexts, drunkenness is expected as a demonstration of one's masculinity. In others, as mentioned under reasons why people drink, it is an act of religious homage, expected of women as well.

For those who are not taking part, drunkenness is often disparaged as a waste of money, a disgusting spectacle, or a public danger. Icelanders often retort that moderate drinking is the wasteful pattern, inasmuch as the best reason for drinking is to get drunk (Ásmundsson, 1995). The disgust with drunkenness is usually more an esthetic than a moral judgment, more in reaction to profanity, vomit, urination in public, and such, than a blanket condemnation of the act. The public danger is dramatic in instances of DWI, when a driver's vision, judgment, and coordination are so impaired that bystanders may be killed and injured (Gusfield, 1981). An intoxicated pedestrian can pose another kind of hazard. Drownings, falls, fire, and various other kinds of accidents more often occur to intoxicated persons than to sober ones. The dismal list of negative outcomes of excessive drinking has been chronicled in great detail by others (Arria & Gossop, 1998), so the point here is more to set a context for our understanding of those relatively rare occasions when some individuals drink too fast or too much, sometimes by choice and sometimes by accident.

LINKED ACTIVITIES

Although much of what has been said about drinking might imply that it is an isolated pattern of behavior quite apart from other activities, that is only very rarely the case (Room, 1984a). The range of behaviors that accompany drinking is remarkably varied in different cultures, many of them highly esteemed, and others deplored by those in the society who do not take part.

Tasting

Having just dealt with excess, it is important to remember that that is only part of the continuum of drinking styles, although it tends to dominate in the literature. Near the other extreme is that of tasting, a popular practice whereby the esthetics of beverage alcohol are highlighted, and impairment would be lamented as a hindrance rather than welcomed as a respite. In fact, much tasting hardly involves drinking at all, although it is often an esteemed way of deciding what one would like to drink on some subsequent occasion.

A group of people who share an interest in tasting assemble a variety of beverages, usually of the same type (red or white, dry or sweet wines; light, regular, or heavy beers; scotches, bourbons, or brandies; and so forth), often covering the labels or decanting them so as to mask the identity of each item to be sampled. A little is poured into each person's glass. Then each does whatever will best intensify the multisensory experience: most hold it to the light to appreciate color and clarity. The contents are swirled to bring out bouquet or aroma. Most sniff strongly to appreciate successive layers of aroma. A sip in the mouth may be deliberately and systematically moved to impinge on different parts of the tongue. A few breathe in sharply through the nose or mouth. And most spit out rather than swallow the drink. The aim is to understand and be able to describe the distinctive character of each beverage in some detail. Clean (or at least rinsed) glasses are used each time, and many tasters also rinse their mouths with water, or cleanse their palates with dry bread or crackers between samples. There is an intense focus on each beverage in turn, although none is consumed in any appreciable quantity. The qualities to be compared are those that enthusiasts look for in such drinks: aroma, various different layers of taste and mouth sensation. Experienced tasters are able to make fine distinctions that others with less experience do not discriminate.

Such tasting was long considered a recondite, and sometimes affected, kind of connoisseurship, practiced by only a few wealthy and extremely knowledgeable people closely associated with the production or serving of alcoholic beverages. But it has increasingly become an occasion for, or an adjunct to socialization by middle-class drinkers who are willing to invest some time and effort to broaden their horizons and enhance their appreciation.

Games and Contests

The congenial atmosphere that many people associate with drinking is sometimes enhanced by combining drink with other forms of recreation and enjoyment. Sometimes drinking is an accompaniment to card-games, board-games, or other such pastimes. Other times, it provides the stimulus for innovative patterns of interaction that fit with the playful aspect of human sociability but that have not been formalized as games. Three examples are the Quian, Han, and Miao peoples, all in contemporary China, who share the custom of drinking homebrew from a large communal pot using exceptionally long straws. They also are alike in that all celebrate any drinking occasion with song, dance, and the recitation of poetry. In exhibitions that demonstrate control and creativity, it is also commonplace that they, like many other of China's ethnic populations, accompany drinking by elaborate competitive games with dice, dominos, tongue-twisters, general word-play, and riddles, some of which require sophisticated knowledge of history and literature (Xiao, 1995). In Tibet, the offer of a drink is often sung, not spoken, and ideally includes some poetic improvisation appropriate to the immediate situation. In accepting such an offer, the guest is expected to respond in kind. We have already mentioned the game or contest whereby Chinese drinkers compose long and intricate poems by taking turns, under strict time-constraints between drinks, adding a line or two, while having to adhere closely to the theme, rhythm and meter, and complex rhyme-scheme of the overall effort. Simpler, but also creative in a verbal way, is the widespread Latin American pattern of improvising couplets to prolong and elaborate a popular or folk song while drinking, again with the pressure of time and the enthusiasm of continued drinking.

Some games of skill, like tossing coins, balls, or markers at a target on the ground, making cats' cradles or intricate webs of string by manipulating one's hands and fingers, hopping backwards, and such tend often to be associated with drink. Sometimes the "penalty" when a member of the group is less successful than the others is an exhortation to take another drink. These linked activities thus can accelerate or sustain the pace of drinking, which otherwise might flag. Among German soldiers, and soldiers in many other countries, long hours of boredom are sometime relieved by races to see who can first dis- or reassemble a weapon, polish shoes, make a bed, or do any other routine activity, again punctuated with drinking and with the obligation to take an extra drink as penalty to the loser. In Poland, some people joke about popular eagerness to drink by citing the examples of a group of friends' betting on where a fly would land, when a dog would wake up, how soon a bird call would be heard, and such mundane events, with a round of drinks to celebrate each such occasion.

If the only aim of a drinking game or contest is to see who can drink the most or the fastest, excess is to be expected, and the risk of death is a sad reality. In many social and cultural contexts, however, drinking games and contests not only are enjoyable to both participants and the broader audience, but they showcase wit, imagination, and creativity as well.

Other Activities

The variety of other things that people do while drinking is almost infinite. Some are so common and popular that they are more fully discussed in chapter 6 as reasons why people drink: to celebrate, to relax, to enhance food, socializing, political protesting, religious worshipping, curing and medicating, among others.

By the 8th century B.C., Greek popular culture had come to include the *symposion* (symposium) as a ritual drinking party, combining socializing among polite male society, with teaching, learning, discussion, and philosophic exploration, as was amply demonstrated later in the lives of Plato and Socrates.

Drinking while watching sports events on television is a popular pattern throughout Europe and North America, although audiences at the auditorium, ballpark, or other site, are often discouraged from drinking. Despite a long and coordinated campaign to stop people from drinking while operating autos, boats, or other dangerous equipment, many people still do, with disastrous results.

For reasons that are not at all clear, most of the Pacific islands, sometimes referred to collectively as Oceania, had no beverage alcohol until contacted by Europeans. Even then, local reactions differed markedly, with some populations rejecting drink and others embracing it (Casswell, 1985). Some different regional patterns show how native reactions to a foreign product can lead to very different drinking patterns and consequences.

On Tahiti, the idea of fermentation was applied to orange juice and coconut milk, and festive drinking became commonplace. Although participation was limited to married adults, drinking, dancing, and sexual promiscuity were common at parties that would last for days at a time, and occasionally even more, with crowds moving from one village to the next (Lemert, 1964).

Drinking parties used similar drinks but differed markedly in form among the Cook Islanders (Lemert, 1964). Mostly male groups would meet outside of the village to drink, talk, pray, and listen to recitations of genealogies or mythical histories in a sedate ritual with rigid rules of conduct.

Using mostly imported ingredients, Samoans brewed a strong beer, sometimes fortified with distilled spirits, and small groups of young men congregated to drink, talk, and sing in the bush (Lemert, 1964). In such a secular context, disruptive behavior sometimes occurred, although the ritual drinking of other Polynesians tended not to have such outcomes.

The young men of Fiji similarly have no tradition of drinking because alcohol was not used in their culture until contact with Europeans in the 1700s, and the highly ceremonial drinking of kava (Lebot, Merlin, & Lindstrom, 1992) was monopolized by a few prestigious elders. Commercial alcoholic beverages have recently become popular, however, among a group who have few jobs, few interests or aspirations, and few culturally sanctioned outlets for their energies.

Most of their drinking is with the intention of becoming intoxicated, which gives them an excuse for such antisocial, amoral and criminal behaviors as rape, fighting, and stealing (Plange, 1998). Indo-Fijians of the same age tend more often to have jobs and money so that when they drink to excess, the deleterious outcomes are more often auto accidents.

Other dangerous associations with drinking can be found in many parts of the world. Although contemporary Maya drinking has a great many important social functions at a community level, its abuse also has significant costs in terms of interpersonal relations, especially spouse abuse (Eber, 1995) as a commonly linked activity. Among Mohave Indians in the U.S., arguing and fighting are rare when sober, but common while drinking (Devereux, 1948, 1961). The links between drinking and aggression are so dramatic that many people presume that alcohol provides a pharmacological trigger for violence. Such a view wholly ignores the almost equally common (but less dramatic) pattern in which drinking is linked with passivity, good humor, and sociable enjoyment. Evidence is increasing that aggressive people tend to be more aggressive in a setting where alcohol provides time-out and gives an excuse for asocial or antisocial behavior, but it does nothing to foster violence on the part of nonaggressive people (Fagan, 1990). In much the same way, it has recently been demonstrated that much of what has been viewed as drunken hooliganism among soccer-fans and others who sometimes demonstrate after sports events tends often to be reactions by sober fans to abuses by the police (Scott & Reicher, 1998).

WHY DOES IT MATTER?

The question of how people drink is crucial in terms of understanding why it is that so much attention is paid to alcohol in the first place. There has been nowhere near a comparable volume of research, legislation, or speculation about eating as a behavior, about milk as a beverage, or about the roles of sweat in cultures around the world, for example.

Our focus on drinking as behavior has the advantage of treating actions in the context of motives, meanings, and values, allowing us to identify and interpret patterns and regularities. In doing so, it becomes evident that the far more prevalent way of focusing on drinking—that is, by simply paying attention to numerical counts of quantity of alcohol ingested and frequency of drinking occasions—omits much that is important in shaping the outcomes of drinking, as well as much that is needed for understanding the drinking in the first place (Grant & Litvak, 1998; Rehm et al., 1996).

A simple quantity-frequency approach is exemplified by the VolMax scale devised by Clark & Hilton (1991, pp. 108–109) to typologize all drinkers encountered in the U.S. national survey. They created a 10-point scale by taking into account not only the number of drinks consumed per occasion, but also the number of drinks per month. The eighth-highest type are called High Volume-Low Maximum drinkers, defined as "those who drink forty-five or more drinks per month and who never have more than two drinks per occasion." The 8th category on a 10-point scale would be interpreted by most as representing (or at least strongly implying) heavy, if not excessive, drinking. And yet that category is where a male would fall who abided by the Dietary Guidelines for Americans (U.S. Department of Agriculture & Department of Health and Human Services, 1995), having two drinks daily—moderate drinking, according to the guidelines.

Survey data are peculiarly skewed to provide abundant information about the majority of people, who drink very little and so they provide very little information about the tiny minority who drink a great deal. Such investigators complain that "the cells are too small" in terms of tabulation, which means there are too few heavy drinkers to yield statistically significant information in most respects (Room, 1993).

Researchers increasingly agree that it is those few excessive drinkers who are responsible for most of the alcohol-related accidents and pathologies, and most of the problems that tend to be associated with alcohol in the first place (Giesbrecht et al., 1989; Hilton, 1991c; Midanik, Tam, Greenfield, & Caetano, 1996). Thus, it is increasingly ironic that research, as well as efforts at control, prevention, and education, are all so predominantly focused on moderate drinkers, and not much targeted at heavy drinkers.

Another example of the way in which ignoring the context of how people drink can result in counterproductive advice on the part of health authorities has to do with tasting as a kind of drinking. One of the most common guidelines or warnings by those who are outspoken in wanting to curtail excessive drinking is that drink should never be the focus of an activity. That caution is based on the way of thinking that equates availability with risk, on the assumptions that people will automatically drink more if it is readily accessible and less if alcohol is difficult to acquire. Most of the regulations about hours of sale, taxation, age-limits, and licensing are based on those premises which are disproven every time that a bottle is re-closed and shelved, a single can is taken from a carton, or a single bottle from a cellar. Certainly tasting, the form of drinking in which the beverage itself is the primary if not the only focus of attention for all participants, is probably the least risky of all possible behaviors in the drinking repertoire.

Everyone who has ever had a drink probably knows that two drinks a day have very different effects and consequences than 14 drinks on Saturday night. Nevertheless those very different patterns are usually treated as if they were the same, when analyzed in relation to epidemiology, problems, attitudes, and outcomes. One of the most fundamental truths that can be learnt from a cross-cultural comparison of drinking occasions is that, within limits, it matters less how much you drink than it does how you drink.

Chapter 5

A Rose by Any Other Name:
What Do People Drink?

At a wedding in Hong Kong, the bride and groom join in a festive toast with champagne. An effervescent wine from northeastern France, champagne is widely used as a special celebratory drink. © *Jodi Cobb/NGS Image Collection.*

Before we pay too much attention to the great variety of alcohol beverages that people drink, it is important that we get some better idea of just what is meant by a drink, or beverage alcohol, or alcoholic beverages. The category is vast, with different drinks having very different meanings and uses and with people

135

reacting very differently to them in various contexts throughout the world. Let us start from the premise that a drink is any beverage that contains enough ethanol (or alcohol) to be psychoactive, that is, to affect the mind if taken in sufficient quantity. Virtually any fruit juice, like most vegetables, contains some alcohol, but so little that one could fill one's stomach before feeling it. Even within such a broad definition, there is a host of different drinks around the world that could command our attention.

We have already been reminded, in the introduction to this book, that ethanol is a simple chemical compound that occurs through the natural process of fermentation. There are many other alcohols known to chemists but none of them is customarily drunk by people anywhere. Shortly after a person drinks ethanol, it enters the bloodstream and is diffused throughout the body. (Details on the physiology of this process and its effects on perception, cognition, and behavior are fascinating, but have been so thoroughly discussed elsewhere that they need no further elaboration in a book that has drinking occasions as its focus.)

In this chapter, we will be looking at drink from a variety of points of view. First, there is a brief discussion of the nature of alcohol itself. Then we turn to the question of types of drinks containing alcohol that have been recognized by different peoples. Because English has become the universal scientific language, and because the overwhelming majority of systematic research on drinking has been conducted or published in the United States, we pay special attention to that country's tripartite typology of drinks, based on the mode of manufacturing and taxing alcohol: fermented, distilled, and fortified. But even that system of classification does not cover all of beverage alcohol, so we also look at mixed and other drinks. Because different types of drinks are so often used and thought of in different ways (Waugh, 1968), it is worth briefly talking about types in relation to types. And, as in each of our chapters, we end with some brief comments about why what is said here may matter even to a reader who never much knew or even cared about world cultures as such.

Our case study in this chapter deals with an African society in which beer is so intrinsic, important, and pervasive that it influences how people think about time, how they order social relationships, and even how they conceive of the good life in reality, in folklore, and after death. Beer is nothing less to the Kofyar than a "locus of value."

Case Study: Beer and the Kofyar

The fundamental importance of homebrewed beer in African agricultural societies is clearly demonstrated with a specific case, the Kofyar, subsistence farmers in northern Nigeria. The ethnographer who studied them went so far as to call beer "a locus of value" (Netting, 1964) and a "focus of cultural concern and activity" (p. 376). Just as the giving of beer is a mark of esteem, exclusion from beer drinking occasions is the harshest punishment that the community metes out to those who break the rules. During courtship, gifts of beer signify affection, just as larger gifts of beer later are part of the bride-price. Harvest, hunting, and other festivals are occasions for widespread distribution of beer, sometimes paid for by public subscription. A newly married man or one who has just paid his taxes is entitled to beer from whoever brewed that day, just as nursing mothers are given extra beer to augment and enrich lactation.

The brewhouse is a sacred place, and a portion of every brew is set aside for the village chieftain and for any diviner who may want some. As among the Tonga, reciprocal labor exchanges are usually enhanced with beer, as are funerals, curing rituals, and frequent commemoration of ancestral spirits.

"Beer is both the symbol and the essence of the good life" (Netting, 1964, p. 378), with a jar of beer inside a magic stone analogous to the European pot of gold that a folkloric hero finds at the end of the rainbow. Short periods of time are even named for steps in the brewing process. Made primarily from millet, Kofyar beer is tasty and nutritious, a valuable addition to the monotonous local diet, providing scarce ascorbic acid, B-vitamins, and microbial proteins which are concentrated by fermentation.

Drinking is not restricted to men; women join equally in drinking parties; a nursing mother is encouraged to drink more than usual, and children are allowed to drink small quantities, even before they are weaned. Parties include slow drinking, resulting in animated talk; singing and dancing are unimaginable without beer. An individual is always held responsible for his or her actions, so drunkenness is rare and frowned upon.

Magnanimity and selfishness are phrased in terms of giving or withholding beer. Communal agricultural work is always an occasion for beer drinking, and small informal beer parties are common when the ingredients are abundant. Fines are paid in beer, and beer is offered to dead ancestors periodically, just as it is to friends at a funeral. So integral a part of social life has beer become that, even though other drinks are known and available,

> as beer becomes increasingly an instrumental entity and a medium which lends itself to the expression of social relationships, the derived values assume a greater importance than the primarily personal satisfactions. The distribution of beer in many ways parallels the flow of money in commercial societies, and beer like money has become through time less dependent on such value as may inhere in its substance and increasingly an accepted symbol of social values and a currency of interpersonal relations (Netting, 1964, p. 383).

Because everyone has access to the ingredients, simple equipment, and know-how, the production of this currency for interpersonal relations is widespread. Because it spoils readily, it cannot be accumulated, so distribution is both an economic leveler and a social lubricant. It would be difficult to avoid the conclusion that beer is more than a primary symbol or locus of value in Kofyar culture.

TYPES OF DRINKS

For different analytic purposes, it may be convenient to distinguish among types of beverages on many different bases. Governmental authorities are often most concerned about taxed as contrasted with untaxed drinks, inasmuch as excise taxes on beverage alcohol are often quite substantial, comprising either a large part of the overall price, or a large part of the political unit's overall budget, or both. There have been several times in Russian history when taxes on drink made up 60% of the national budget (Vroublevsky & Harwin, 1998). Drinks that are untaxed are not necessarily illegal, illicit, or clandestine (although they are often thought of in those terms). In addition to those conveniently subsumed in English as moonshine, other untaxed alcohol may be imported by individuals from abroad, tax-free to a diplomatic entity or a military base, or otherwise exempted.

Another way in which alcohols are distinguished is between potable and nonpotable or nonbeverage. The difference does not mean that one cannot drink the latter, but only that most individuals will be discomfited by doing so, and some may even die. In spite of gastric disturbances, the risk of blindness, and other risks, it is not at all unknown for some people, sometimes routinely, to drink nonbeverage alcohol. One example was the rapid disappearance from stores and bakeries of vanilla extract during the days when President Gorbachev sharply curtailed the production and sale of drink in the hope of stimulating temperance in the final days of the Soviet Union. Before long, people were drinking cologne, after-shave, shoe polish, paint remover, antifreeze, and any other source of alcohol they knew. In the U.S. during federal Prohibition, denatured alcohol was devised for solvent and other industrial purposes; it is simply ethanol with a toxic substance added deliberately to make it unattractive as a drink.

The Chinese have traditionally distinguished between natural and manufactured alcohol, on the basis of human intent (Xiao, 1995). Whereas natural alcohol can and does occur whenever fermentation takes place, even in the absence of any human intervention, manufactured alcohol, in their terms, is the deliberate product of someone's ingenuity and effort. There is even a corpus of folklore that gives two different explanations for the invention of the latter on the basis of discovery of the former. One version tells how, during the reign of Emperor Yu (around 2140 B.C.), one of his daughters' maidservants discovered just how good a taste and feeling could be had from a bowl of gruel that had been left for a few days and accidentally fermented. When the Emperor found out about it, he foresaw trouble, exiled her (Yi Di), and declared a prohibition on drinking. Another legend about the discovery of beverage alcohol tells how Du Kang, a young shepherd around 1800 B.C., abandoned his lunch of sorghum when he ran home in a rainstorm one day and found it wonderfully transformed when he returned later. Drink was viewed as such a contribution to humankind that the deity Jade Emperor invited Du Kang, after his death, to join the celestial court and named him god of alcohol. It is still commonplace in China to hear the proverb: "What can relieve sorrow? Nothing but Du Kang."

Another effective way to illustrate the point that the nomenclature of drinks is not clear-cut is to look at the terminologies that were offered by various authors to characterize types of drinks in the large geographic regions about which they were writing in a single recent book. With reference to Africa, Haworth and Acuda (1998) classified the several specific drinks into five groups: "factory-produced, home-brewed, factory-brewed, homemade, and illicit." By contrast, Shen and Wang (1998) listed three main types in China: "distilled spirits, fermented wine, and compound wine"; for India, Isaac (1998) listed three very different types: "country liquor, Indian-made foreign liquor, and illicitly distilled liquor."

Given such international variation, without even touching on the functional typologizing by nonliterate peoples who, as will be explained below, sometimes talk about hidden beer, seven-day beer, child's beer, or stomach wine, this is not the place to try to arrive at definitive labels.

It is true that beers are fermented, and so are wines, whereas spirits or liquor are distilled. Most beers are made from grain and most wines are made from grapes. But beers can also be made from fruits, tree saps, tubers, honey, and other components, whereas wines can also be made from most of those same ingredients. Japanese sake is usually called rice wine, just as birch beer or spruce beer are made from sap, whereas palm wine derives from sap or the fleshy covering of a nut. Terminology on this front is not only inconsistent but can be positively misleading. What is called malt liquor in the U.S. is not liquor at all. Not distilled, it comes close to being the equivalent of what northern Europeans refer to as strong beer, a simple fermented drink with an alcohol content of only about 6%. Mead is the term most often applied to a fermented drink that has honey as its base, just as ale tends most often to refer to a beer without hops, or to a beer produced by top fermentation, as contrasted with bottom fermentation. There is no clear reason why various authors have referred to palm wine fermented from the sap of palm trees, whereas the fermented sap of agave is almost always called by its Mexican name pulque, and the fermented sap of maple or birch trees is usually called maple or birch beer. Fermented mares' milk seems consistently to be called by the local name kumiss, and the word chicha recurs throughout much of Latin America, regardless of whether that homebrew has fruits, berries, grain, or tubers as its base. One might also wonder why palm wine becomes gin (and not brandy) when it is distilled, or why sugarcane produces rum but maize produces whiskey through distillation.

There are already dictionaries, technical manuals, and more specialized books that provide what appear superficially to be rigorous definitions and distinctions among many kinds of drinks, but few are even internally consistent, much less do they address historical and cross-cultural variations (Halley, 1996; Keller, McCormick, & Efron, 1982). When one considers the bewildering variety of ingredients that people have chosen to ferment into some drinks, or to distill into other drinks, perhaps more fruitful than looking for consistent terminology will be our quest for an appreciation of how these products are used and what they mean.

With all of these caveats in mind, it still seems both useful and convenient to talk about three types of alcoholic beverages in terms of how the alcohol got to be there: fermented, distilled, or fortified.

FERMENTED DRINKS

Fermentation is a natural process, as we have seen, often occurring without any human intervention. But having discovered this fascinating and useful process, humankind was quick to harness it (Braidwood, 1953), domesticate it, and eventually to elaborate it in many ways that afford greater control over the outcome (Hartman & Oppenheim, 1950). Fermented drinks are products of the process of fermentation (the conversion of carbohydrates to sugars by yeasts). Fermentation is usually completed in a few days, and the product often spoils by souring or rotting within a few more days, unless pasteurized or kept in an anaerobic environment such as a sealed can, bottle or keg. Because the yeasts themselves become intoxicated or die when ethanol reaches a concentration near 20% by volume, there is a natural ceiling to the strength of fermented drinks. Fermented beverages are probably the oldest and most widespread means of altering consciousness that is known to humankind.

One of the most rudimentary of drinks containing alcohol is simply called yeast. It is prepared by just letting some commercial yeast ferment for a day or so in water containing a little bit of sugar or molasses. Vaguely sweet and slightly alcoholic (3–6% by volume), it is drunk plain or with some flavoring by the adolescent Micronesian males who make it (Nason, 1975).

Beer

In general, fermented drinks that are based on grain are called beers in English; the malt that plays so important a role in some manufactured beers refers simply to the sprouted seed of a grain, but, in many parts of the world, sprouting is unimportant and beers are fermented from cracked or ground grains, whether fresh or dried. By contrast, drinks that are made from the fermented juice of fruits or berries are generally called wines. There are enough exceptions to

Haya men drink banana beer from gourds while resting from building a traditional house near Bukoba, Tanzania, in 1986. Drinking is often an integral part of cooperative work-activities and typically involves beer brewed from a broad range of fruits, grains, or tubers. © *Robert Carlson.*

this generalization however, such as rice wine or cherry beer, that the simple dichotomy based on primary ingredients should not be construed as strictly logical or certain.

Throughout much of history, and still in some areas, it is with considerable justification that beer has been called liquid bread (Katz & Voigt, 1986). Not only are they often produced from the same ingredients, but also often they are used in very similar manners. When we speak of homebrewed beer, we are also talking about products in which fermentation yields the same process of "biological ennoblement" (Gastineau, Darby, & Turner, 1979; Platt & Webb, 1946), whereby the sum is more nutritious than its component parts. To be specific, yeasts synthesize B-complex vitamins (which are often in short supply in native diets in tropical regions), and they contain several trace minerals that are essential to life, such as chromium, copper, and selenium. The remarkably high level of glucose tolerance factor that is found in brewers' yeast helps the body to utilize glucose more efficiently, reducing cholesterol and triglyceride levels. Yeasts also are rich in vitamins B_{12} (which few vegetables have), niacin (which is low in maize), riboflavin and thiamine (low in rice diets), and C (lack of which can lead to scurvy).

Beer remains the most important beverage throughout most of Africa today, only occasionally displaced by cows' milk in those groups where pastoralism predominates, and it is drunk and enjoyed by all (Nelson, Novellie, Reader, Renning, & Sachs, 1964). Almost as important as the food value in the minds of local people are the social and ceremonial usages of beer discussed in chapter 1. Fermented from many different basic ingredients, such homebrew is variously known as Bantu beer, "Kaffir" (the term is a disparaging one referring to Blacks) beer, millet beer, sorghum beer, maize beer, or palm wine. The product itself is generally dark and thick, often like a porridge, with a considerable amount of the ingredients vaguely distinguishable. For this reason, it is often generically classed as opaque or native beer, in contrast with clear, light, or European beer.

Grain, water, and yeast are the basic ingredients in most European or American beers, with hops added (since about the 1400s) to sharpen or give an edge to the taste. An early law in what is now Germany specified that no other ingredients be used, and several breweries still pride themselves on holding to that simple ancient recipe today (Bickerdyke, 1886).

For the past 100 years or so, barley has been the principal grain used in mass-producing commercial beer in the United States and Europe. Rice and wheat yield strikingly similar products, and other grains come into play from time to time. Local variants that deserve mention include, for example, the many flavors of beer (especially fruits and berries) that have long been popular in Belgium, and that are recently gaining some market among microbrewery products in the U.S. (Buhner, 1998). The Great American Beer Fest, an annual exhibition held in Denver, in the U.S. state of Colorado, has over 52 types or categories of beers (e.g., lager, pilsner, bock, light, etc.) and ales (e.g., India pale, Scotch, brown, small, etc.) in competition for gold, silver, and bronze medals. Beyond these, special flavors abound (such as smoke, cranberry, loganberry, and a host of others). When this author attended in 1997, he was amazed to find 1448 brews from 365 breweries; each year, during the 15 years of that event, there have been more entrants and more entries. Many varieties of beer, ale, and cider have been described and analyzed in some detail in separate books by different authors. For our purposes, a couple of general surveys should be useful as introductions to the subject (Finch, 1989; Jackson, 1977, 1988; Weiner, 1977).

Even such an abbreviated account as this should not, however, ignore the many drinks (specifically beers) that are made domestically rather than in factories. Homebrew is one generic term for such beers, that are produced on a small scale (albeit sometimes for the commercial market), with principal ingredients ranging from millet to sorghum, manioc to taro, potato to bread. Throughout much of central and eastern sub-Saharan Africa (Platt, 1955), the grains millet and sorghum are routinely brewed into traditional products (opaque or native beers), which are being increasingly complemented or displaced by factory-made beers (usually lager, or light beers), that tend to be like their European counterparts, often produced by the same international companies. Central and western sub-Saharan African peoples, more often produce wine from palm-sap (Ngokwey, 1987), or cassava-beer, from the tuber sometimes also called manioc and tapioca (Partanen, 1991). In the 1960s, traditional beers accounted for fully 85% of all of the beverage alcohol consumed in all of Africa, and in the 1980s it was still 50% (Kortteinen, 1989). Homebrew remains important not just for ritual and other traditional uses but as a beverage appreciated by newcomers to the rapidly growing cities as well as by the rural folk (Epstein, 1958). As such, it continues to play an important role in the informal economy, especially as a means by which women, as brewsters, can gain access to cash (Maula, 1997).

There are well over 300 different native names for specific homebrews that are listed in the scientific literature, and often the distinctions between them are important locally in terms of the principal ingredient(s), the process by which brewing or fermentation takes place, or even the uses to which the finished drink is put. But in this volume, it seems appropriate to avoid confusion by using only a few such names, and choosing those that tend to be applied in several cultures throughout a region.

Mexican pulque is like a homebrewed beer fermented from the sap of the maguey (century-plant) (Fundación de Investigaciones Sociales, 1997, 1999). Somewhat milky in appearance, it has subtle distinctions in flavor that are a focus of local pride and connoisseurship, not only among peasants and Indians but even among many of the middle-class urbanites who pride themselves on being of a superior "race" or caste (Natera, 1995). Pulque provides nearly half of the key vitamins and minerals in the Otomi diet (Anderson, Calvo, Serrano, & Payne, 1946). The Nahua Indians, linguistic and biological heirs of the Aztecs, rely heavily on pulque which is part of every meal, for men, women, and children alike (Madsen & Madsen, 1969). A pregnant female is exhorted to drink more pulque to nourish her unborn child; the nursing infant is also given pulque to feed and strengthen it. Children and adults continue to drink it regularly, and tend to think about it more as food than as a drink containing alcohol. The esteem that pulque enjoys is reflected in its often being called "the milk of our Mother" (referring to the Christian Virgin Mary), although there are still some who care enough about their mythological history to say firmly that pulque was given to humankind by the 20-breasted Aztec goddess, Mayahuel (Gonçalves de Lima, 1956). Although pulque has as much ethanol as many other homebrews throughout the world, about 3%, the Nahua are quick to distinguish it from commercial beer or distilled drinks, which they think of as alcohol and which they think are drunk by alcoholics.

Another homebrewed beer in Mexico is mezcal, sometimes including small amounts of mescaline derived from the peyote cactus, quasisacred because of the way in which it enhances sensory perceptions and may even occasionally induce hallucinations, an important form of religious experience.

Throughout the Andean highlands of Latin America, the term chicha refers to a wide range of homebrews that are fermented from such varied ingredients as maize, palm-nut, mango, banana, yuca, or strawberry (Cutler & Cardenas, 1947). The same term is used, perhaps somewhat more rarely, for unfermented drinks, especially in the lowland regions of Central and South America (Cooper, 1949; Hartmann, 1958). Chicha was an important commodity even before the time of the Spanish Conquest, with special breweries where selected "Virgins of the Sun" (young women dedicated to serve the Inca himself) lived together and produced chicha with which he rewarded successful warriors and other leaders (Morris, 1979). To this day, chicha plays important roles in religion, hospitality, and medicine (Allen, 1988; Doughty, 1971; Mangin, 1957).

Toddy, or palm-toddy is common in a narrow swath in the tropics, where the sap of various species of palm trees is fermented to yield a sweetish beer (3–5% alcohol). Often too, it is called palm-wine. India, southeastern Asia, Brazil, and western Africa are areas where such palm-beer (although it seems never to be called that) is popular. In Russia and throughout the former Soviet Union kvas is a low-alcohol beer made from wheat bread or rye bread, sometimes with honey, hops, raisins, or other additives. Rarely exceeding 4% alcohol, it is treated in some respects as a soft drink and also as a tonic.

In the last quarter of the 20th century, beer appears to be displacing wine in popularity among both women and youth throughout most of Europe, and European-style beer is gaining popularity throughout the developing world (Jernigan, 1997; Pedlow, 1998). Although we have already seen that beer and wine are remarkably indistinguishable in some respects, it is evident that they are thought about and treated differently by most people in ways that seem important. Let us turn now to wine to see some of the meanings, uses, and functions that it has as a different kind of fermented drink.

Wine

Another huge class of beverages made by the relatively simple method of fermentation is wines. Although the bulk of the world's wines are made from grapes, the term applies equally to those that are made from other fruits or berries, and that have anywhere from 5 to 18% alcohol with the average well between those extremes.

Just as with beer, many of the ancients thought of wine as a gift from the gods. Dionysus was said to have brought it to the Greeks (Dodds, 1956), who continued to celebrate him and his gifts with dionysian revels, profoundly religious rites that were also clearly sensual and carnal in their enactment (Sournia, 1990). Later, the classic Romans said that their god Bacchus had introduced wine, and they were like the Greeks in holding bacchanalia in his honor, similarly combining sacred and secular celebration in a licentious and orgiastic way. The deity Orisis was credited by the ancient Egyptians with also having introduced wine to them (Darby, Ghalioungui, & Grivetti, 1977), and their art, in many media, portrays wine as central to the luxurious life (and burial for afterlife) of the incredibly wealthy and powerful ruling class.

The earliest evidence for wine-making and wine use is archeological, dating from the latter part of the fourth millennium B.C. (McGovern, Fleming, & Katz, 1996). The identification was of residue in pottery jars at the site of what was then a major community in the mountains of Iran near Greater Mesopotamia on the major thoroughfare that later became the Silk Route (Badler, 1996). Evidence of beer was also found in the same room. Although older remains have not yet been identified it is presumed that both beverages were made and drunk at earlier times (Lutz, 1922).

A number of ancient sayings indicate that wine was appreciated in different ways, by different age groups (Grivetti, 1996). For example, the distinguished physician Hippocrates held that

> Infants should be bathed for long periods in warm water and given their wine diluted and not at all cold. . . . This should be done to prevent the occurrence of convulsions and to make the children grow and get good complections.

The great philosopher Plato called wine "the cure for the crabbedness of old age, whereby we may renew our youth and enjoy forgetfulness of despair." Even the Talmud, ancient repository of Jewish commentary, prophetically pronounced "Wine taken in moderation induces appetite and is beneficial to health. . . . Wine is the greatest of medicines. Where wine is lacking, drugs are necessary." Maimonides called wine "a very good nutrient . . . [that] generates praiseworthy blood." And Omar Khayyam said, "I wonder often what the vintners buy one-half so precious as the stuff they sell."

Grape vines must grow for several years before they bear enough fruit to make the pressing of wine a feasible enterprise. Ideally, a vineyard should be kept weeded and the vines pruned to maintain production. The equipment for processing grapes into wine is bulky, even if the pressing is done by people's treading without a press. It is not a venture to be undertaken lightly, as the brewing of beer can be, and thus, wine was not cheap until a century or so ago. For sheer economic reasons, it is little wonder that nobles and monasteries played major roles in the emerging wine industry for centuries before access to land and wealth become more widely diffused.

As we look around the world at various kinds of drink that are, in English, called wine, it is often difficult to tell how they differ from beer. Barley-wine and rice-wine are arresting examples, because each has a counterpart, also produced by simple fermentation from the same principal ingredient, that is commonly called beer. Other problematic examples are wines made from dates in North Africa or the Near East, palm nuts in western Africa or the Amazon Basin, algarroba in the South American chaco, or cactus fruit in northern Mexico, all of which seem to have little in common that would significantly distinguish them from beers with the same ingredients.

Wines were popular in China (Xiao, 1995), Persia (Modi, 1888), and India (Bose, 1922; Mitra, 1873), both as adjuncts to food and polite conversation, and as stimulants to artistic creativity. At certain eras in the history of each country, drunkenness was viewed as an honorable state, likely to enhance one's skill in poetry or music; at other times, each area had prohibition and austerity as a goal.

Viticulture was diffused through Europe by the Roman legions, and centuries later wherever Catholic missionaries went, to provide for Communion and conversion. Treated as food in France and Italy, grapes and wine became important in the diet when they were cheap enough for those other than the wealthy. Their popularity in recent decades has included both esthetic and prestige considerations, although the increasing evidence of health benefits may have influenced some drinkers (Johnson, 1994, 1998; Robinson, 1986, 1994).

Those who wanted stronger drinks than could be achieved by fermentation eventually turned to distillation.

DISTILLED DRINKS

In the same way that almost any fruit, berry, vegetable, tuber, or grain can be fermented to produce beer or wine, they (or their fermented products) can subsequently be distilled to produce spirits or liquor. Some of the more popular are sugarcane or molasses, yielding rum; potatoes as a base for vodka (although sugarbeets, turnips, and other ingredients also serve); rye for rye whiskey; maize or barley for bourbon; and grapes for brandy, pisco, or grappa (Jeffers, 1997).

It appears as if the Arabs, who were scientifically advanced in many respects, were the first to learn about distillation around 800 A.D. In this connection, it is noteworthy that the word alcohol is derived from the Arabic al-koh'l, originally an exceptionally fine powder but in a more general sense, the essence or spirit of a substance. The term spirits has persisted, especially when alcohol is used as a solvent, antiseptic, analgesic, or anesthetic, and sometimes is applied to that entire class of beverage alcohol that is the product of distillation. There is a mystique that still hovers around distillation as a process in many cultures. It is far simpler than most people believe; that mystique may in part be a heritage of the traditional secrecy with which alchemists and monks worked in the many centuries when they monopolized that special knowledge in the Western world.

On the arid plains of Mongolia, mares' milk is fermented to produce kumiss, a popular beverage. Like many homebrews, it is occasionally distilled later, yielding a strong liquor. © *Dean Conger/NGS Image Collection.*

The term *eau de vie* (literally, water of life) is still used as the name for colorless highly refined fruit-flavored drinks that are popular after dinner in France. Pear, peach, strawberry, and raspberry tend to be favored, in tiny quantities or mixed with other drinks. Similar in appearance and even more potent (89%) is the favorite drink of the Camba (Heath, 1958), a rum distilled from sugarcane that they call by the Spanish name *alcohol*. In many other sugar-producing areas, including Brazil and many of the Caribbean islands, rum is the standard drink, taken straight at least as often as it is mixed with other beverages. The raw taste and burning sensation that it gives are construed as proofs of its purity, its value in killing intestinal parasites, and of the valor of the drinkers.

"The gin epidemic" of England in the mid-1700s saw gin reach such low prices that many of the unemployed poor in the dirty crowded slums of mushrooming cities found drinking cheaper than eating. Subsequent changes in taxes eventually resulted in beer's returning to dominance over gin, and people's gradually adjusting to the many dislocations of the Industrial Revolution made English cities far more habitable.

In Russia, vodka has long been the popular drink, providing the illusion of warmth and solace to an oppressed peasantry who made a virtue of drunkenness as a temporary escape from their dismal situations. Swedish and Finnish drinkers enjoyed better economic and social conditions but similarly sought oblivion periodically through vodka. The pattern of continuous drinking once a Russian vodka bottle is opened has a long tradition, and it certainly has not been discouraged by producers who sealed them, not with a screw top or cork, but with a crown cap that can only be replaced using a machine. The customary gesture of throwing the cap away with a broad toss right after opening the bottle still underscores the unlikelihood of any such thing as moderate drinking or the saving of any for another day.

Brandy was popular as an energizing drink in France and Spain, or as a luxury elsewhere. Variations in small-batch production often yield remarkably subtle and distinctive flavors. Grappa served the same dual purposes in Italy, as did tequila and mezcal in Mexico, or pisco in Peru.

Spirits made from rice, grapes, and various fruits are popular in China (Xiao, 1995), and are used largely for medicinal purposes with such exotic additives as rhinoceros horn as an aphrodisiac, tiger bones to instill bravery, or certain snakes to drive poisons from the system. The gin that is usually distilled from palm wine continues to be sought by those throughout sub-Saharan Africa who want a more potent drink than beer but can not afford European-style spirits (Leis, 1964). Distilled by the Tonga from their village beer that has a maize or millet base (Colson & Scudder, 1988), their gin with 20% alcohol has been made only since the 1970s, but rapidly became popular among men, joining bottled beer as drinks preferred over the traditional opaque beer. As Africans drink more, they are also generally turning to stronger drinks.

In the Caribbean, Yawney (1969) speaks of rum distilled from sugarcane juice or molasses, as the symbol of national identity for Trinidad, as it might well be for some of the other islands as well. Rum was much more widely popular in the 18th century, when it played a major role in the infamous "triangle trade," by which rum was taken to western Africa and traded for captives who became slaves and were then shipped to the West Indies and traded for molasses. That, in turn, was shipped to New England, the northeastern part of the U.S., where it was made into rum, which was then shipped to Africa. The system was premised on an elaborate division of labor that bound the British Empire together, and North Americans were quick to substitute native-grown maize and its derivative whiskey once they gained independence from England.

Among the spirituous drinks that are common in the U.S. and Europe, and increasingly throughout the world are whiskeys (or, in reference to Scotch, whisky) mostly derived from grains, and vodka mostly from tubers. Multiple successive distillations, aging for different periods in various kinds of containers, and a number of additives can each convey special and distinctive flavors, just as they affect the colors of what begins as a colorless transparent liquid.

Commercial mezcal is distilled in Mexico from the sap of the agave and has about 45% alcohol. It is often distinguished by the inclusion in each bottle of an agave worm, a caterpillar that feeds on that massive century-plant. Ouzo is a Greek brandy flavored with herbs, usually with caraway or anis dominant. Slivovitz, a fiery plum brandy, is popular in the Balkans. Calvados is distilled cider, especially popular in northern France and Spain.

Gin is usually a spirit distilled from unmalted grain or from molasses. It is subsequently steeped in juniper berries, coriander, and/or other herbs and rectified (that is, redistilled), yielding a clear but flavorful drink that used to be extremely popular alone but that has tended, in the past 50 years, more often to be mixed. When kumiss is distilled, the Mongols have different names for several different strengths of the resulting "milk liquor," all of which are thought to stimulate circulation, relax muscles, mend internal organs, stimulate the appetite, and strengthen the spleen and bones (Williams, 1998).

Like many other technological processes, distillation is remarkably simple once the principle is understood. Those who are not intimidated by the mystique of distillation make frequent use of it to produce strong drinks, often under very primitive conditions. During the brief season when ripe pineapples are cheap and abundant in Costa Rica, there are often more inmates in the national prison who are distilling pineapple-jack on their slightly adapted electric coffee-percolators than who are not. Russians and Ukrainians fondly reminisce about how they used to use anything to make samogon (moonshine) on the kitchen stove, especially at times when commercial supplies of liquor were low. That practice appears again to be becoming popular in the former Soviet Union as fiscal miscalculations and galloping inflation have so debased the official currency that moonshine is informally being used as the medium of exchange for many kinds of transactions.

Moonshine has come to be an almost universal name applied to illegally distilled alcohol as a class (Wilkinson, 1985), although varieties of it are generally known by several local designations even within a single country. For example, Guatemalans distinguish regionally between guaro, kuxa, and boj (Adams, 1995) whereas nearby Hondurans speak of making charamila, gato, pachanga, or cususa (Vittetoe, 1995), all in the same way and from the same ingredients. In some areas, or at some times, moonshine has a bad reputation for poisoning people. One common cause of this is the presence of excessive lead in the cooling apparatus; another is the grossly unsanitary conditions under which it is made, often including dead rodents in the mash. Another common problem is using too low a heat, which results in producing methanol rather than ethanol.

Another unexpected danger was discovered in Costa Rica in the 1970s while the author was there as consultant to World Health Organization. At that time, it was a country small enough to have only one morgue. The chief medical examiner remarked that an inordinate number of middle-aged men from rural areas were dying from what appeared to be alcohol poisoning, but with no indication that they had been drinking more or faster than usual. Postmortem examinations revealed traces of natural toxins in each instance, but they were different poisons in almost every case. Acting on a hunch, I sought out the moonshiners (part-time distillers of illegal and untaxed liquor) and collected samples of their products.

It was a happy accident that some of them were already friends, known on the basis of my having earlier studied one of their other part-time occupations; as commercial archeologists, many were grave-robbers plundering pre-Columbian graves to find ancient gold, jade, stone, or ceramic artifacts that have a lucrative place in the international art-market. Having already earned their trust in connection with that research provided a foot in the door and rapport; they then passed me from one acquaintance to another through personal networks that spread throughout the country, a good example of how ethnographic research methods can yield data that are simply not available by other means.

When the samples of Costa Rica moonshine (guaro) were subjected to gas-chromatographic analysis, they revealed small amounts of the same toxins that had been found in the blood of the dead men, correlated by region. Observation of the distilling process then revealed that a moonshiner often added a little something extra (his signature) to give distinctive flavor or impact to his product. In some instances, the additive was the root of a particular jungle vine or the bark of a tree; in others, a few mushroom/toadstools, or some such.

Although many customers appreciated those signatures, the unique chemical balance of other individuals apparently made them susceptible to even small doses of the same toxic substances (remember how dangerous sugar can be to a diabetic). Once the dangerous additives had been identified, it was simply a matter of convincing moonshiners that it was in their best interest to find new signatures that wouldn't kill their customers. Few people would expect to find an ethnographer teaching moonshiners how to make a better product, but, in what may still be a unique experiment in applying anthropological findings to the practical field of public health, that is just what happened.

In Finland, Norway, and Sweden, survey researchers have for years been concerned that nearly half of the spirits people drink are products of illegal distillation. In Sri Lanka, that figure is estimated to be 30% of overall consumption (Hettige, 1990); in India, 50% (Singh, 1989), and in Tanzania, at least 80% and maybe closer to 90% (Maula, 1990). Those who advocate raising taxes and other formal controls as ways to lessen alcohol-related problems ignore the ease with which people manufacture their own beverage alcohol when legal sources are diminished.

The period since 1950 has been remarkable for the worldwide popularization of distilled spirits of the European and North American styles. Whiskey has become for many a badge of having joined the cosmopolitan capitalist way of life even if only at a low level. Bottles, labels, and even their contents are counterfeited or bought dearly, often more as displays of conspicuous consumption than to satisfy the tastes of people in the developing world (Grant, 1998).

FORTIFIED, MIXED, AND OTHER DRINKS

Although this heading may appear to refer to a hopelessly jumbled residual category of drinks that are neither fermented nor distilled, it actually comprises some that are both but that tend to be conceptualized in different ways in many different cultures.

The yeasts that promote fermentation are themselves living organisms and, as such are affected by ethanol. In a solution above 18–20%, they become grossly ineffective or die, setting a ceiling on the concentration of alcohol in naturally fermented beverages. Just as the addition of water can dilute a drink, the addition of new yeast or of distilled alcohol can strengthen it. Such is the origin of a spectrum of drinks that are intermediate between beers and wines on the one hand, and distilled spirits on the other.

Mixed drinks is a generic term for drinks that are made up of any alcoholic beverage when mixed or diluted with water, ice, fruit juice, carbonated soda, or some other drink. Some are simple and others complex; some are world-famous and many enjoy only regional popularity. Without attempting an encyclopedic inventory, it seems appropriate in this context to illustrate the range of these as yet another exemplification of the variety and imagination that humankind has lavished on the world of drink.

The broad spectrum of fortified drinks is probably best known as encompassing cordials, liqueurs, vermouth, port, or sherry, ranging from around 17–40% (by volume). Each tends to be drunk in relatively small quantities at a time, often after a meal. Such preparations are often highly flavored, with the addition of herbs or fruit essences; some brands are said to be the result of a highly complex blending of ingredients that is supposedly known to only one or two persons in a generation. For reasons that are not at all clear, sherry has gained special popularity as a component in cooking. In Arabic-speaking areas of Africa and the Near East, arrack, a cordial based on figs or dates, is popular. Many liqueurs have only very local distribution, but others are appreciated by affluent fans almost anywhere. Their strong flavors, high prices, and higher alcohol content make them less popular than wines and beer, although some have captured the imagination of different populations for years.

Mixed drinks are not a recent innovation. Many Europeans are amazed and appalled at the way in which North Americans drink wine without using carbonated water to dilute it. The addition of quinine to water in drinks mixed with spirits probably originated as a means by which European colonialists could take small doses of anti-malarial drugs in a relatively painless manner while serving in tropical areas where they were exposed to the vector. Bitters is a complex blend of herbs and wood derivatives that may have served a similarly antiseptic purpose, and simple syrup, made of sugared water, was probably developed to counter the unpleasant taste of either or both of those additives.

The addition of a slice or wedge of lemon, lime, or orange to an alcoholic drink can be a visual enhancement at the same time that it lends a pleasant variation to the taste. The addition of ice to any drink was a luxury, especially in hot climates. Long before refrigeration allowed the manufacture of ice anywhere, natural ice was cut in winter from ponds and rivers in northern regions, stored in straw or sawdust for months, and shipped around the world.

Carbonated drinks, with or without natural and artificial flavors, became popular in the late 1800s and served to provide new variety, taste, and zest to alcohol beverages. Some drinks lend themselves to blending with others, such as vermouth, gin, or vodka. Some combinations may have resulted from random experimentation with what came readily to hand, as with a small glass of whiskey dropped into a large mug of beer.

It has been said that "A first-rate bartender of one of the great hotels of the last century was expected to maintain a working repertory of at least 150 cocktails, shrubs, slings, punches, cobblers, juleps, smashes, flips, and nogs . . . at all hours of the day and night" (Batterberry & Batterberry, 1999), and an amateur can consult any of numerous books that give detailed recipes for hundreds of drinks with fanciful names and sometimes strange ingredients.

Many drinkers enjoy different kinds of spirits, sometimes unadulterated (neat, plain, or straight up); others prefer to have them iced (or on the rocks). The addition of water, seltzer, or some kind of soft drink (soda, tonic, pop, etc.) both dilutes and adds a different flavor to any distilled drink. Beyond those relatively simple variations, there is an encyclopedic variety of further blends that yield drinks that are variously colorful, visually attractive, flavorful, or otherwise remarkable, generally grouped under the broad rubric of cocktails (Spalding, 1988). The art of producing such drinks is sometimes jokingly referred to as "the science of mixology," and there are numerous compilations of recipes that are more voluminous than this book. Fruit, fruit juices, sorbets, bitters, various proportions of different drinks, can all come into play. For some, it makes a major difference whether the ice is broken, crushed, or not, whether the drink is stirred or shaken, the shape of the glass, and so forth. The addition of sugar, salt, or lemon juice on the rim of a glass can be meaningful, and so can the addition of an onion or an olive in the glass.

Some such mixed drinks are novel and short-lived; others are remarkably durable. Some are strongly identified with a particular place: for example, the Singapore sling. Others tend to be associated with a particular type of drinker: for example, the Depth Charge with workingmen, or the *pousse café* with wealthy women. The "3-martini lunch" became emblematic in the 1980s of the dissolute extravagance of a newly wealthy group of entrepreneurs in Europe and North America, and there was a large move from various kinds of cocktails to white wine, in situations of group hospitality, in drinking with meals, and in simply drinking. By the late 1990s, the martini was enjoying a new flush of popularity (Edmunds, 1998).

In the 1970s, a whole new category of drinks appeared, called wine-coolers in the U.S. and in the 1990s alco-pops in Great Britain. Generally sweet and fruit-flavored, these were packaged in small units, with an ethanol content of

A group of young men and women in Scotland share a drink. Mixed drinks or cocktails are fashionable in many parts of the world.

approximately 6% by volume. They were quickly immensely popular for a year or so and were also criticized as having been devised in order to increase drinking among women, children, young people, or all of these. A major change in tax laws in the U.S. prompted manufacturers to shift from a wine-base to a malt-base, but few people outside of the industry seem to have noticed. The rapid growth of sales resulted in wildly speculative predictions that this new category might surpass beer or wine in popularity, but the fad was short-lived.

A cocktail waitress or bartender is likely to earn sizable gratuities if she or he remembers what is "the usual" for a regular customer and produces it without having to be told (Spradley & Mann, 1975). Beginning drinkers tend to experiment, especially when in a situation where drinks are relatively inexpensive, whereas more experienced drinkers tend to have narrowed their repertory to one or a few favorites.

In the 18th and 19th centuries, mixed drinks of a different sort were also available (Smith, 1995). Various flips were produced, combining beer, or rum, or whiskey with eggs, or milk, or spices; a hot poker was often thrust into the blend to warm it, while also producing a dramatic hiss of steam and diffusing the smell around the room. Eggnog or syllabub, with elaborate blends of eggs, whipped cream, nutmeg, and cinnamon, are still popular drinks for large groups on wintry festive occasions. Punches, combining wines with spirits and often also with generous helpings of fruit, have similarly been popular for hundreds of years, usually served in times when the weather is warmer. In Spain, sangría is a punch based on wine and fruit but it is often served with more substantial food.

Mixed drinks have become so dominant a part of the drinking scene that some public outlets provide "mocktails," which look like cocktails but without the alcohol, for patrons who do not want it known that they are not drinking. It is a strong commentary on the social importance of drinking together that people go to such expense and bother to dissimulate in such a manner.

In view of all the readiness there is to mix drinks with each other or with other substances, we must not lose track of those who feel strongly that the adulteration of their favorite drink would be a waste, or inappropriate. This includes not just wealthy snobs who boast about rare and expensive beverages that have been aged for decades; a Camba peasant at the headwaters of the Amazon (Heath, 1958) is just as likely to poke fun at people he considers too weak, on the basis that they dilute the rum he drinks (while others use it as a laboratory tissue-fixative). Having looked successively at the variety of types of beverage alcohol that people drink around the world, we can now learn more about drinking occasions and drinking patterns by looking at types in relation to types.

TYPES IN RELATION TO TYPES

It is evident that any typology, whether of drinks or anything else, is a conceptual scheme reflecting ways of thinking about things more than it reflects the reality of the things themselves. Although our preceding discussion of types of drinks may have helped in thinking about certain drinks or what people drink in certain places, it should be clear by now that few populations, and probably no individuals other than analysts who pay special attention to comparative drinking patterns, restrict their attention to a single type.

A brief look at how the types of drinks relate to each other should provide a more helpful understanding of how and why researchers sometimes prefer to deal with the commonalties among beverages that contain alcohol, rather than always focusing on specific details about any drink, no matter how popular or prevalent it may be.

Table 1 is a simple but dramatic illustration of how different drinking patterns result in very different rates of consumption among three basic types of

Table 1 Countries with highest and lower per capita consumption, 1994

Total		Spirits[a]		Beer		Wine	
Lowest 8	Highest 8	Lowest 8	Highest 8	Lowest 8	Highest 8	Lowest 8	Highest 8
Morocco	Luxembourg	Malaysia	Russia	Morocco	Czech Rep.	Thailand	France
Malaysia	France	Thailand	China	Tunisia	Germany	China	Luxembourg
Tunisia	Portugal	Argentina	Poland	Turkey	Rep. Ireland	Mexico	Italy
Thailand	Germany	Turkey	Cyprus	Israel	Luxembourg	Singapore	Portugal
Israel	Hungary	Singapore	Hungary	Malaysia	Denmark	Peru	Switzerland
Turkey	Czech Rep.	Norway	Bulgaria	Thailand	Austria	Cuba	Argentina
Peru	Austria	Portugal	Greece	Ukraine	Slovakia	Turkey	Greece
Singapore	Denmark	Mexico	Spain	China	Hungary	Venezuela	Hungary

Source: Adapted from *World Drink Trends 1995.*

[a] No statistics were available on Peru, Israel, Tunisia, and Morocco for spirits.

Note: Reprinted from *Drinking Patterns and Their Consequences* (p. 16), by M. Grant & J. Litvak, 1998, Philadelphia: Taylor & Francis.

beverages, beer, wine, and spirits. In addition to comparing quantities of different beverages sold in the countries with highest and lowest consumption records, it is also important to compare how the consumption of each beverage type compares to the overall consumption in that country (*Productschap von Gestilleerde Dranken*, 1997). For example, Luxembourg and France are the two countries highest in both overall consumption and wine consumption, but neither appears among the top eight countries in beer consumption. Russia is highest in spirits, but does not even appear on any of the other lists. China is high for spirits but low for both wine and beer. Argentina is high for wine but not for anything else. Denmark is among the highest in overall consumption but not for any of the three types (Single & Leino, 1998).

When one is comparing the consumption of various kinds of beverage alcohol, it is important to keep in mind the vast difference between volumes of the various beverages, and the volumes of ethanol contained in those beverages. For example, beer is by far the most popular drink in the U.S., accounting for 53% of the volume people drank in 1995. However, commercial beers usually contain only about 5% and rarely over 6% ethanol by volume, meaning that spirits (drunk in relatively tiny quantities, but containing around 30–40% ethanol by volume) accounted for more of the alcohol intake. Wine was drunk in much smaller quantities than beer, but its 10–13% strength means that it made up nearly half of the alcohol.

Throughout much of the world, the drinks of Europe and North America have become the drinks most popular among those who are educated, or who wish to demonstrate how cosmopolitan they are (Armyr et al., 1982). In part, this is a function of the extent to which a few major producers have come to dominate the world market (Cavanagh & Clairmonte, 1985). But local manufacturers often imitate well-known brands or types of beverages. No matter how expensive it may be, no Japanese product should be dignified by being labeled Scotch, according to the Scotch Whisky Distillers who insist that the distinctive quality of local water, peat, and barley makes for regional uniqueness.

In addition to such commonalties, however, there are also significant differences. In recent years, tequila has gained considerable popularity internationally, although that distillate of maguey (century-plant) was virtually unknown outside of Mexico before the 1980s. Vodka, the dominant distilled drink in the former Soviet Union and in much of eastern Europe, had little distribution for centuries, although it is now immensely popular elsewhere. Pisco is a grape-based brandy in Peru, as singani is in Bolivia; locally popular, neither has yet caught the imagination of drinkers elsewhere. Sugarcane-based rums of the Caribbean enjoy worldwide popularity, although those of Brazil are generally ignored. An almost infinite variety of distilled drinks enjoy local popularity in various regions, but they are unknown elsewhere.

There are a few populations in which a major historical shift in drinking patterns has occurred within the past century or so. In Australia, for example, distilled spirits overwhelmingly predominated until late in the 1800s, when a fairly rapid shift to beer took place (Hall & Hunter, 1995). That change was the direct opposite of what had happened somewhat earlier in both Denmark (Schiøler, 1995) and Iceland (Ásmundsson, 1995), both of which had gone from a taste for beer to favoring spirits. Curiously, both countries have since reverted to an overwhelming preference for beer. If any generalization is warranted about changes in preference for specific beverages, perhaps the safest is that such changes are difficult to predict. Taking a longer historical perspective, it should be noted that beer had been a staple in the daily diet of Egyptians for centuries before it became taboo under Islam (Ashour, 1995). In much the same way, poets and songsters had long been eloquent about the joys of wine and even drunkenness in much of the Middle and Near East before Islam.

In most of the countries where attention has been paid to the subject, it is evident that traditional drinks (such as homebrewed beer, palm wine, chicha, pulque, or moonshine) tend to be drunk predominantly in traditional contexts, whereas modern drinks (such as factory-bottled beer, imported spirits, and labeled wine) tend to be drunk in nontraditional settings. The meanings and uses of drinks are also differentiated, with traditional drinks used for rituals, offerings and general sociability, whereas modern drinks are more associated with prestige, hedonism, or escape. It should not be thought that only tradition-oriented people use traditional drinks, while progressives favor drinks from industrial sources. It is commonplace that the same individuals use both, in different contexts and for different purposes. So much is this the case that some authors who have paid attention to drinking patterns in developing societies over time have remarked that they tend to be additive rather than substitutive (Skog, 1983).

WHY DOES IT MATTER?

There are many reasons why it matters what people drink. A fundamental one is health. Although most investigators who write about beverage alcohol tend to do so in predominantly numerical terms, there are important qualitative differences among the several ways in which a standard dose of ethanol can be taken. The nutritional value of each drink can be appreciable, or it can be nil. The acute short-term impact on the nervous system can be abrupt and harsh, or it can be gradual and slight. The chronic long-term impact on the nervous system and many organ systems can be irritating, harmful, and deleterious, or it can be harmless or even salutary.

Although the ethanol contained in any standard drink may be approximately uniform (cf. p. 177), the other contents of drinks differ markedly. This also affects the way in which people react and respond to a standard dose of alcohol. Because of the rapidity with which alcohol diffuses throughout the body, a second strong drink will have considerably more effect than a second weak drink in the same time-frame. The importance of pacing one's drinks depends on what one is drinking. So does the likelihood that drinking will have a discernible

impact on visual acuity, manual dexterity, coordination, balance, and other behaviors.

We have already seen in earlier chapters that how people think about, talk
about, and use different beverages is by no means the same. It is certainly
convenient for survey-researchers to say that "A drink is a drink is a drink,"
in strictly quantitative terms, while counting supposed consumption. In reality,
there are few people for whom that statement holds in the workaday world. In
qualitative or behavioral terms, one might say with equal conviction that "A
drink is not a drink is not a drink."

Different drinks and types of drinks are used by different people. Or they
are used by some of the same people at different times. Or they are used in
different places, with different confederates, for different purposes, while doing
different things (Heath, 1995).

The Kofyar in our case study live in a culture that is suffused by beer,
at meals, in social relationships, in folklore, marking stages in the life-cycle,
in association with taxes or work, socialization or hospitality. Wine or spirits
would have no place in any of those routine contexts; without beer, they would
be awkward to manage and difficult to comprehend. In various ways, the other
peoples whose drinking we have mentioned are not indifferent in terms of what
they drink.

If we are to understand more about the many roles that alcohol plays in
human culture, it is crucial that attention be paid to what it is that people drink
in any given situation.

It may be more difficult to do, but a serious social scientist should also try
to understand why it is that people drink.

Chapter 6

The Heart Has its Reasons:
Why Do People Drink?

Old and new friends exchange toasts in the Extremadura region of Spain. The secular ritual of toasting is a way of expressing social solidarity and camaraderie. © *Thad Samuels Abell II/NGS Image Collection.*

Although it is true that every animal has to drink, in the generic sense of imbibing some liquid in order to survive, it is also true that no animal has to drink, in the specific sense of ingesting any alcoholic beverage. And yet most people in most societies throughout the world do choose to drink from time to time. Having already explored the questions of who drinks, what, when, where and how they drink, it now seems appropriate to look at why they drink and, correlatively, why some others choose not to drink.

The reasons that people give for drinking are many and varied (Cox, 1990). Their statements are always subject to some reservations with respect to accuracy or validity. Even when an individual is not trying to misrepresent his or her motivations, there remains the question of how much insight one may have or how thorough one has been in the introspection or explanation. Within those limitations, however, it is striking that drinking often seems to serve similar purposes in very different cultures and contexts. The Bondo and Muria tribal populations of India are like some of the tribal populations of Mexico in thinking of liquor as "Mother Earth's milk," and in considering drinking both a pleasure and a duty (Mohan & Sharma, 1995), but few societies are so frank or so articulate.

It is not always easy to shift from observing behavior to attempting to discern motivations that lie behind it. This is not to say that there is anything mystical about motives. They are just as real as are actions, and they play important roles in shaping the world as we know it. But the fact that people have motives and act upon them does not mean that they can be studied with the scientific precision and accuracy with which we count and describe other patterns of behavior. There are occasions when people purposely misrepresent their reasons for doing things, sometimes in order to present themselves in a better light, and sometimes in order to avoid some stigma or cautioning that they expect might be associated with admitting to certain kinds of motives. Beyond that, there are other occasions in which an individual is honestly quite unaware of his or her own reasons for doing something and truly cannot articulate them clearly or adequately.

A social scientist does not usually pretend to penetrate the psyche of the actors whose behavior is being observed. Much of what is learned about motives comes from what people say. But there is a filtering process in which the plausibility of such statements is measured against a broad range of alternative interpretations. The models for such tests of plausibility are not vague subconscious urges but rather functions that, in turn, can be observed as well as inferred. By functions, we refer, quite simply to what a behavior does—how it changes the situation for the actor or the actors. A skilled and insightful observer can often analyze changing dynamics within a social or cultural system that get things done that are important to an individual or a group, whether those changes were intended or not.

This does not mean that the analyst is brighter than the actors. It only means that the analyst is observant in different ways, attuned to different cues, and, with broad cross-cultural experience, able to compare the given situation with others that may be far removed in time or space. In case this sounds like a closed system in which whatever the observed says must be accepted on blind faith, that really is not the case. One of the simplest ways to check the reality of such a functional interpretation is to present it, in simple terms, to the principals, the actors themselves, and to get their reactions. When that was done with our case study, changing drinking patterns among the Bolivian Camba, the reaction of the Camba was uniformly supportive. Often they preceded their agreement with a contemplative "You know, I never really thought of it that way…" or "You'd have to be an outsider to come up with that…." And then followed unanimously the smiling reassurance that "It really makes sense," or "You're right, that's how it worked, although we never knew it at the time."

There is a very brief discussion about why the question of why people drink is so often a sensitive one, and how investigators have dealt with it or neglected to do so. Next, we outline a few of the types of reasons that have been proposed to account for cultural patterns of drinking. Remember that our focus is on customary habits that are widespread in groups, and not the complex combination of hereditary factors, biological makeup, personal and familial history, and private motives that make for the idiosyncrasies of any individual drinker. Next, the reasons that people give for drinking and not drinking are shown to be many and varied, but remarkably consistent with the other things we know about drinking as behavior. Apart from the reasons that drinkers give, there is also some discussion of reasons that we infer, using logical induction based on detailed understanding of the social and cultural context. The final section deals, as usual, with why the focal question for this chapter deserved to be asked in the first place.

Case Study: Changing Camba Drinking Patterns

A small group whose reasons for drinking well illustrate the value of an anthropological approach are the Camba, who live at the headwaters of the Amazon in eastern Bolivia. Their drinking patterns are exceptional in worldwide perspective, partly because they drink so much more than most other people (Heath, 1958) and partly because they are so free of virtually all of the so-called alcohol-related problems that might be expected to plague a population in which most adults drink to the point of oblivion just about every weekend, using a rum that is stronger than most beverages that are in customary use anywhere (Heath, 1962). We are also fortunate in having periodic restudies (Heath, 1971, 1994) that show dramatic changes over time, as well as some remarkable continuity, by a reporter who has attempted to address all of the questions that others have raised with respect to Camba drinking (Heath 1991a, b).

When first studied, the Camba were economically marginal and living dispersed in widely scattered thatched huts, lacking the tight social bonds that often characterize tribal or peasant groups. There was little sense of community, and even kinship, other than that between mother and children, meant little. Their prodigious drinking was not a daily occurrence; mostly it happened on weekends and holidays. In fact, almost the only context in which any Camba drank was a drinking party, but there were plenty of them at different homesteads, starting Friday evening and continuing until Monday morning, or lasting throughout any official holiday and usually extending through the following day.

Drinking itself was so formalized as to be a secular ritual. With only one bottle and a single glass in use at any time, person A (the host, who had bought the first couple of bottles) would pour a tumblerful (about 300 g.) of alcohol (the 178-proof raw fuel produced by local sugar refineries and sold as primer for the popular stoves and lanterns that operated on kerosene vapor and silk mantles). He would then stand in front of person B, and neither the Camba nor I could discern any recurrent pattern in that choice; sex, age, reputation, and other logical variables didn't hold consistently. After nodding slightly, A would say in the local dialect, "Health" or "To your health," drink half of the glass in one quick draft, and hand it to B. B returned the toast and emptied the glass in a single gulp, after which A would sit down. B would refill the glass and toast C. And so it went, hour after hour, day and night, until either the supply ran out or people would be called to work. After the first few rounds, toasting was not continuous but sporadic, with long pauses during which people talked quietly with others seated near them, played music (on guitar, flute, and/or drum), or apparently did nothing. As many as 20 or as few as eight people would be involved, seated in a rough circle around a fire; children were behind them, looking on or playing. When a participant passed out, he or she was simply left while the party continued; on waking up or coming to, that person rejoined without comment.

With so high a concentration of ethanol (about 89% by volume), people were taking in plenty of calories but no food value, and one could smell the alcohol in everyone's sweat which stung their eyes, as the drinking irritated their throats. Just as it was unthinkable that anyone would drink in any other context (except that of a funeral), it was also unthinkable that anyone would have negative consequences from drinking. Drunkenness was a quiet affair of simply staring into space or passing out for a while. Aggression, whether verbal, physical, sexual, or other, was virtually unknown among the Camba, drunk or sober. Similarly absent were boisterousness, clowning, maudlin sentimentality, or other exaggerated comportment such as tends to be associated with intoxication in other cultures.

No Camba suffered or could even imagine such a thing as a hangover, and people worked at difficult and dangerous tasks (such as harvesting sugarcane) just a few hours after a party ended. Accidents were rare, and the drinking problems that are common elsewhere, such as trouble with the police, absenteeism, guilt, psychological or social discomfort, were meaningless to them. In an area of short life-expectancy and several endemic diseases, I was unable to discern any physical effects; although not formally trained in medicine, I am familiar with the physiological impact of long-term excessive drinking. In sum, it is difficult to point to any way in which the Camba pattern of drinking, which almost anyone would consider excessive, and which was frequent enough to be long-term in anyone over 35 years of age, was harmful or risky. Many did complain of liver discomfort, but so did most of the Spanish-speaking townspeople in the region, who called themselves "white," many of whom prided themselves on not drinking.

On the basis of the first year's experience with them, I wrote: "[Such] fiestas provide occasions for intense interaction, and drinking groups constitute primary reference groups which are lacking in other phases of Camba life" (Heath, 1958, p. 504). The small but highly valued sense of conviviality and sociability that they enjoyed in drinking parties seemed to be reason enough, from the point of view of the Camba, and from this social scientist's interpretation. Alcohol serve[d] to facilitate rapport between individuals who are normally isolated and introverted" (Heath, 1958, p. 507). Hints of such an interpretation of drinking elsewhere had been given by Simmel (1949), and Partanen (1991) subsequently developed the functionalist idea in considerably more detail on the basis of his studies concentrating on social organization in Africa. With the arrival of a paved highway and railroads connecting the Camba region to more populated areas and with growing awareness of recent land reform, the Camba were prompted to form *sindicatos*, localized peasant unions that were government-sponsored corporate plaintiffs in appeals for the expropriation and reallocation of large estates (Heath, 1972). Such organizations quickly became strong and meaningful reference groups for Camba peasants who previously had had none. For a brief moment in Bolivian history, grass-roots community action flourished, contrasting markedly with the atomistic pattern that had preceded it.

That was the beginning of a heady time in which the landed oligarchy had been deposed and there was the promise of universal education and suffrage. Cambas who had never before been allowed to carry firearms were given rifles and ammunition from the demobilized army, and it looked as if participatory democracy was soon to become a reality. With a keen sense of liberation, neighbors worked together to carry out the tedious mechanics of laying legal claim to land that they had worked as unofficial tenants, and they called each other *compañero* (comrade), as prescribed by the revolutionary movement that had made them feel like citizens as never before.

As social interrelatedness increased, drinking decreased. There were fewer and fewer parties, and they did not last as long. Class consciousness reached the point where "In many respects, the *sindicato* now serve[d] as a primary reference group for most Camba farmers.... The coordinate decline in drinking bouts [was] striking, and sindical activity [had] replaced frequent heavy drinking in the lives of many individuals" (Heath, 1965, p. 290). Once again it looked as if drinking patterns were mirroring social organization.

In subsequent years the Camba were subjected to a flood of changes in many aspects of their lives, including the very ecology that had been the source of so many things that they hunted, fished, or made. The first paved highway provided closer contact, first with the state capital and then with the densely populated highland portion of the country, which in turn was linked by rail with neighboring countries and eventually with seaports that Bolivia itself totally lacked. At the same time, the Camba region was the goal of large numbers of newcomers seeking free or inexpensive land in that counterfeit paradise of lush green, but basically fragile and unproductive, soil of the tropical forest. The new migrants brought different languages and cultures, and they destroyed the jungle with logging and farming, both of which brought short-term booms that upset the local economy without helping the Camba. Quechua and Aymara Indians took over local markets with their more assertive entrepreneurial vigor, and made the Camba feel crowded and besieged in what was hardly recognizable as their old territory. Cattle herding by outsiders brought new pressures on the land but provided no new jobs before it too crashed. Drug-traffickers polluted the rivers with chemicals that they used to convert coca leaves to cocaine paste, killing the fish just as the game had earlier been destroyed.

Major political changes also resulted from a military coup. Peasant leaders were killed or exiled, and the *sindicatos* were dissolved and outlawed. It is striking that drinking in the old manner returned (Heath, 1994). Lacking the sense of social interrelatedness that they had enjoyed before with the *sindicatos*, and beset by bewildering and damaging changes in all aspects of their own daily lives, the remaining Camba, older and diminished in numbers, have resumed their earlier patterns of episodic heavy drinking, in the same secular ritual manner as before. The drinking party appears to serve as an adaptation from their fragmented cultural past that once again fits with their newly atomistic social situation. The pendulum-like swing of change in Camba drinking styles contradicts some of the most popular views about the ways in which people's drinking patterns evolve, and it reinforces one's confidence in an interpretation that stresses aspects of the social structure and organization. Although the Camba do not loom large in world history, they provide an important case-study for our discussion of drinking occasions.

A SENSITIVE ISSUE

We have emphasized the fact that this book is descriptive rather than prescriptive, dealing with drinking as an observable behavioral phenomenon, without focusing on neurological, physicochemical, pharmacological processes, nor on any long-term outcomes. After having looked at the when, where, who, what, and how of drinking, that still leaves open the question of why. In all candor, it would be easier just to leave that question aside, and there would be some justification in that motives are not quite so readily accessible as are other aspects of behavior. But it would be an error that could too easily be misconstrued as indicating that behavioral science is ill-equipped or reluctant to come to grips with meanings and values, as if they were some mystical or intrapsychic epiphenomena beyond our comprehension.

On the contrary, social and epidemiological researchers have for years been innovative and imaginative in dealing with why people drink, and some of the resulting theories have earned wide acceptance among colleagues in other sciences and academic disciplines. Motives are not necessarily mysterious, buried deeply under layers of the subconscious or unconscious in the minds of individuals. Often they are behavioral in the sense that people think about them, talk about them, and act upon them, in ways that are socially patterned. Sometimes also the social patterning itself is so consistent as to suggest very strongly reasons that people may not clearly articulate, functions that are evidently served by the drinking or by not drinking, as the case may be. It is wholly appropriate that we address here both the reasons people give and the reasons that we can unequivocally infer, without having to detour far into psychology.

There are many fields in which social scientists have been reluctant to address questions of causality, or explanations about why people behave as they do. For better or for worse, the study of drinking often puts the investigator in a situation where reasons are expected or even demanded, and a broad range of theories have been proposed (Heath, 1988a). It also happens to be a realm of behavior about which people may be reluctant to discuss their motivations frankly.

We have already seen how difficult it is for researchers to get what they consider reliable responses to such ostensibly objective questions as when people last drank and how much they drank at that time. How much more difficult it is to elicit meaningful data about such intrinsically subjective a question as why they drink, or continue to drink, or have chosen not to do so.

Despite the difficulties, numerous investigators have tried to do just that with varying degrees of success. One of the most obvious obstacles at the outset is that many people are presumably quite unaware of their motivations beyond a very superficial level, and they may respond in a stylized way that fits with popularly shared stereotypes but that may not actually be revelatory of their own feelings. This is not to imply that everyone must have deeply submerged unconscious or subconscious motivations for drinking, but that they are apt initially to volunteer little more than the glib reasons that are used among those with whom they most often drink, or reasons that they think will be most acceptable to the interviewer. Many survey instruments and questionnaires include lists of reasons, among which a respondent may choose. Such lists can be as short as six to eight reasons or as long as 40, with instructions to indicate those that most nearly approximate one's own reasons. The common problem that persists throughout the construction of such an instrument is the need to compromise between not asking enough, which can result in inadequate data, or asking too much, which can annoy, confuse, and tire the respondents as well as costing dearly in both time and money (Room, 1990). Besides, if the exact wording does not coincide with what a person would volunteer, there may be some reluctance to agree with the reason offered.

On those rare occasions when the question about why people drink has been posed in an open-ended manner, the deluge of responses has been so huge that investigators have been reluctant to deal with them. Presumably, they could be classified, categorized, or sorted into meaningful types, but that would do violence to the richness of the data, and it may be a futile exercise, because there is rarely any indication that there was any probing to get beyond the initial responses in an attempt to elicit a more comprehensive or exhaustive list of reasons.

As is common in epidemiological research, cultural variation is a confounding variable, especially inasmuch as the cluster of reasons for drinking tends to be fairly consistent among the members of a given population, and often quite different from those given by members of another. Nevertheless, the cost in time, effort, and money of preparing and pretesting any research instrument is such that relatively few individuals or agencies take such an initiative, and it is infinitely easier to use, translate, or slightly adapt one that someone else has already prepared.

Unlike survey researchers, ethnographers and other observational researchers are often dissatisfied with instruments that allow for only limited forced-choices, often among alternatives that have been devised and phrased by people with a very different view of the world. The concern is that they may miss some of the most important responses, those that have not been anticipated. Especially when dealing with different cultures, it is important to be open to the unforeseen nuances of individual responses couched in the language of the actor. Again, the fullness of qualitative data constitutes a rich resource that may be mined for meaning. But it is difficult to analyze, more difficult to summarize, and often next to impossible to communicate such data in quantity. The expository format is often construed as time-consuming and less than scientific. Precoded responses to a survey instrument are easily converted to numbers, which in turn can be easily aggregated, compared, contrasted, statistically manipulated, vividly presented in visual graphs, and have the convincingly authoritative dimension of quantification, which some mistake for scientific accuracy.

Mayan dancers in Tenejapa, Mexico, punctuate their Carnaval festivities with drinking. Drinking is often an integral part of religious rituals worldwide. © *Lorenzo Armendariz-Latin Focus.com*

With respect to why people drink, as with all of the other questions raised in this book, the most fruitful way to look for answers is undoubtedly to combine the qualitative and quantitative approaches. As we turn to a closer examination of reasons people give for drinking, it is once more clear that these should not be thought of as mutually exclusive or alternative methodologies but rather as necessarily complementary tools that together make easier the complex job of understanding drinking as behavior.

REASONS PEOPLE GIVE

A fundamental curiosity about most of what is written about beverage alcohol, especially by scientists, health professionals, and other researchers, is that so little acknowledgment is made that the great majority of people who drink do so because they find it enjoyable and pleasurable. There are a few individuals whose long-term heavy drinking has made them "dependent" on alcohol (American Psychiatric Association, 1980; World Health Organization, 1997), meaning that they need it to feel normal, and that it interferes with other parts of their life. The overwhelming majority of those who drink, however, choose to do so for at least partially hedonistic reasons. This may, in fact, be one of the major reasons why some anhedonic religious groups not only abstain but decry drinking on the part of others. A recent conference on the linkages between drinking and pleasure has recently been published as a book (Peele & Grant, 1999), but it only begins to redress a long-term imbalance in the scientific literature. Some major types of reasons tend to be mentioned in the literature about drinking patterns around the world: taste, celebration, relaxation, mood alteration, hospitality, sociability, food and enhancement, pastime, religion, medicine, and other.

Taste

There appears to be little reason to doubt most drinkers when they say that they enjoy the taste of what they drink. This can range from subtle nuanced layers of flavor that complement each other in intricate ways and that tasters love to discuss at length, to a straightforward hearty appreciation of a familiar and distinctive taste that no one ever tries to analyze.

In the same way, taste can be a basic reason for some people not to drink. The hops and carbonation in mass-produced commercial beer is often "bitter" to those who first encounter it, and some never come back to it. Many homebrews, as much as they may be appreciated by local people, are rejected by outsiders on the basis of flavor or other aesthetic grounds: sour, putrid, disgusting, rotten, and dirty are only a few of the responses that people typically give to a chicha, pulque, or beer with which they are not familiar.

At the other end of the spectrum are connoisseurs who vie for an opportunity to sample a given cru of a particular vintage wine from just the right property. They may describe it ecstatically as "nectar of the gods." Or they pub crawl from one establishment to the next in an unending quest for the perfect beer, ale, or stout. Although the numbers of fans may be fewer, there are many brands of spirits, cordials, and liqueurs that people cherish and savor. Even moonshine is often esteemed for its special smoothness or flavor, and individual makers can sometimes be identified by their product.

Some individuals find that spirits cause an uncomfortable burning sensation in the mouth or throat; others esteem just that as a sign of potency. Sweeter drinks are often favored by younger drinkers or by females. Most people in the U.S. prefer beer cold; in the U.K., many feel that cold kills the flavor.

No matter what the beverage, there are some for whom it is the favorite taste and some for whom it is repugnant. But those who do appreciate a drink will often quietly savor it for some time, perhaps simultaneously studying its color and texture, enjoying its aroma, and paying more attention to details of its esthetics than they do to a favorite food.

Celebration

In chapter 1 we have already seen the large number and diversity of occasions that different peoples celebrate with drinking. Almost universal is New Year's; wedding and birthdays are commonplace, as are a host of rites marking holidays, anniversaries, initiations, and other special events. The Asante are another population who have a festival, unrelated to the life-stages of any individual, that is celebrated like Catholic carnaval with the inversion of many normal social roles, humorous to all as a kind of topsy-turvy representation of life (Akyeampong, 1996).

Some people make their lives more enjoyable by celebrating small things, such as the completion of a household task, the receipt of a message from a friend, a break in bad weather, or simply having lived through another day. If this is done to provide an excuse for drinking when one should not, it might be problematic. But if it does no harm to the drinker or anyone else, it may be psychologically beneficial. For some, of course, the very act of having a drink is itself celebratory. It has been said that champagne can turn any occasion into a celebration. Peruvian mestizos treat the availability of beer or whiskey as an occasion for celebrating (Doughty, 1971). With homebrews, the availability of that important substance may be an occasion for celebration in itself, and toasting the completed preparation of a beer or wine is a widespread custom. Those who are suspicious of celebration as frivolous behavior can cite it also as a good reason not to drink.

Relaxation

Alcohol is unusual in having a dual effect on the central nervous system, first as a stimulant, but only briefly on the upswing of the curve of BAC. Subsequently, and often tellingly, it acts as a depressant. This is why most drinkers feel slightly stimulated by the first drink or two, and most can even perform better in tests of eye-hand coordination. But relaxation is another common reason for drinking, especially when it is framed (in sociological terms) as leisure, a little time set aside from whatever demands may be routine. Another phrasing of this might be refreshment—a cold drink on a hot day, an opportunity to quench one's thirst, a time for contemplation rather than hectic action. Iteso men taking a break around the communal beer pot after the day's work and before going home epitomize this reason for drinking; so does a North American commuter, settling into a favorite chair to listen to some music at home for a few minutes before beginning to work in the garden, preparing dinner, or doing something else.

Some people say that drinking lets them relax, as if it were something difficult to do without that cue. Presumably, this is close to what some people mean when they say they need a drink to get through the day. Of course, some who interpret relaxation as slothful and demoralizing see it as another reason not to drink.

Mood Alteration

For most people a drink or two is sufficient to cause some alteration of mood. For the vast majority, such a change is pleasant and agreeable, to a point. For example, it is often cited as a means of overcoming shyness or gaining courage, as among tribal populations in Polynesia, highland Colombia, or western Mexico, and among many (especially youths) in much of modern Europe and North America. Tarahumara Indians are said to be so bashful that married couples often feel the need to drink before engaging in sexual intercourse (Zingg, 1942). The Lepcha of Nepal believe that drinking together will settle an argument, and they are confident that a shared drink will seal any settlement or agreement (Gorer, 1930). The Swiss are cautious drinkers for fear that they might somehow lose control and do something that would make them feel guilty.

A Confucian tradition that persists in China is the concept of "moral drinking," moderate drinking that is thought to emphasize and strengthen all that is good in a person, and to contribute to his or her well-being. According to some devout Confucians, even drunkenness is a virtue if it relaxes and refreshes a person, without costing too much and without resulting in a fight (Xiao, 1995).

Presumably mood alteration is what many respondents have in mind when they say that the reason they drink is to forget, or to get away from troubles or simply to feel better. On the negative side, it may also be what is meant by disinhibition, letting one's hair down, "being the real me," as if one spent most of one's time acting in ways that are contrary to one's nature and that alcohol somehow released one from such pretense.

There is a hint of that in the institution of happy hour, in some public drinking establishments in urban and cosmopolitan settings. For an hour or more, usually late in the afternoon, one can drink at reduced prices, presumably with the aim or result of being or becoming happy. Some critics have voiced their complaint that drinking should not be touted as the key to happiness; in response, some bars have instituted an "attitude-adjustment hour." Apaches and many other Native American peoples value the exhilarating sense of heightened awareness that comes with a couple of drinks, just as others are fearful of it.

Sometimes an alcoholic drink has been the medium for ingestion of other substances that make for even more dramatic mood alteration. Mead, like beer, was often the vehicle for ecstatic drug experiences in northern Europe (Rätsch, 1994). Commonplace additives that, in minute amounts, were used to produce sexual excitement, intense pleasure, inspiration, and even hallucinations include morning glory seeds, fly agaric, datura, henbane, hemp, poppy, rosemary, myrtle, hemlock, mandrake, and belladonna. Unfortunately, the very same additives, in only slightly larger amounts, are toxic and deadly, which is not always sufficiently emphasized (Buhner, 1998). Fly agaric was sometimes added to beer or kumiss in Siberia (Jochelson, 1906); some Andean Indians apparently put coca in their chicha (Wassén, 1972); and both morning glory and datura appear to have been used in pulque on special occasions. In each instance, use was not general among the population but restricted to a few shamans or diviners whose spirits were thought to leave their bodies during their special intoxication. Some say the reason they drink is to increase the effect of drugs; others to decrease it.

For some, the mood that is sought is precisely no mood, or oblivion. Unfortunately, loss of consciousness appears to be attractive to some, especially the young, for whom it may be just a part of their eager experimenting to test the limits of the human experience. Others who claim to drink "just to get drunk" or "to be totally out of it" subsequently take great pleasure in recounting their outlandish behavior, suggesting that they may instead have been drinking primarily in order to misbehave while enjoying the temporary suspension of certain social expectations (time-out) that is often accorded to the inebriate. Attitudes toward drink, drinkers, and drunkenness are so ambivalent in some societies that alcohol can be treated as exculpatory for some inappropriate actions but incriminating for others.

As with most of the other reasons for drinking, mood alteration can also be given, with full plausibility, as a reason for not drinking. Some individuals would argue that no one should rely on a foreign substance to alter their mood. Others would scoff at the idea that one should want or strive to be happy. If one's body is a sacred temple, then drink might be an extraneous distraction or even a pollutant.

For a minority of people, the mood alteration that comes from even a few drinks can be a negative rather than a positive change. There is some indication that depressed or aggressive people tend to become more so after drinking. Perhaps this has something to do with the intimate association between drinking and war that obtains in many societies. Jivaro, Tupinamba, and Araucanian warriors drink to fuel their strength and courage as well as to sharpen their wits before going on a war-party. Legends tell of Vikings, Scythians, and other hit-and-run bands as often drinking and carousing before undertaking the episodic raids that brought them wealth and made them objects of fear and dread among more peaceful and sedentary populations. The aim was supposedly to give them courage. Many North American and European veterans of World War I also tell of having been issued rations of liquor, both to make them feel warmer and to allay some fears just prior to being sent "over the top" to attack the well-entrenched enemy nearby. At the end of the 20th century, international courts concerned with genocide and ethnocide are hearing reports from soldiers in the former-Yugoslavia that they were plied with drink by their officers to steel them for the atrocities that they were obliged to commit on innocent civilian populations, especially when entire villages were destroyed. In the Desert Storm War, U.S. pilots were often issued distilled spirits from the ship's medical stores as a calmant when they returned to an aircraft carrier from a bombing mission.

Many observers have chosen to explain a large part of the high correlation between drinking and crime or violence by pointing to a high proportion of perpetrators who claim to have intended to commit such acts but first had a few drinks "to screw up their confidence," rather than to any causal linkage between alcohol and such behavior. For better or for worse, drinking often serves to alter one's mood.

That fact in itself is ample justification to many abstainers that they should avoid the risk of drinking. Some fear that becoming more affable or relaxed among others will make them vulnerable; others may fear that a drink or more would aggravate depression or violent tendencies. In much that has been written about alcohol, the tendency toward loss of control or disinhibition has loomed large and, while some find that an attraction, others consider even the prospect an abomination.

Hospitality

In every one of the 27 countries described in a recent volume on alcohol and culture (Heath, 1995), one of the most prevalent among drinking occasions was hospitality, the welcoming of a guest, often in a wide variety of contexts. This is often extravagant in "wet cultures" but it is also very common in relatively "dry cultures" that have remarkably low average per capita rates of consumption. In large segments of the U.S. population, the second or third utterance of a host or hostess to a visitor is likely to be the offer or invitation to a drink. In any of the "wine culture" countries of southern Europe or South America, one would be thought miserly or antisocial if at least wine, and preferably also some food, were not produced in the course of a visit.

And the visit need not be primarily a social one between long-term friends or acquaintances. It is a normal courtesy in much of rural Scotland that a commercial person who delivers anything to a farmstead be offered "a wee dram of whisky." In households where homebrew or wine is produced in any quantity, a visitor is often invited to sample it. Such invitations are not casually extended, and the norms of social interaction make acceptance almost obligatory. In many Chinese groups, it is quite offensive to decline the offer of a drink in such a context. Whether ritualized or not, the offer of a drink as a gesture of hospitality is an ancient and widespread custom in almost every culture that is at all permissive with respect to alcohol.

Sociability

The same international survey of drinking patterns and alcohol policies (Heath, 1995) included virtually universal agreement that the reason most often given for drinking was sociability. Most people know from their own experience that drinking together enhances sociability, helping to put people at ease, giving them something to do with their hands, and providing, if necessary, a common initial focus for conversation.

Not so many people realize that drinking together can actually create sociability. It is for many a pleasant and immediate shared experience, usually in a setting that the drinkers have chosen. In small doses, ethanol is a relaxant, easing both physical and mental stress. At a level that may not even be conscious, it provides a kind of communion in which each drinker is sharing with others, incorporating into his or her body material from a common source. If all of these are reinforced with the expectation that a drink will be a social lubricant, or that it helps one to talk with others or to be less reserved and more outgoing, the stage is set for drinking to be viewed as a quintessentially social act, and one that makes people even more sociable than they usually are.

Throughout most of sub-Saharan Africa, beer is a significant part of any social exchange, drunk whenever people visit, meet, talk, or transact any business (Partanen, 1991). For the Camba and Sikaiana, alcohol appears to be the elixir without which there would be little sociability.

Not only do most people feel more sociable after a drink or two; experiments under conditions that approach a natural context but that include enough controls to be scientifically accurate have shown that most people are judged by others to be more sociable (Lowe, 1994). In situations where being sociable has increasing adaptive value—not just in terms of self-concept but also in terms of economic, political, sexual, and other forms of status—sociability can be a strong motivation for some to drink.

Another widespread reason given for drinking is to foster or express social unity; toasting is perhaps the quintessential expression of this. There are many contexts in which a crucial sign of acceptance is to be invited to drink with a group or to be congratulated that "you drink like us." It is commonplace in such situations that invidious comparisons are made with the ways in which other people drink, or the drinks they use, as if these were emblematic of membership in an in-group, or of separation from an out-group. Some say they drink to fit in with "a group" or "the group."

It should not be assumed that drinking, in itself, is any golden key to one's becoming a social cynosure, or that drinks will guarantee the amicability of any group of people. Often the most sociable drinking occasions are those that include other activities, with alcohol as more an adjunct than a focus of attention. The reception, when a large group of strangers meet for the first time to deal with some subject of shared interest such as at a conference, is one such common occasion. The opening of an exhibition at a museum, a gallery, a library, or an exposition is another. The drinking of toasts during a large meal can often serve to signal, by punctuation, the social unity of the larger group, even though conversation and other exchanges take place within several smaller groups at scattered tables.

Sociability among drinkers may even be enhanced when another activity is closely linked with both. The fun of competitive drinking, the creative enjoyment of playing word-games, doing puzzles, or collectively composing poetry are all illustrative of how sociability can be expressed and even enhanced by drinking in the context of other ludic or recreational activities.

Closely linked with sociability as a reason for drinking is reciprocity or social credit. By this, we refer to the frequent use of beverage alcohol as a refreshment and social equalizer on occasions of joint community action. Periodic work on public projects (corvée) such as maintaining roads, trails, bridges, irrigation ditches, or water systems often includes a session of drinking, as a break or at the end as a reward. Similarly, work by an ephemeral gang of neighbors on private projects that involve reciprocal labor-exchange, such as plowing, planting, weeding, harvesting, house building, or barn-raising, are commonly drinking occasions that stress sociability among individuals who do not necessarily spend much time together otherwise.

In some circles, drinking almost serves as emblematic of membership in a social group, as happens in some occupational groups, bands of Irish-American males, or American Indians while sojourning in an alien cultural ambiance.

The links between drinking and sociability can also serve as a reason for some people not to drink. "If people need drink to be sociable, we want nothing to do with such people" is one such negative reaction. The implicit risk of losing control or committing a faux pas in a social setting may be a fear that prompts others to avoid drinking.

Food and Food Enhancement

Beer and related homebrews are often staples in the diet of populations who derive significant portions of their basic nutrients from beverages that contain alcohol, and in other instances, a few key vitamins or minerals may be provided (Gastineau et al., 1979). Even though beer is sometimes characterized as liquid bread, people rarely try to subsist on it alone. There are some among the Mongols who claim that they drink Chinese whiskey "because it's cheaper than food" (Williams, 1998). In view of the high price of food there, it may be true on a per-calorie basis, although clearly one could not long survive on a diet of whiskey alone.

Far more commonplace around the world is the use of alcoholic beverages as an accompaniment and enhancement of food. For many French and Italian adults, no meal is complete without wine. Throughout much of Latin America, people feel the same way about chicha or pulque. Even in medieval England, where ale and beer had long been favored drinks, if the documents are to be believed, one of the more extravagant feasts included 1300 deer, 170 boars, 7000 hens, tens of thousands of fish, and 68,500 loaves of bread, all washed down with 25,000 gallons of wine (Hammond, 1993). The perfect matching of food and drink is an activity that some treat as an art form, and people pay enormous prices to eat such elaborately orchestrated meals. For others, a pizza just tastes better with a cold beer.

The gastronomic experience is sometimes enhanced by an aperitif (usually distilled or fortified) drunk before the meal, ostensibly to enhance one's appetite, or a digestive (similarly distilled or fortified) drunk afterward, ostensibly to ease one's digestion, or both. The specific beverages that are used for these purposes differ markedly in terms of regional or idiosyncratic tastes, but the general pattern is widespread and on its way to becoming cosmopolitan.

A family in Zangla, India, proffers an alcoholic barley drink to a guest. The serving of alcohol is in many cultures an important element in hospitality and other sociable occasions. © *CORBIS/Earl Kowall.*

Whether it be construed as a rationalization or taken at face value, there are many people in many cultures who give reasons for drinking that could easily be interpreted as the enhancement of food. Others who claim to abhor indulgence and sensory enjoyment view drinking in such a context as vicious gluttony, inappropriate sensualism, or just plain evil.

Pastime

It is a sad commentary on the worldview of a few people that they claim to drink out of boredom, or because there's nothing else to do. An unimaginable statement from the point of view of most, it appears to be a sincere complaint from some poor and disadvantaged European or Asian youths, some scattered groups of Eskimos and Indians in North America, and others, most of whom are chronically unemployed and living on the fringes of a capitalist economy. Those who drink to get drunk are probably seeking a mood alteration or time-out as noted earlier.

Religion

There are few cultures in which many people will volunteer that the reason they drink is religion, yet there are many specific contexts in which that evidently is the case. Although not many Christians think of the wine of the Eucharist as being an alcoholic drink, it often is, whatever else it may also be, to them or others. We have mentioned Native American priests or shamans for whom the drinking of rum is an integral part of several stages in the elaborate prayers and rituals that they perform. Drinking and even drunkenness were expected, if not required, by devotees of certain deities in ancient Greece, Rome, India, and Babylonia; that is still the case in parts of southern and central Asia. In most of the many cultures that consider homebrew to be the ideal offering to gods and supernatural forces or spirits, it is usually requisite that the worshipper first drink at least a little, to demonstrate the value of the gift. Libations are rarely just poured out on the ground, a figure, or a shrine without first being sampled in a devout way by the donor.

Drunkenness was mentioned as one of the "varieties of religious experience" (James, 1909) that allows one literally to transcend one's mundane secular existence and become, unite with, or participate in the divine. Few religions formally agree (Felice, 1936), but folk-Catholicism as it is practiced at the grass roots—the little or folk tradition as contrasted with the great or formal tradition that is codified by official teachings of the church—has very similar beliefs and practices, mostly associated with homage to patron saints. It is common that women as well as men devoutly drink themselves into oblivion, comfortable that doing so is a proof of their dedication to Catholicism. Doctrinal opposition to such drinking has been loud and clear for centuries, but has had little impact on what happens outside of the church building.

Although the celebration or debauch of pre-Lenten Carnaval (culminating in Mardi Gras) throughout the Hispanic and Latin worlds is hardly religious in its overtones, it is clearly a part of the Church calendar, and some devout Catholics are equally serious about the raucously celebratory prelude as they are about the austere and ascetic holy time that follows.

Confucian and Buddhist concerns about drink include the unusual concept of "moral drinking," in which the proper amount of alcohol, taken in the proper way, is supposed to provide a transformation that betters a person in a manner very like a religious experience. Wine is so important a part of domestic religious practices for devout Jews that some social scientists have likened its sacred status to a sort of immunization that protects Jews from alcohol abuse and dependence.

In all of these comments about religion and drinking, it should be evident that nominal affiliation with a religious group counts for little; survey researchers often wrestle with the thorny methodological problem of how to learn about a respondent's devoutness, or degree of serious commitment to the tenets of the group to which he or she declares affiliation.

It should surprise no one that religion is also one of the reasons most frequently cited for not drinking. The Islamic and ascetic Protestant mandates for abstinence were already discussed in the section on abstainers in chapter 3. The Muslim injunction against drink remains controversial, but it appears to be based largely on the imperative that nothing be allowed to interfere with one's commitment to Allah. Pentecostal, evangelical, and other fundamentalist Protestants, by contrast, tend to emphasize the sanctity of the human body and soul, in defense of which one should renounce earthly pleasures with the aim of achieving blessed immortality.

Medicine

The medicinal value of alcohol is widely recognized, although the reasons given for its efficacy are not the same in different cultures. In Malaysia, for example, drink is important in achieving balance among the humors (much as in the ancient Galen's view), with spirits being hot or heating, and beer generally being cold or cooling. The aim is to achieve a proper balance, correcting any surplus or deficit within the bodily system. Although the terminology is akin to that of temperature, the terms relate to another kind of inherent quality which cannot be easily expressed in English. Interestingly, a similar view of humoral medicine occurs throughout much of Spain and Latin America, and the roles played by beverages (including but not restricted to those with ethanol) are very similar. For example, spirits provide warmth to counter the cold of old age, arthritis, rheumatism, influenza, and other ailments, whereas light-colored beer or pulque are thought to cool the humors when they are overheated as from measles, chicken pox, or venereal diseases (Foster, 1994). Dark beers tend to be thought of as hot in this scheme.

In ancient civilizations, beverage alcohol often played a variety of important roles in medicine (Keller, 1958), as a relaxant, food supplement, relatively sanitary drink, analgesic, and for other reasons, not all of which conform to current medical thinking. Until the development of ether, chloroform, and many other anesthetics in the latter part of the 19th century, it was often used to render a patient unconscious, or at least oblivious, for surgery, including amputations, even in the Western world. In fact, ethanol is still listed in the U.S. pharmacopeia (U.S. Pharmacopeial Convention, 1995), although it is not so widely used in patent medicines or readily available tonics as it was in the late 1800s (Armstrong, 1991), with a wide variety of purposes (Williams, 1980; Wright-St. Clair, 1962). Medicinal beers, both historical and contemporary, are numerous and versatile (Buhner, 1998; Rätsch, 1994), each attributed with very specific healing properties. An old Chinese proverb holds that "Alcohol is the best of medicines." Among the many medical uses of wine by many peoples in contemporary China, that with realgar is supposed to protect against several poisons and even more diseases, whereas that based on calamus is believed to purify the blood. In Peru, it is widely believed that rum can combat a cold, and vermouth relieves a stomachache or intestinal disorders. Mongolian kumiss is generally believed to prolong life by suppressing the growth of many kinds of pathogens within the body, and specifically to provide defense against rheumatism, tuberculosis, hypertension, and coronary heart disease.

Many African homebrews are not only thought to provide good general nourishment, but also to stimulate hair growth, relieve high blood pressure, and lessen dysmenorrhea. During the colonial period, many such folk beliefs were tested and proven by Western scientific methods. The use of alcohol as a water purifier, topical antiseptic for wounds, defense against intestinal upset, and diarrhea, vermifuge, and tranquilizer are sporadically reported by laypeople and soldiers throughout much of European and American history as well. Many rely on a nightcap to help them fall asleep or to sleep well.

European and North American medical researchers are currently providing compelling evidence, from large populations, that moderate drinkers do have significantly lower risk of coronary heart disease and atherosclerosis than do abstainers, but many physicians are still hesitant to recommend drinking because of the risk it holds for other problems. The evidence is not yet clear whether ethanol itself is the major protective factor, by lessening LDL (the "bad" cholesterol), raising HDL (the "good" cholesterol), and combating platelet aggregation (clotting), or whether these effects are due more to some of the many complex microcomponents of wine. Other long-term health benefits that appear to derive from moderate drinking of wine or other beverage alcohol are strengthening of the bones, improvement of memory, lessened risk of gallstones, among others (Meister, 1999). In each instance, the distribution curve is J- or U-shaped, meaning that drinking more than two drinks a day is risky, in the same way that abstinence is.

Just as some choose to drink for medical reasons, there are others who choose not to drink for medical reasons. Too much drinking can raise the blood pressure, and if that pattern is continued over several years, it can do serious damage to the liver, throat, peripheral nerves, and many other parts of the body. Much of what is said and written about drinking, at least in recent years, has strongly emphasized such negative outcomes and virtually ignored any positive outcomes, so many people give concern for their health as a primary reason for not drinking. There are many others who are taking various medications and give that as a reason for their not drinking. To be sure, there are several medications that interact in dangerous ways with ethanol so such caution is well advised. In some cultures, women abstain throughout pregnancy for fear of damaging the fetus, a genuine risk in the event of long-term heavy drinking. Some have the strange idea that beverage alcohol is somehow vaguely unnatural and for that reason deleterious to the health, and they avoid drinking for that reason. Others have accepted admonitions that it is "bad for you," or that it is a dangerous and addictive drug to which anyone should "just say no." The medical reasons that people give for not drinking are often no more scientifically valid than some of the medical reasons that others give to justify their drinking.

Other Reasons

People give literally hundreds of other reasons for drinking, if asked in a way that lets them respond freely. Some say it is because they like the smell, or the feel, or the appearance of a drink. Others, most notably young people, say that it makes them feel stronger, more mature, more masculine (or feminine), more independent, more sophisticated, or at least they hope that drinking may make them appear to be any or all of those things.

For the Lacandon Maya, the special honey beer balché is believed to be needed to purify people so that they can approach the gods that inhabit a special outbuilding (Gonçalves de Lima et al., 1977; McGee, 1990). Among the many things that Chinese drinkers think that they achieve by "moral drinking" is to "harmonize the blood" and to instill or enhance virtue. For the Lepcha of Tibet, beer is the only proper medium in which a teacher should be paid for the valuable service of imparting knowledge. Similarly, those small groups of iron-workers who produced tools for almost all of the sub-Saharan populations often insisted on being paid with beer, just as many chieftains collected taxes in beer. Following the burial of a friend, mourners in some African societies wash their hands in beer, before drinking it as a salute.

The drinking that takes place at communal or reciprocal work projects is not just refreshing and sociable; those who are involved are often earnest in stressing the symbolic bonds of mutual obligation and social credit that are expressed in the act of drinking together in that context.

Farmers in the Tuscany region of Italy harvest grapes in two stages, first selecting the finest bunches and storing them on racks to be made into *vin santo* (Calabresi, 1987), unlike the general harvest, which is used for ordinary wine. *Vin santo*, unlike other wine, is not to be part of a meal, but rather it is a special nectar reserved for extraordinary uses. A special friend may be given the homage of sharing a sip of *vin santo*, or it may be a special treat when one wants to relax and savor one's good fortune. It is also a fortifier, to be taken before setting out on a long or difficult trek or task. Some is devoted to use in church, but most is hoarded as a rare and precious good, even though made by rustic methods from homegrown fruit.

In national surveys that specifically asked about drinking in various contexts, it was found in the U.S. that most men sometimes have a drink while spending an evening at home and nearly half do while watching television, whereas the rates for women were only 39% and 27% respectively. Fully 71% of men said that they sometimes drank when friends visited and 13% almost always, in comparison with 57% and 8% of women in similar circumstances (Clark & Hilton, 1991). Those who say, "I need a drink because I'm hooked" or who joke raucously about being addicted to drink are not very likely to be among the few for whom that is actually the case. Whether because of denial or simply lack of insight, few who have the alcohol-dependence syndrome give such reasons for drinking, although they often come up with numerous imaginative alternative reasons.

"It's time for a drink!" is often used not only to signal the conclusion of work activities for a while, but in some respects, also as a call for time-out in the sense in which MacAndrew and Edgerton (1969) used the term, a respite from the usual rules of behavior. In that sense, drinking provides an excuse for lapses of responsibility, and even a somewhat festive air. In this, drinking can provide a degree of license for slightly inappropriate behavior, although it does not excuse any serious transgression. For example, a sarcastic remark may be excusable in a drinking situation, although an insult would not be. An off-color joke or remark may be acceptable from someone who has been drinking, although sexual advances might not be tolerated. The idea of occasional time-out is attractive to many who chafe under a variety of social constraints, and it is a commonplace feature of drinking, drinking places, and drinking occasions. Clearly, however, the degrees of freedom that drinking allows must be understood as highly variable; usually there is a strict within-limits clause that will be abruptly invoked to warn or stop anyone who may be on the verge of trespassing beyond the bounds of whatever local people consider appropriate or acceptable behavior, even while intoxicated.

Beer can play an important role in enforcing as well as loosing certain kinds of social control, as when a Chagga man fears that he has been lied to or otherwise wronged. He may quietly but dramatically confront the suspected offender by offering beer that has been mixed with the blood of a recently sacrificed goat. The belief that a liar would be poisoned by that combination prompts some who are guilty to confess rather than take a drink (Washburne, 1961).

We have already looked at toasting and tasting as special reasons for drinking, each with its own elaborate set of rules that differ from one culture to the next. The idea of drinking as emblematic can be another important reason. When a population are renowned for drinking, whether for better or for worse, members of that group will often fit themselves to the stereotype as a matter of pride or identity. "If people expect us to be irresponsible, we may as well be," seems to be their rationalization.

Among the reasons that people give for not drinking, some are decidedly personal, such as not liking the smell or taste that they associate with beverage alcohol (although ethanol itself tends to be both odorless and tasteless). Others do not like the effect that drinking has on them, whether that means flushing, warming, impairment of vision, or some other physical cue.

The affirmation that drinking is bad, evil, or wrong, when inculcated by a loved, respected or dominant person may be enough to convince some, especially when it is couched in strongly moral, ethical, or religious terms. Fear of losing control is another commonly cited reason, whether that refers to the ability to stop drinking, or to control over emotions or behavior. Fear of loss of reputation or of status prompts others to abstain. For some, their body is sacrosanct and they see no reason to ingest any substance that may be damaging to it; for others, drinking seems an inappropriate and unnecessary expense.

A person who has suffered abuse, embarrassment, or inconvenience in a household torn by problem drinking may not want to risk replicating that pattern. This is especially the case when parents, grandparents, or too many other kinpersons are known to have shown alcohol abuse or dependence. It is evident that such problems run in families, and there may even be some as-yet-unknown genetic predisposing factor. Caution about the possibility of being susceptible to excessive drinking is the reason many people give for never starting.

Even more acute is the concern in someone who has already experienced problems with drinking. A portion of abstainers everywhere are probably people who earlier were heavy or even excessive drinkers. In fact, most who are in the popular movement Alcoholics Anonymous fervently believe that abstention is the cornerstone of their sobriety. Their supposed allergy to alcohol is thought to mean that they cannot be cured of alcoholism, but are only in remission as long as they avoid the vector. Precariously "one drink away from a drunk," many former drinkers pride themselves on abstention and are quick to tell anyone who might be interested just how many years, months, days, and hours have passed since they chose not to drink.

Undoubtedly, there are many more valid reasons, some arrived at first-hand and some accepted from others, to explain why so many people choose to drink or not to drink. From the point of view of public health and social welfare, it is important that so many reasons, often diametrically conflicting, can be found in so many cultures throughout history. If we measure the importance of drinking as a behavior by the affect that it generates, positive or negative, there can be no doubt that alcohol has a firm place in the human experience. And all of the reasons dealt with so far are reasons that people volunteer when they are simply asked about why they drink, or not.

REASONS WE INFER

It is of crucial importance that we pay close attention to what people say when we are trying to understand any behavior. But it is equally important that we not rely solely on what they say. One reason why this is the case is that they may not be fully aware of their own motivations, or of how those motivations relate to other parts of the complex social and cultural reality in which they are imbedded. Another is that they may have no conception of alternative ways of thinking or acting, viewing what they know and do as human nature, not recognizing how other populations have other human natures, and how any one may relate (or not) to other cultures and worldviews. Beyond that, an important part of the role of the social scientist is to try to understand how such systems work: how social relations are perpetuated; how ideas diffuse, how groups form, evolve, break up, are reconstituted, or reform. And how all this happens beyond the ken of actors who, while intimately affected by such changes, may have no idea about how or why they happen. Among the reasons that we infer for why people drink, again it is both convenient and appropriate, as with their explicit reasons, to look at types or categories: health, psychological, political, social, economic, religious, and other.

Health

It would be futile to try to guess how often a drink or two has served importantly to relieve tension, to calm nerves, or to lessen overexertion. In cultures where a homebrew is either a principal food or the dominant beverage or both, we can feel safe in assuming that, whether the people know why or not, it is likely to be nutritious and healthful. Until less than two centuries ago, little attention was paid in most parts of the world to assuring that drinking water was pure, and beverage alcohol was often safer than other things that one might drink. Wine kills some bacilli that cause dysentery, and the heating that is part of the manufacture of beer, ale, or spirits kills other potentially dangerous microorganisms. The fact that drinks often provide precisely those vitamins or minerals that are in short supply in the rest of the local diet suggests that health played some role in their selection, whether consciously or not. The fact that fermentation often enhances the food value of a liquid means that a given quantity of grain can be worth more as beer, in terms of human nutrition.

Although it is difficult to quantify the specific benefits that derive from occasional enjoyment, relaxation, relief of tension, or general enhancement of life-satisfaction that some drinkers enjoy periodically from beverage alcohol, there is consensus in the medical community that the highly subjective factor "quality of life" is positively and strongly correlated with overall state of health. Long before scientifically trained internists had learned in detail about the role of ethanol in relation to cholesterol and coronary heart disease, insurance actuaries were aware that moderate drinkers have a lower death rate from all causes than do abstainers. Health could well be one of the latent or unrecognized reasons why people, and peoples, drink as they do.

Psychological

Reasons for drinking can be just as valid if they are subconscious or unconscious as if they were fully conscious and articulated. Projective tests, thematic analysis of speech, folklore, proverbs, writings, and other indirect methods can provide clues to reasons that the actors themselves do not, or perhaps even cannot, explicitly voice, and they may well be of concern to anyone who is trying to understand behavior. For example, McClelland and his colleagues (1972) and Kalin and his (1966) examined themes in folktales in a great many different cultures. By comparing them with drinking patterns in a systematic way,

Sidewalk cafés offer their patrons the opportunity to relax during a jazz festival on Copenhagen's waterfront. A drink at a pub or café often serves as a moment of respite or simple enjoyment. © *CORBIS/Steve Raymer.*

they concluded that a major reason why men drink was to enjoy a subjective feeling of power, based on the interplay of physiological (a feeling of warmth imparted by alcohol), psychological (a sense of strength and superiority felt after drinking), and sociological (deference on the part of others) factors.

In the 1940s, Horton (1943) pioneered a novel cross-cultural methodology, treating societies as units of analysis and comparing them (without regard to size, location, or historical importance) in terms of a large number of different variables that are described in various ethnographic monographs. His specific methods have been widely criticized, modified, and elaborated by two generations of scholars since then, but the fundamental idea of focusing on how specific traits covary among a sample of the world's cultures is still valued as a quasi-experimental technique, in the sense that the whole of human experience is taken as a natural laboratory, and the history of each people can be treated as a natural experiment.

It may well have been fortuitous that Horton chose to examine drinking (instead of marriage, hunting, slavery, or a host of other topics that have subsequently been studied by the method that he devised), but that first cross-cultural effort resulted in what became probably the most widely quoted generalization about drinking: "... the primary function of alcoholic beverages in all societies is the reduction of anxiety" (Horton, 1943, p. 223).

Conflict with a dominant alien culture is often cited as a rationale for drinking, and that, in turn, is treated as almost an obligatory response. Sometimes referred to as "despair drinking," this pattern is widespread around the world in colonial and quasi-colonial situations where the social hierarchy tends to be rigid, and those who are dominated tend to be resentful or otherwise stressed by pressures that derive from social and cultural conflict. It seems to be a characteristic of such drinking that it has quick intoxication as a goal, supposedly to forget one's troubles, or to seek oblivion. Whether those specific aims are realized, or whether frictions are merely aggravated, heavy drinkers often act (and sometimes speak) as if they had no meaningful alternative. Such drinking tends to be associated with a wide range of problems, and is usually recognized as inappropriate within the drinker's subgroup as well as by others. It is important to recognize that such a reaction to cultural deprivation is counterproductive in aggravating the poverty and powerlessness of the drinker, alienating friends and family, and often resulting in arrest or incarceration. Nevertheless, in the face of a belief that they "will never make it" in a capitalistic world that they never intended to join but had imposed upon them, such despair drinkers are creating rural equivalents of Skid Row on the fringes of some Australian, African, and Native American communities. A special irony attaches to the fact that such problem drinking tends to be most common in areas where drinking was unknown or unimportant in traditional native life.

But that outcome is by no means inevitable. Long before the theory of cultural deprivation was even proposed (Dozier, 1966), an interesting study in Sarawak described a situation very different from what one might expect along a continuum of differential exposure to Western cultures. Banks (1932) showed variation among five tribes, but in exactly the opposite manner. This continuum showed the degree of insobriety increasing in direct proportion to the degree of isolation.

An elaborate effort to refine the cross-cultural findings about alcohol resulted in the conflict-over-dependency theory. Not content to rely on the extant published literature, those authors sought out researchers who were willing to answer their questions and to expand on the descriptions they had published earlier. This step provided a pool of data that was larger, more pointed to the issue, and presumably more valid. They paid special attention to child-rearing as a crucial shaper of people's predispositions and found that those societies in which people's lives showed marked continuity in terms of responsibility had few alcohol-related problems. By contrast, societies in which a relatively carefree childhood was followed by abruptly increased demands for independence, resulted in insecurity that found one predominant form of expression in drink. According to them (Keller, 1965, p. 31), ". . . as a reaction to dependency conflict, alcohol has a triple function: it reduces anxiety and tensions; it permits the satisfaction of desires for dependence; it permits uncritical indulgence of unrealistic fantasies of achievement."

Most efforts at interpretation by social scientists are much more modest in scale, however, paying especially close attention to the details of life in a specific social and cultural milieu that shapes the experience and expectancies of those who live there, in ways that are often very different from the influences that are felt by individuals in other societies, even those nearby. It is from such efforts at culture-specific interpretation that we get discussion of *machismo* (exaggerated emphasis on masculinity), cultural deprivation, acculturative stress, competitiveness, and others as causes, reasons, motives, or explanations of drinking. It is as if the analyst were dealing with a culture as personality-writ-large (or, conversely, with the individual as a microcosmic reflection of themes that can be seen in the culture). For example, although young Swedish bureaucrats may seem an unlikely group to associate with orgiastic heavy episodic drinking, that is precisely what Lalander (1997) found. Periodic parties provide them an opportunity to overturn established norms, to invert the rules, make fun of social hierarchy, and express suppressed desires, all in a safe context before an appreciative audience. What they call "breaking away" or "cutting loose" is just another manifestation, extreme, to be sure, of the value of a drinking occasion as providing psychological time-out. For every individual who is willing to admit that the reason for drinking is to feel (or to appear) more mature, more masculine, more sophisticated, or more endowed with whatever the enviable attribute, there are probably several for whom that can be easily, and probably accurately, inferred. Motives and reasons need not be mysterious, even when the actors are unable or unwilling to talk about them.

Political

During the early days of civilization, the production and distribution of beverage alcohol appears to have been an important part of the process by which emerging elites expanded their control over craft production, established symbols, and created and manipulated surpluses. Because of their irregular availability and scarcity value, such drinks took on diacritical symbolic functions as a new way to define status, and they were strategically used by elites to differentiate themselves. Not only was this the case in Egypt and the Levant (Joffe, 1998), but also in China (Pirazzoli-t'Serstevens, 1991), among Incas in the Andes (Morris, 1979), and on the part of German tribal chiefs as they gradually came to dominate Iron Age Europe (Dietler, 1990, 1996). Drinks were used to recognize and reward success and to instill or reinforce solidarity and loyalty among subordinates.

Just as drinking and the apportioning of drink were important ways to symbolize political power in ancient times, they still play visible roles today. Patronage, generosity, and access, whether to politicians, entrepreneurs, or others, often involve alcohol as a mediator or a medium. It may be more obvious when an African chief insists that taxes be paid in beer, but it is just as plausible when a "big man" in Papua New Guinea treats a case of beer almost exactly as he would have treated a donated pig some years ago, both in the context of regional trade-fairs and feasting.

We see patterns that are not too different among Japanese office workers at the end of the workday, or at office parties throughout Europe and America that are usually linked with holidays. Elaborate toasting is usually an important part of protocol at state banquets, just as it is when an unknown stranger asks for shelter in a Mongol yurt.

Although the popular stereotype of the drunken Indian is demonstrably inaccurate with reference to a number of entire tribes in the U.S., just as it is inaccurate with respect to many individuals even in those tribes where drinking is commonplace (Westermeyer, 1974), Lurie (1971) has suggested that the myth becomes an excuse for some who feel that, if people expect them to behave that way, they might as well use it to make a political statement, and so drink to assert and validate their Indianness.

A century ago, a U.S. politician could go into a saloon and buy as many votes as he wanted, at the cost of a mug of beer for each. Although the tone of fund-raising dinners, election night parties, and such events is very different today, the political functions of drink may still be strongly inferred.

Social

For many African populations, a tribal council or a local court could not, or would not be held without abundant beer, at least for the authorities (Beidelmann, 1961), and preferably for all participants (Haworth & Acuda, 1998). Several of the tribal populations in India are similarly governed by a community council that also serves as their tribunal for adjudicating disputes. Many of them mark the end of a session with drinks at the expense of whoever has been found guilty, and the public drinking signifies acceptance of the settlement (Mohan & Sharma, 1995).

Occasional beer-dances among the Azande bring together large groups of people who most of the time live widely dispersed. Such dances, sponsored by a few of the more affluent and powerful men, provide important opportunities for young people to meet with others from distant communities, sometimes to flirt, and to find potential mates in a context that involves people of all ages from diverse backgrounds. The same dances are enjoyed as opportunities for trade, visiting and recreation by their elders. Toward the end of a 3- or 4-day party, they sometimes also serve as occasions for the airing of grievances in a way that appears to satisfy those who have complaints, without offending those who are complained about (Washburne, 1961).

If a drink is an affordable luxury, it can be an emblem of membership, or at least of earnest aspiration, with respect to a privileged group. Like so many other things, wealth is relative, and among people who are unaccustomed to having much disposable income, just a couple of bottled beers, or a beer with a foreign label, may be impressive signals than one has a job or some other income. Presumably that display function would help to explain why young men in much of Latin America (or in southern Africa, or eastern Asia) let the containers accumulate rather than having them cleared at a bar or restaurant.

A people who are proud of their distinctive drink, or of their distinctive pattern of drinking, may take some pains to display, preserve, and make much of either or both. At the same time, in much the same way that the ancients apparently used exotic and imported alcoholic beverages for feasting, to cement clientage, and to secure authority as a domestic type of politico-symbolic drama, we now find just the reverse occurring. In a cosmopolitan capitalistic economy, exotic or imported drinks are sometimes flaunted by those who have little wealth or power, apparently to deny or euphemize social inequality. Time after time, we have seen colonized peoples eagerly embrace the drinks and drinking patterns of the colonizers.

Economic

The act of drinking is clearly one of consumption, so any effort to infer economic reasons is more likely to be successful if we shift our focus from the actor to those around, who are supplying or encouraging the drinking. Most acts of drinking have a fairly immediate cost that can be measured pretty closely, and it is not too difficult to trace where the money goes. Of course, in many systems of exchange the cost may not be in money, but in labor, other goods, good will, or the expectation of some other benefit in the future. And the cost need not be borne by the drinker: patrons often use drink to attract or to reward clients; a host who lavishly serves drinks usually anticipates some sort of eventual reciprocity; and even potlatch feasts, buying rounds, or sponsoring parties produce returns in terms of prestige or social standing, often in ways that could not easily be bought without the use of drink as an intermediate commodity.

Historically, it has been typical to see that, as brewing becomes progressively remunerative, it tends to pass from the control of women and quickly becomes dominated by men. That transition was well documented in medieval England (Bennett, 1996) and has often been reported more recently in sub-Saharan Africa and in Asia.

The way in which serving alcohol translates into local social standing is rarely so clearly evident as in the case of Latin American *cargos*, the festive and yet onerous political-religious hierarchical systems that often entail the spending of more than a household's annual income on rum and music (Cancian, 1965) to be enjoyed by all one's townspeople. Another kind of economic calculus is involved in making the decision whether to use scarce foodstuffs in the preparation of alcohol, especially in times of general famine (Harwood, 1964).

The economic significance of drink is enormous, especially when one considers the amount of land and labor devoted to producing and gathering the ingredients, the inputs of time and additives involved in preparation, packaging, storage, and distribution, no matter what kind of beverage or what the final value may be. Other costs and benefits include the making of containers, or the provision of service in different kinds of outlets, without even touching on such large-scale aspects as advertising, treatment for alcohol abuse, costs of accidents or diminished productivity, and such systemic features as would be requisite to a thorough economic analysis (Heien & Pittman, 1989). None of these reasons is likely to be in the mind of any individual when choosing to drink or not to drink, but they cannot be ignored when we consider drinking occasions in their full social and cultural context.

Religious

Wine was specified in the Old Testament as appropriate for libations (Numbers, 15:5–10; 28:7–8), and in the New Testament for medication (Luke, 10:34; 1 Timothy, 5:23). Its importance to those who wrote the Bible is reflected in numerous ways (O'Brien & Seller, 1982; Seller, 1984). According to the story of the flood that was said to have engulfed nearly all of life on earth, the first thing Noah did after the Ark came to rest on dry land was to plant a vineyard (Cohen, 1974). The first miracle credited to Jesus was his changing of water into wine for a wedding at Cana (John, 2:1–12), and wine was chosen to represent his blood as he laid out the conceptual basis for what has become the rite of Communion throughout Christianity (Matt., 26:26–29).

Beer, wine, and various homebrews have been touted in many cultures as gifts that the gods originally gave to mankind, and people are still expected to return them to the gods from time to time as offerings or libations.

The very fact of choosing not to drink is often an important badge of faith. Similarly, drinking in a specific way, at a specific time or place, can signal social boundaries that are connected with systems of belief and practice that we call religions. Just as some populations are under a sacred covenant to stay away from drink, others use it to symbolize their participation and commitment to supernatural beings or forces. Even in times of general prohibition, exceptions have often been made for sacramental beverage alcohol, as in the U.S. in the 1920s and 30s.

Religious specialists are often engaged in the production of alcohol, and many use it in their spiritual ministrations. Just as drink can be a diacritical marker that distinguishes adherents of one religion from those of another, religion can be a diacritical marker of the boundary between drinkers and abstainers. Although few individuals volunteer religion as a major reason why they drink, it certainly can be a cardinal reason whether they drink.

Other Reasons

The classical Greek *symposion*, or leisurely drinking party with wide-ranging philosophical discussion, was an institution that, however sociable it may have seemed to the individual participants, can probably most accurately be assessed from the societal perspective as a means of gradually transforming male warriors into an urban aristocratic social class (Murray, 1983). Its contrast with the contemporaneous Macedonian pattern of drinking, both in terms of form and in terms of outcome, is vividly exemplified in the hectic and damaging bouts that characterized the life of Alexander the Great (O'Brien, 1980).

Moonshine may have a special appeal to assertively masculine drinkers not just because of its relative cheapness and the mystique of being hand-crafted in small batches. There is real symbolic value in that beverage that has to do with cheating the government of taxes, a small but clear defiance of authority. This pattern, incidentally, refers not only to the several kinds of moonshine that one encounters throughout Central and South America, but also to that in Ireland (poteen) and in southern U.S. (mountain dew or white lightning).

For all of the talk and writing about the correlation of alcohol with aggression, even its severest critics must be aware that no causal link has been scientifically established. Contrary to earlier ideas about disinhibition, it is evident that ethanol is not a pharmacological trigger, and there are probably more societies and situations in which drinking lessens the likelihood of a violent outcome than in which it increases that probability (Pernanen, 1991). One of the most common ways in which the two are linked is the fact that drinking or drunkenness can often be used as an excuse for behavior that is socially disapproved or normally controlled in most contexts (Fagan, 1990; Rossow, 1996).

Those who uncritically accept the common belief that cold weather, severe winters, long confinement indoors, higher latitudes, or any combination of those factors are reasons for alcohol abuse, would do well to consider the experience of the U.S. Antarctic Program. Several kinds of beer, wine, and spirits are available for purchase, without limit and at reasonable prices, at each of their stations (two of which are virtually isolated for nine months of the year). The populations are about one-third each of research scientists, civilian support-personnel, and military in aviation or logistics. Among those who drink, the norm is responsible drinking and the National Science Foundation, which administers the entire program, rejects even the need for rationing (Mahar, 1999).

The search for reasons that we could plausibly infer for why people drink could be a never-ending task. The sampling we have touched on is only meant to illustrate the range of ways in which beverage alcohol fits into the rest of culture for many peoples, and to show dramatically how its very lack of acceptability is an integral part of the way of life and thinking of others who reject it.

WHY DOES IT MATTER?

When we try to deal with the reasons for any behavior—why some people do and others do not—we are invariably confronted with the multiplicity of factors that may be determinant, and with the complexity of interrelationships among them. While trying to bring that complexity closer to manageable proportions, many of those who talk and write about alcohol make an initial grandiose clustering by affirming that biological, psychological, and social factors are all important, and that none should be treated without at least some reference to the others (Zinberg, 1984). In some senses, this comes back to our earlier discussion of the fact that, in different ways, each human being is like all other human beings, but also and simultaneously, like some others, and yet undeniably also like no others.

Throughout this book, we have consistently tried to strike a middle ground in emphasizing the social and the cultural aspects of human behavior, customs, beliefs, and practices that are shared with others in various reference groups (be they societal, within the community, family, occupation, or other), but that often differ markedly from those shared by others whose various reference groups are distinct.

In this chapter, we have tried to deal with what is often the most obscure aspect of any behavior, that is, reasons or motivations. Each of us knows from experience that answers to the question "why?" lie only rarely near the surface of our consciousness. We also know that when they do, those answers may be only partial, or misleading, or both. Beyond that, we also know that, while some people are very private about such answers, others may not be, whereas a third group may be ill equipped even to think about such things.

With such reservations commonly held and commonly known, even in a culture that is relatively open about discussing personal matters, it seems highly unlikely that any short list of reasons, no matter how typical or representative they may be of a given population, could capture the range and emphasis of any respondent. If no individual person's reasons are likely to be communicated by means of their making a forced choice among a few alternatives, it seems utterly improbable that such data would have much validity when aggregated, no matter how sophisticated the statistical manipulations to which they might be subjected.

Artists, authors, playwrights, and others have for centuries been grappling with questions about why people drink. It is likely to be a long time yet before scientific investigation sheds much new light on the subject, although its fascination holds.

Chapter 7

Conclusions and Implications

The gin shops that were fashionable in London of the 1830s were the subject of essays by Charles Dickens in his *Sketches by Boz*, with illustrations by George Cruikshank.

The preceding chapters have presented a broadly cross-cultural and international view of beverage alcohol by focusing on drinking as a form of behavior that some people choose and others reject, always in the context of norms, values, attitudes, and relations with other people and with institutions. Looking at variations in the ways in which different peoples might answer the basic concerns about when, where, who, how, what, and why, with respect to drinking occasions, we always came back to the very immediate and practical question of "Why does it matter?" with special reference to further research and the development of policies.

An anthropological perspective on alcohol is different from most (Heath & Cooper, 1981). By using beverage alcohol as a window through which to look at other aspects of life, we can see how parts of a sociocultural system work in relation to other parts. By looking at a number of populations throughout the world and during all of history, we avoid the dual pitfalls of assuming that a few neighboring communities or countries represent normal human nature, or that patterns of belief and behavior are fixed by tradition and immutable (Heath, 1998a). By being consistently descriptive rather than prescriptive, we encounter a truly startling array of variations in how people think, feel, and act with regard to drink and drinking, without our imposing moral judgments that would be inappropriate to each context. By comparing evidence collected by different research methods, we are better able to understand, through a process analogous to triangulation, how different patterns function in different social and cultural environments. By looking at some social and psychological benefits of drinking, which are generally ignored, we partially redress the emphasis on costs and problems that characterizes most writing on the subject.

WHEN DO PEOPLE DRINK?

In many societies, beverage alcohol plays many different roles, and its use in everyday life is far more common than its being banned or relegated to a few special occasions scattered throughout the year. The acceptability, or expectation, of drinking at different times of the day, week, month, or year ranges from low to high, just as the propriety of drinking for people of different stages of life varies across a broad spectrum. Over the course of history, attitudes toward drinking have changed, at different rates and in different ways, in many societies, with customs similarly very different from time to time. Among such changes have been episodic rejections and prohibitions of drinking, even in societies where earlier it was accepted. When laws fly in the face of popular opinion and practice, they are unlikely to be effective for long, and when public sentiment is strong, people are likely to find ways around the laws.

Efforts to make an inventory of occasions "when it is all right to drink" have repeatedly, and in very different cultures, run up against the problem that there are simply too many to list and analyze in any of the ways that are generally acceptable in scientific research. A clear trend is discernible, however,

The raising of the ridge-pole of a Japanese house at New York's Museum of Modern Art is marked by celebratory cups of sake among the carpenters. Secular ceremonies are sometimes important in connection with work.   © *CORBIS/BETTMANN-UPI.*

supporting earlier investigations that used more narrowly focused questions and more restricted responses. Most people drink for pleasure, and view drinking in a positive light. They associate drinking with friendship, good times, sociability, hospitality, and celebration, although they are aware that excess can be problematic or risky. While there are some cultures in which no time is acceptable for drinking, most recognize many such, and even provide for the act of drinking to endow some times with a special celebratory quality.

WHERE DO PEOPLE DRINK?

As we turn to the place of drinking, in spatial terms, again the variation is more striking than most of the patterns that can be discerned. Private or public, indoors or out, rural or urban, cultivated or bucolic, no place is dry unless custom makes it so, and there are few such places on which different populations agree. Similar places may be viewed in very different ways, and people drink in different manners, for different reasons, and with very different outcomes, in those many settings. Whatever place that people strongly feel should be kept free from drink should be respected, but there is no universal agreement on such places. The pervasiveness of drinking, even when it plays no dominant role in a culture, is evidence of the degree to which it fits with other kinds of behavior.

WHO DRINKS?

In some societies, it is generally agreed that no one should drink, and those who do are treated as deviant or abnormal. In other societies, it is acceptable and expected that everyone will drink, so those who do not are unusual and sometimes suspect. More commonly, we find that rights and expectations about drinking differ according to various statuses and roles that are recognized as important for various purposes. Males tend to drink more than females, and adults more than children, but within those broad parameters exceptions can be many and diverse, depending largely on personal choice. The category of abstainers is far from uniform, and they deserve special attention for choosing not to drink, sometimes even in a context where that choice is not an easy one.

HOW DO PEOPLE DRINK?

Our emphasis on drinking as behavior calls for attention to be paid to more than the usual measures of quantity and frequency. Context and drinking pattern are aspects of drinking that have rarely been described by those who seek to understand what alcoholic beverages mean, or how they fit into the social, economic, political, religious, and other systems that make up a culture. In anthropological terms, it is the interrelationships among such traits and institutions that best reveal the place and functioning of any item of behavior. The theme of excess, which dominates in much that is written about alcohol, fits here because it is a variant style of drinking. Although recognized in most societies, it is only embraced in some, for various reasons, and deplored in others, for risks that it poses both to the drinker and to others. The range of variation that we find cross-culturally with regard to the propriety and the impropriety of drinking, is yet another dramatic illustration of the strikingly different ways in which ethanol has been treated and viewed in the human experience.

WHAT DO PEOPLE DRINK?

Although alcohol is a common denominator in all of the behavior that is dealt with in this book, we must add a crucial qualifier to the alcohol researchers' convenient convention in saying that "a drink is a drink is a drink." Equivalence in terms of measured content of the predominant psychoactive chemical component is admittedly importantly for certain analytical purposes, but the fact is that most people, most of the time, treat different kinds of drinks in very different ways. They drink them at different paces, in different places, for different reasons, with or without food, while doing different things, and clearly with very different expectations and intentions of what will be achieved by the drinking.

A closer look at the beverages themselves helps to account for some of the drinking patterns that can be observed, and for some of the outcomes of drinking, in different contexts. Beliefs and practices with respect to various

In Inner Mongolia in the People's Republic of China, women enjoy a drink of liquor after a long day of work. © *CORBIS/Earl Kowall*.

types of drinks show intracultural diversity as well as differences from one population to another. Differences in the ways in which drinks are used, as well as differences in their composition, have clear and important implications for how they should be viewed and treated from a public health standpoint as well as by each individual.

WHY DO PEOPLE DRINK?

As with any other behavior, a social scientist studying drinking would be remiss to ignore the difficult but basic question of reasons or motives. Because of subjectivity and sensibilities, social surveys have yielded results in this connection that their strongest proponents generally consider less than satisfactory. However time-consuming and imprecise the methods may appear to be, qualitative observation, interviewing, and analysis tend to provide more valid and reliable insights in this crucial realm. The reasons that people give for drinking are neither recondite nor hidden—nor are they necessarily fully accurate. Similarly, the reasons that can be inferred from analyzing the interplay among actions and the functioning of people within systems provide another perspective on motivations that, while not necessarily fully accurate, is an invaluable complement that can significantly increase our understanding of any given individual, institution, or drinking occasion. Reasons tend to be as varied as any other of the major aspects of drinking that were brought into question in this book, but they, too, are crucial to our understanding of drinking and not drinking as important parts of culture.

WHERE DO WE GO FROM HERE?

An anthropological perspective is usually more likely to raise complex questions than to provide simple answers. That is especially the case where cross-cultural variation has been the theme rather than close scrutiny of a specific local situation. In alcohol studies, the situation may be more difficult than in most others because such reports as we have tend to deal with the subject in a tangential rather than a clearly focused way. Much of what we do know about drinking in various cultures is a by-product of research that had very different aims and emphases, and it is still unusual for a granting-agency to fund investigations other than fairly narrow ones aimed at meeting priorities that have been set by people who are not themselves conversant with the theory, methods, or literature of anthropology.

Nevertheless, a few general points and implications deserve to be mentioned.

- Variation is as important a characteristic of drinking as it is of most other forms of behavior. It should never be assumed that forms, meanings, or functions associated with it in one population will be similar in another.
- Variation within a given population can be as important as that between populations. It is important to be sensitive to rules and norms for different demographic groups and other social categories, rather than presuming homogeneity with respect to drinking.
- Drinking is normally a social act, and the quality of social relations tends often to be significantly enhanced by the act of drinking.
- Most people expect drinking to be enjoyable, and usually they find it so. Meanings and expectations are shaped in large part by the consensus that has grown out of widespread experience within a given society.
- For that reason, new drinks can be problematic because lack of societal experience leaves expectations more in the hands or minds of experimenting individuals. If new drinks are treated as were old ones, such problems may be minimized.
- The predominant association with drinking for many populations is celebratory, and drinking itself of often treated as a joyous occasion.
- Some risk or danger is often recognized as a possible outcome of drinking, but it can usually be avoided by careful avoidance of excess, however that may be defined by the local community.
- Drunkenness, or gross physical impairment, is usually viewed as risky for the individual, and sometimes as dangerous for the group. Ways of avoiding it, or of reducing the risks of associated harm, differ in various cultures, but

Germans drinking beer and dressed in traditional *Lederhosen* (leather shorts and suspenders) of the Bavarian region are illustrative of how both drink and dress can serve as symbolic references to a person's chosen ethnic or other identity. © *CORBIS/ Bob Krist.*

few condone unfettered excessive drinking (except in a few specific and limited contexts, usually by specific persons and for specific limited purposes).

• Temporary suspension of a few of the normal rules of everyday behavior (time-out) is often allowed as an accompaniment to drinking, but it is always subject to strict limitations. The exculpatory quality of such rules implies culturally shared expectations and permissiveness, not a generalized phamacokinetic disinhibition.

• Alcoholism, alcohol abuse, and alcohol dependence, even in the general sense of acute or chronic problem drinking, are rare in most societies throughout the world, and have been throughout history. The nature of problems that are associated with alcohol is a matter of social construction, negotiated differently by various constituencies, at various times.

• Societies in which drinking is disallowed for many years and alcohol has a mystique of holding the implicit promise of imparting power, sexiness, social skills, or other special qualities, tend often to have young people who drink too much, too fast, or for inappropriate and unrealistic reasons.

- Where drunkenness is viewed as stupid, disgusting, or inappropriate behavior, it tends to be avoided. By contrast, where it is deemed "heroic," masculine, or desirable, it tends to be embraced. The positive evaluations that may be held by a subcultural reference group provide little defense against the risks and dangers that inhere in either acute or chronic excessive drinking.

- The quantity and frequency of drinking, as routinely measured in social surveys, fails accurately to represent the meanings or effects of drinking. By numerically equating moderate but regular drinkers with infrequent heavy drinkers, they tend to make unproblematic drinking appear risky, and trivialize our need to learn more about heavy drinking.

- Greater attention to drinking patterns should provide a better understanding of the many roles that ethanol plays in the normal routine or of the many people for whom it is a pleasant adjunct to, but not a necessary part of, their way of life.

- A wide variety of social and psychological benefits of moderate drinking have long been widely recognized cross-culturally. In recent years, evidence of various physiological benefits of moderate drinking is being recognized as well. Such benefits, of course, cannot accurately be predicted for any given individual, so the choice about whether to drink or not remains an important one, no matter on what basis an individual may make it.

- Those who want nothing to do with alcohol should be free to leave it alone, with no pressures to drink.

- But those who want to drink moderately, for whatever among the many benefits of ethanol may suit them at a given time, should be confident that their behavior is neither deviant nor drug-addicted, but fits well in the vivid panorama of human history.

References

Aaron, P., & Musto, D. (1981). Temperance and prohibition in America: A historical overview. In M. H. Moore & D. R. Gerstein (Eds.), *Alcohol and public policy: Beyond the shadow of prohibition* (pp. 127–181). Washington: National Academy Press.

Abel, E. L., & Hannigan, J. H. (1995). Maternal risk factors in fetal alcohol syndrome: Provocative and permissive influences. *Neurotoxicology and Teratology, 17*, 445–462.

Acuda, W., & Alexander, B. (1997). Individual characteristics and drinking patterns. In M. Grant & J. Litvak (Eds.), *Drinking patterns and their consequences* (pp. 43–62). Washington: Taylor & Francis.

Adams, W. R. (1995). Guatemala. In D. B. Heath (Ed.), *International handbook on alcohol and culture* (pp. 99–109). Westport, CT: Greenwood.

Akyeampong, E. K. (1996). *Drink, power, and cultural change: A social history of alcohol in Ghana, c.1800 to recent times.* Portsmouth, NH: Heinemann.

Alasuutari, P. (1992). *Desire and craving: A cultural theory of alcoholism.* Albany, NY: State University of New York Press.

Allen, C. J. (1988). *The hold life has: Coca and cultural identity in an Andean community.* Washington, DC: Smithsonian Institution Press.

Allen, J. P., & Columbus, M. (Eds.). (1995). *Assessing alcohol problems: A guide for clinicians and researchers* (NIAAA Treatment Handbook Series 4, NIH Publ. 95-3745). Rockville, MD: National Institute on Alcohol Abuse and Alcoholism.

Ambler, C. H. (1987). *Alcohol and disorder in precolonial Africa* (Boston University Working Papers in African Studies 126). Boston: Boston University.

American Psychiatric Association. (1980). *Diagnostic and statistical manual of mental disorders* (3rd ed., rev.). Washington, DC: American Psychiatric Association.

Ames, G. M., & Janes, C. R. (1987). Heavy and problem drinking in an American blue-collar population: Implications for prevention. *Social Science and Medicine, 25*, 949–960.

Andersen, A. T., Grønbaek, M., Becker, U., Thorsen, T., & Sørensen, T. I. A. (1998). Personal communication; 1 June.

Anderson, B. G. (1968). How French children learn to drink. *Trans-action, 5*, 20–22.

Anderson, R. K., Calvo, J., Serrano, G., & Payne, G. (1946). A study of the nutritional status and food habits of Otomi Indians in the Mezquital Valley of Mexico. *American Journal of Public Health, 36*, 883–903.

Armstrong, D. (1991). *The great American medicine show: Being an illustrated history of hucksters, healers, health evangelists, and heroes from Plymouth Rock to the present.* New York: Prentice Hall.

Armstrong, R. W. (1985). Tobacco and alcohol use among urban Malaysians in 1980. *International Journal of the Addictions, 20*, 1803–1808.

Armyr, G., Elmer, A., & Herz, U. (1982). *Alcohol in the world of the 80s: Habits, attitudes, preventive policies and voluntary efforts*. Stockholm: Sober Forlags.

Arokiasamy, C. V. (1995). Malaysia. In D. B. Heath (Ed.), *International handbook on alcohol and culture* (pp. 163–178). Westport, CT: Greenwood.

Arria, A. M., & Gossop, M. (1998). Health issues and drinking patterns. In M. Grant & J. Litvak (Eds.), *Drinking patterns and their consequences* (pp. 63–87). Washington: Taylor & Francis.

Ashour, A. M. (1995). Egypt. In D. B. Heath (Ed.), *International handbook on alcohol and culture* (pp. 63–74). Westport, CT: Greenwood.

Ásmundsson, G. (1995). Iceland. In D. B. Heath (Ed.), *International handbook on alcohol and culture* (pp. 117–127). Westport, CT: Greenwood.

Bach, P. J., & Schaefer, J. M. (1979). The tempo of country music and the rate of drinking in bars. *Journal of Studies on Alcohol, 40*, 1058–1064.

Bacon, S. D. (1943). Sociology and the problems of alcohol: Foundations for a sociological study of drinking behavior. *Quarterly Journal of Studies on Alcohol, 4*, 399–445.

Bacon, S. D. (1973). The process of addiction to alcohol; social aspects. *Quarterly Journal of Studies on Alcohol, 34*, 1–27.

Badler, V. R. (1996). The archeological evidence for winemaking, distribution, and consumption at proto-historic Godin Tepe, Iran. In P. E. McGovern, S. J. Fleming, & S. H. Katz (Eds.), *The origins and ancient history of wine* (pp. 45–56). Amsterdam: Gordon and Breach.

Badri, M. B. (1976). *Islam and alcoholism*. Indianapolis: American Trust Publications.

Bahrampour, T. (1999). *To see and see again: A life in Iran and America*. New York: Farrar, Straus & Giroux.

Bailey, J., & Seftel, A. (Eds.). (1994). *Shebeens take a bow! A celebration of South Africa's shebeen lifestyles*. Johannesburg, South Africa: Bailey's African History Archive.

Bales, R. F. (1946). Cultural differences in rates of alcoholism. *Quarterly Journal of Studies on Alcohol, 6*, 480–499.

Banks, E. (1932). Native drink in Sarawak. *Sarawak Museum Journal, 4*, 439–447.

Barlett, P. F. (1980). Reciprocity and the San Juan fiesta. *Journal of Anthropological Research, 36*, 116–130.

Batchelor, J. (1892). *The Ainu of Japan: The religion, superstitions, and general history of the hairy aborigines of Japan*. London: Religious Tract Society.

Batterberry, M., & Batterberry, A. (1999). *On the town in New York* (2nd ed.). New York: Routledge.

Beck, S. (1992). *Manny Almeida's ringside lounge: The Cape Verdeans' struggle for their neighborhood*. Providence, RI: Gavea-Brown.

Beck, K. H., Summons, T. G., & Thombs, D. L. (1991). A factor analytic study of social context of drinking in a high school population. *Psychology of Addictive Behavior, 5*, 66–77.

Beidelmann, T. O. (1961). Beer drinking and cattle theft in Ukaguru: Intertribal relations in a Tanganyikan chiefdom. *American Anthropologist, 63*, 534–549.

Bennett, J. M. (1996). *Ale, beer, and brewsters in England: Women's work in a changing world, 1300–1600*. New York: Oxford University Press.

Bennett, L. A., Janca, A., Grant, B. F., & Sartorius, N. (1993). Boundaries between normal and pathological drinking: A cross-cultural comparison. *Alcohol Health and Research World, 17*, 190–195.

Bennett, W. C., & Zingg, R. M. (1935). *The Tarahumara*. Chicago: University of Chicago Press.

Bickerdyke, J. (1886). *The curiosities of ale and beer: An entertaining history*. London: Field and Tuer.

Bing, J. (1997). Personal communication, 15 August.

Blocker, J. S., Jr. (1989). *American temperance movements: Cycles of reform* (Rev. ed.). Boston: Twayne.

Blum, R. H., & Blum, E. M. (1964). Drinking practices and controls in rural Greece. *British Journal of Addictions, 60*, 93–108.

Bose, D. K. (1922). *Wine in ancient India*. Calcutta: K. M. Connor.

Brady, M. (Ed.). (1998). *Giving away the grog: Aboriginal accounts of drinking and not drinking.* Canberra: Commonwealth Department of Health and Family Services.

Braidwood, R. J. (1953). Did man once live by beer alone? [with comments by J. D. Sauer, H. Helbaek, P. C. Mangelsdorf, H. C. Cutler, C. S. Coon, R. Linton, J. Steward, & A. L. Oppenheim]. *American Anthropologist, 55,* 515–526.

Brandes, S. (1979). Drinking patterns and alcohol control in a Castillian mountain village. *Anthropology* (Stony Brook, NY), *3,* 1–16.

Bruun, K., Edwards, G., Lumio, M., Mäkelä, K., Pan, L., Popham, R. E., Room, R., Schmidt, W., Skog, O-J., Sulkunen, P., & Österberg, E. (1975). *Alcohol control policies in public health perspective.* Helsinki: Finnish Foundation for Alcohol Studies.

Buhner, S. H. (1998). *Sacred and herbal healing beers: The secrets of ancient fermentation.* Boulder, CO: Siris.

Burns, T. F. (1980). Getting rowdy with the boys. *Journal of Drug Issues, 10,* 273–286.

Caetano, R. (1991). Findings from the 1984 National Survey of Alcohol Use among U.S. Hispanics. In W. B. Clark & M. E. Hilton (Eds.), *Alcohol in America: Drinking practices and problems* (pp. 293–307), Albany: State University of New York Press.

Cahalan, D., Cisin, I. H., & Crossley, H. M. (1969). *American drinking practices: A national study of drinking behavior and attitudes* (Monograph 6). New Brunswick, NJ: Rutgers Center of Alcohol Studies.

Calabresi, A. T. (1987). Vin santo and wine in a Tuscan farmhouse. In M. Douglas (Ed.), *Constructive drinking: Perspectives on drink from anthropology* (pp. 122–134). Cambridge: Cambridge University Press.

Cancian, F. (1965). *Economics and prestige in a Maya community: The religious cargo system in Zinacantan.* Stanford, CA: Stanford University Press.

Carpenter, E. S. (1959). Alcohol in the Iroquois dream quest. *American Journal of Psychiatry, 116,* 148–151.

Carstairs, G. M. (1954). *Daru* and *bhang:* Cultural factors in the choice of intoxicant. *Quarterly Journal of Studies on Alcohol, 15,* 220–237.

Carter, W. E. (1977). Ritual, the Aymara, and the role of alcohol in human society. In B. du Toit (Ed.), *Drugs, rituals, and altered states of consciousness,* (pp. 101–110). Rotterdam: A. A. Halkema.

Casswell, S. (1985). *Alcohol in Oceania.* Auckland, NZ: University of Aukland Alcohol Research Unit.

Cavan, S. (1966). *Liquor license: An ethnography of a bar.* Chicago: Aldine.

Cavanagh, J., & Clairmonte, F. F. (1985). *Alcoholic beverages: Dimensions of corporate power.* New York: St. Martin's Press.

Cheung, Y. W., & Erickson, P. G. (1995). Canada. In D. B. Heath (Ed.), *International handbook on alcohol and culture* (pp. 20–30). Westport, CT: Greenwood.

Clark, P. (1983). *The English alehouse: A social history, 1200–1830.* London: Longman.

Clark, W. B. (1991). Some comments on methods. In W. B. Clark & M. E. Hilton (Eds.), *Alcohol in America: Drinking practices and problems* (pp. 19–25). Albany: State University of New York Press.

Clark, W. B., & Hilton, M. E. (Eds.). (1991). *Alcohol in America: Drinking practices and problems.* Albany: State University of New York Press.

Cohen, H. H. (1974). *The drunkenness of Noah.* University, AL: University of Alabama Press.

Colby, B. N., & Colby, L. M. (1981). *The daykeeper: The life and discourse of an Ixil diviner.* Cambridge: Harvard University Press.

Collmann, J. (1979). Social order and the exchange of liquor: A theory of drinking among Australian Aborigines. *Journal of Anthropological Research, 35,* 208–224.

Colson, E., & Scudder, T. (1988). *For prayer and profit: The ritual, economic, and social importance of beer in Gwembe District, Zambia, 1950–1982.* Stanford: Stanford University Press.

Conroy, D. W. (1997). *In public houses: Drink and the revolution of authority in colonial Massachusetts.* Chapel Hill: University of North Carolina Press.

Cooper, J. M. (1949). Stimulants and narcotics. In J. H. Steward (Ed.), *Handbook of South American Indians* (Bulletin 143, vol. 5) (pp. 525–558), Washington: Bureau of American Ethnology.

Cottino, A. (1995). Italy. In D. B. Heath (Ed.), *International handbook on alcohol and culture* (pp. 156–167). Westport, CT: Greenwood.

Cox, W. M. (Ed.). (1990). *Why people drink: Parameters of alcohol as a reinforcer.* New York: Gardner.

Csikszentmihalyi, M. (1968). A cross-cultural comparison of some structural characteristics of group drinking. *Human Development* (Basel), *11*, 201–216.

Cutler, H. C., & Cardenas, M. (1947). Chicha: A native South American beer. *Harvard University Botanical Museum Association Leaflet, 3*, 33–60.

Dailey, R. C. (1968). The role of alcohol among North American Indian tribes as reported in the Jesuit relations. *Anthropologica, 10*, 45–59.

Darby, W. J., Ghalioungui, P., & Grivetti, L. (1977). *Food: The gift of Osiris* (2 vols.). London: Academic Press.

Davies, C. S. (1927). Customs governing beer drinking among the Ama-Bomuana. *South African Journal of Science, 24*, 521–524.

de Castro, J. M., & Pearcey, A. M. (1995). Lunar rhythms of the meal and alcohol intake of humans. *Physiology and Behavior, 57*, 439–444.

de Certau, M., Giard, L., & Mayol, P. (1998). *The practice of everyday life* (vol. 2, Living and Cooking) (trans.). Minneapolis: University of Minnesota Press.

de Lint, J. (1988). Alcohol data in longitudinal research. *Themes in Alcohol and Drug Problems, 1*, 18–32.

Devereux, G. (1948). The function of alcohol in Mohave society. *Quarterly Journal of Studies on Alcohol, 9*, 207–251.

Devereux, G. (1961). *Mohave ethnopsychiatry and suicide: The psychiatric knowledge and the psychic disturbances of an Indian tribe* (Bureau of American Ethnology Bulletin 175). Washington: Government Printing Office.

Dietler, M. (1990). Driven by drink: The role of drinking in the political economy and the case of early Iron Age France. *Journal of Anthropological Archaeology, 9*, 352–406.

Dietler, M. (1996). Feasts and commensal politics in the political economy: Food, power, and status in prehistoric Europe. In P. Wiessner & W. Schiefenhövel (Eds.), *Food and the status quest: An interdisciplinary perspective* (pp. 87–125). Oxford: Berghahn.

Dionysos: The Journal of Literature and Addiction. semi- annual, since 1989.

Dobrizhoffer, M. (1822). *An account of the Abipones, An equestrian people of Paraguay* (4 vols.). London: John Murray.

Dodds, E. R. (1956). *The Greeks and the irrational.* Berkeley: University of California Press.

Doll, R. (1998). The benefit of alcohol in moderation. *Drug and Alcohol Review, 17*, 353–363.

Donnor, W. (1994). Alcohol, community, and modernity: The social organization of toddy drinking in a Polynesian society. *Ethnology, 33*, 245–260.

Doughty, P. L. (1971). The social uses of alcoholic beverages in a Peruvian community. *Human Organization, 30*, 187–197.

Downes, R. M. (1933). *The Tiv tribe.* Kaduna, Nigeria: The Government Printer.

Dozier, E. P. (1966). Problem drinking among American Indians: The role of sociocultural deprivation. *Quarterly Journal of Studies on Alcohol, 27*, 72–87.

Dumett, R. E. (1974). The social impact of the European liquor trade on the Akan of Ghana (Gold Coast and Asante), 1875–1910. *Journal of Interdisciplinary History, 5*, 69–101.

Duster, T. (1983). Commentary. In R. Room & G. Collins (Eds.), *Alcohol and disinhibition: Nature and meaning of the link* (NIAAA Research Monograph 12) (pp. 326–330). Washington: National Institute on Alcohol Abuse and Alcoholism.

Eber, C. E. (1995). *Women and alcohol in a Highland Maya Town: Water of hope, water of sorrow.* Austin: University of Texas Press.

Edmunds, L. (1998). *Martini, straight up: The classic American cocktail.* Baltimore: Johns Hopkins University Press.

Edwards, G., Anderson, P., Babor, T. F., Casswell, S., Ferrence, R., Giesbrecht, N., Godfrey, C., Holder, H. D., Lemmens, P., Mäkelä, K., Midanik, L. T., Norström, T., Österberg, E., Romelsjö, A., Room, R., Simpura, J., & Skog, O-J. (1994). *Alcohol policy and the public good.* Oxford: Oxford University Press.

Epstein, A. L. (1958). *Politics in an urban African community.* Manchester, UK: Manchester University Press.

Evans-Pritchard, E. E. (1937). *Witchcraft, oracles, and magic among the Azande.* Oxford: Clarendon Press.

Fagan, J. (1990). Intoxication and aggression. In M. Tonry & J. Q. Wilson (Eds.), *Drugs and crime* (vol. 13) (pp. 241–320). Chicago: University of Chicago Press.

Felice, P. (1936). *Poisons sacrés, ivresses divines* [Sacred Poisons, Divine Raptures]. Paris: Albin Michel.

Fillmore, K. M. (1984). Research as a handmaiden of policy: An appraisal of estimates of alcoholism and cost in the workplace. *Journal of Public Health Policy, 5,* 40–64.

Fillmore, K. M. (1988). *Alcohol use across the life course: A critical review of 70 years of international longitudinal research.* Toronto: Addiction Research Foundation.

Fillmore, K. M. (1990). Occupational drinking subcultures: An exploratory epidemiological study. In P. M. Roman (Ed.), *Alcohol problem intervention in the workplace* (pp. 127–153). Westport, CT: Quorum.

Finch, C. (1989). *Connoisseur's guide to the world's best beer.* New York: Abbeville Press.

Forbes, R. J. (1954). Food and drink. In C. Singer (Ed.), *A history of technology* (vol. 2) (pp. 103–146). New York: Oxford University Press.

Foster, G. M. (1994). *Hippocrates' Latin American legacy: Humoral medicine in the New World.* Langhorne, PA: Gordon and Breach.

Fundación de Investigaciones Sociales. (1997). Bebidas nacionales [National drinks]. *Guia México Desconocido, 18,* (entire issue).

Fundación de Investigaciones Sociales. (1999). *Beber de tierra generosa: Historia de las bebidas alcohólicas en México* [To drink from a generous land: History of alcoholic drinks in Mexico]. Mexico: Fundación de Investigaciones Sociales.

Gamella, J. F. (1995). Spain. In D. B. Heath (Ed.), *International handbook on alcohol and culture* (pp. 254–269). Westport, CT: Greenwood.

Gastineau, C. F., Darby, W. J., & Turner, T. B. (Eds.). (1979). *Fermented food beverages in nutrition.* New York: Academic.

Giesbrecht, N., González, R., Grant, M., Österberg, E., Room, R., Rootman, I., & Towle, L. (Eds.). (1989). *Drinking and casualties: Accidents, poisonings, and violence in an international perspective.* London: Tavistock/Routledge.

Golub, A. L., & Johnson, B. D. (1998). Alcohol is not the gateway to hard drug abuse. *Journal of Drug Issues, 28,* 971–894.

Gonçalves de Lima, O. (1956). *El maguey y el pulque en los códices Mexicanos* [Maguey and pulque in the Mexican codices]. Mexico: Fondo de Cultura Económica.

Gonçalves de Lima, O., deMello, J. F., D'Albuquerque, I. L., Monache, F. D., Marini-Bettolo, G. B., & Sousa, M. (1977). Contribution to the knowledge of the Maya ritual wine: Balché. *Lloydia: The Journal of Natural Products, 40,* 195–200.

Gorer, G. (1938). *Himalayan village: An account of the Lepchas of Sikkim.* London: Michael Joseph.

Gose, B. (1996). A license to drink. *The Chronicle of Higher Education,* May 31, A29–A30.

Grant, M. (Ed.). (1998). *Alcohol and emerging markets: Patterns, problems, and responses.* Philadelphia: Taylor & Francis.

Grant, M., & Litvak, J. (Eds). (1998). *Drinking patterns and their consequences.* Washington: Taylor & Francis.

Graves, T. (1971). Drinking and drunkenness among urban Indians. In J. O. Waddell & O. M. Watson (Eds.), *The American Indian in urban society* (pp. 274–311). Boston: Little, Brown.

Greeley, A. M., McCready, W. C., & Thiesen, G. (1980). *Ethnic drinking subcultures.* New York: Praeger.

Greenfield, T. K., & Rogers, J. D. (1999). Who drinks most of the alcohol in the U.S.? The policy implications. *Journal of Studies on Alcohol, 60,* 78–89.

Grivetti, L. E. (1996). Ancient sayings about wine. In P. E. McGovern, S. J. Fleming, & S. H. Katz (Eds.), *The origins and ancient history of wine* (pp. 3–6). Amsterdam: Gordon and Breach.

Gusfield, J. R. (1963). *Symbolic crusade: Status politics and the American temperance movement.* Urbana: University of Illinois Press.

Gusfield, J. R. (1981). *The culture of public problems: Drinking-Driving and the symbolic order.* Chicago: University of Chicago Press.

Gusfield, J. R. (1987). Passage to play: Rituals of drinking time in American society. In M. Douglas (Ed.), *Constructive drinking: Perspectives on drinking from anthropology* (pp. 73–90). Cambridge: Cambridge University Press.

Gusfield, J. R. (1996). *Contested meanings: The construction of alcohol problems.* Madison: University of Wisconsin Press.

Gutmann, B. (1926). *Das Recht der Dschagga* [Chagga Law]. Munich: C. H. Beck.

Gutmann, M. C. (1996). *The meanings of macho: Being a man in Mexico City.* Berkeley: University of California Press.

Gutmann, M. C. (1999). Ethnicity, alcohol, and acculturation. *Social Science and Medicine, 48,* 173–184.

Haine, W. S. (1996). *The world of the Paris café: Sociability among the French working class, 1789–1914.* Baltimore, MD: Johns Hopkins University Press.

Hall, W., & Hunter, E. (1995). Australia. In D. B. Heath (Ed.), *International handbook on alcohol and culture* (pp. 7–19). Westport, CT: Greenwood.

Halley, N. (1996). *The Wordsworth dictionary of drink: An A-Z of alcoholic beverages.* Ware, Eng.: Wordsworth Editions.

Hammond, P. W. (1993). *Food and feast in medieval England.* Gloucestershire, UK: Wrens Park.

Hanson, D. J. (1995a). The United States of America. In D. B. Heath (Ed.), *International handbook on alcohol and culture* (pp. 300–315). Westport, CT: Greenwood.

Hanson, D. J. (1995b.) *Preventing alcohol abuse: Alcohol, culture, and control.* Westport, CT: Praeger.

Hanson, D. J. (1996). *Alcohol education: What we must do.* Westport, CT: Greenwood.

Harford, T. C., Parker, D. A., & Light, L. (Eds.). (1980). *Normative approaches to the prevention of alcohol abuse and alcoholism* (Research Monograph 3). Rockville, MD: National Institute on Alcohol Abuse and Alcoholism.

Harper, F. F. (1904). *The Code of Hammurabi, King of Babylon.* London: Luzac.

Hartman, L. F., & Oppenheim, A. L. (1950). *On beer and brewing techniques in ancient Mesopotamia.* Baltimore: American Oriental Society.

Hartmann, G. (1958). *Alkoholische getränke bei den naturvolkern Sudamerikas* [Alcoholic drink among South American aborigines]. Berlin: Frei Universität Berlin.

Harwood, A. (1964). *Beer drinking and famine in a Safwa village: A case of adaptation in a time of crisis.* Kampala, Tanganyika: East Africa Institute of Social Research.

Haworth, A. (1995). Zambia. In D. B. Heath (Ed.), *International handbook on alcohol and culture* (pp. 316–327). Westport, CT: Greenwood.

Haworth, A., & Acuda, S. W. (1998). Sub-Saharan Africa. In M. Grant (Ed.), *Alcohol and emerging markets: Patterns, problems, and responses* (pp. 19–90). Philadelphia: Taylor & Francis.

Heath, D. B. (1958). Drinking patterns of the Bolivian Camba. *Quarterly Journal of Studies on Alcohol, 19,* 491–508.

Heath, D. B. (1962). Drinking patterns of the Bolivian Camba (revised). In D. J. Pittman & C. R. Snyder (Eds.), *Society, culture, and drinking patterns* (pp. 22–36). New York: John Wiley and Sons.

Heath, D. B. (1964). Prohibition and post-repeal drinking patterns among the Navajo. *Quarterly Journal of Studies on Alcohol, 25,* 119–135.

Heath, D. B. (1965). Comments on David Mandelbaum's "Alcohol and Culture." *Current Anthropology, 6,* 289–290.

Heath, D. B. (1971). Peasants, revolution, and drinking: Interethnic drinking patterns in two Bolivian communities. *Human Organization, 30,* 179–186.

Heath, D. B. (1972). New patrons for old: Changing patron-client relationships in the Bolivian Yungas. In A. Strickon & S. Greenfield (Eds.), *Structure and process in Latin America: Patronage, clientage, and power systems* (pp. 107–137). Albuquerque: University of New Mexico Press.

Heath, D. B. (1975). A critical review of ethnographic studies of alcohol use. In R. J. Gibbins, Y. Israel, H. Kalant, R. E. Popham, W. Schmidt, & R. G. Smart (Eds.), *Research advances in alcohol and drug problems* (vol. 2) (pp. 1–92). New York: Wiley.

Heath, D. B. (1977). *Observational studies into alcohol problems* (Background Document). Geneva: World Health Organization.

Heath, D. B. (1988a). Emerging anthropological theory and models of alcohol use and alcoholism. In C. D. Chaudron & D. A. Wilkinson (Eds.), *Theories on alcoholism* (pp. 353–410). Toronto: Addiction Research Foundation.

Heath, D. B. (1988b). Alcohol control policies and drinking patterns: An international game of politics against science. *Journal of Substance Abuse, 1,* 109–115.

Heath, D. B. (1989). The new temperance movement: Through the looking glass. *Drugs and Society, 3,* 143–168.

Heath, D. B. (1991a). Drinking patterns of the Bolivian Camba (Rev.). In D. J. Pittman & H. R. White (Eds.), *Society, culture, and drinking patterns reexamined* (pp. 62–77). New Brunswick, NJ: Rutgers Center of Alcohol Studies.

Heath, D. B. (1991b). Continuity and change in drinking patterns of the Bolivian Camba. In D. J. Pittman & H. R. White (Eds.), *Society, culture and drinking patterns reexamined* (pp. 78–86). New Brunswick, NJ: Rutgers Center of Alcohol Studies.

Heath, D. B. (1991c.) Uses and misuses of the concept of ethnicity in alcohol studies: An essay in deconstruction. *International Journal of the Addictions, 25,* 609–630.

Heath, D. B. (1994). Agricultural changes and drinking among the Bolivian Camba. *Human Organization, 53,* 357–361.

Heath, D. B. (Ed.). (1995). *International handbook on alcohol and culture.* Westport, CT: Greenwood.

Heath, D. B. (1998a.) Cultural variations among drinking patterns. In M. Grant & J. Litvak (Eds.), *Drinking patterns and their consquences* (pp. 103–125). Washington: Taylor & Francis.

Heath, D. B. (1998b.) Beverage alcohol in developing regions: An anthropological and epidemiological perspective on public health issues. In M. Grant (Ed.), *Alcohol and emerging markets: Patterns, problems, and responses* (pp. 287–309). Philadelphia: Taylor & Francis.

Heath, D. B., & Cooper, A. M. (1981). *Alcohol use and world cultures: A comprehensive bibliography of anthropological sources* (Bibliographic Series 15). Toronto: Addiction Research Foundation.

Heien, D. M., & Pittman, D. J. (1989). The economic cost of alcohol abuse: An assessment of current methods and estimates. *Journal of Studies on Alcohol, 50,* 567–579.

Hellmann, E. (1934). The importance of beer-brewing in an urban native yard. *Bantu Studies, 8,* 38–60.

Helzer, J. E., & Canino, G. J. (Eds.). (1992). *Alcoholism in North America, Europe, and Asia.* New York: Oxford University Press.

Henderson, E. (1997). Personal communication; 11 August.

Herd, D. (1991). Drinking patterns in the Black population. In W. B. Clark & M. E. Hilton (Eds.), *Alcohol in America: Drinking practices and problems* (pp. 308–328). Albany: State University of New York Press.

Hester, R. K. (1995). Behavioral self-control training. In R. K. Hester & W. R. Miller (Eds.), *Handbook of alcoholism treatment approaches: Effective alternatives* (2nd ed.) (pp. 148–159). Boston: Allyn and Bacon.

Hettige, S. T. (1990). Social research on alcohol in Sri Lanka: Background issues and prospects. In J. Maula, M. Lindblad, & C. Tigerstedt (Eds.), *Alcohol in developing countries* (pp. 206–223). Helsinki: Nordic Council for Alcohol and Drug Research.

Hill, T. W. (1974). From hell-raiser to family man. In J. P. Spradley & D. M. McCurdy (Eds.), *Conformity and conflict: Readings in cultural anthropology* (2nd ed.) (pp. 186–200). Boston: Little, Brown.

Hilton, M. E. (1991a). A note on measuring drinking problems in the 1984 National Alcohol Survey. In W. B. Clark & M. E. Hilton (Eds.), *Alcohol in America: Drinking practices and problems* (pp. 51–70). Albany: State University of New York Press.

Hilton, M. E. (1991b). Demographic characteristics and frequency of heavy drinking as predictors of self-reported drinking. In W. B. Clark & M. E. Hilton (Eds.), *Alcohol in America: Drinking practices and problems* (pp. 194–212). Albany: State University of New York Press.

Hilton, M. E. (1991c). Higher and lower levels of self-reported problems among heavy drinkers. In W. B. Clark & M. E. Hilton (Eds.), *Alcohol in America: Drinking practices and problems* (pp. 238–246). Albany: State University of New York Press.

Hilton, M. E. (1991d). The demographic distribution of drinking patterns in 1984. In W. B. Clark & M. E. Hilton (Eds.), *Alcohol in America: Drinking practices and problems* (pp. 73–86). Albany: State University of New York Press.

Hilton, M. E. (1991e). The demographic distribution of drinking problems in 1984. In W. B. Clark & M. E. Hilton (Eds.), *Alcohol in America: Drinking practices and problems* (pp. 87–101). Albany State University of New York Press.

Hilton, M. E. (1991f). Trends in U.S. drinking patterns: Further evidence from the past twenty years. In W. B. Clark & M. E. Hilton (Eds.), *Alcohol in America: Drinking practices and problems* (pp. 121–148). Albany: State University of New York Press.

Honigmann, J. J. (1963). Dynamics of drinking in an Austrian village. *Ethnology, 2,* 157–169.

Honigmann, J., & Honigmann, I. (1945). Drinking in an Indian-White community. *Quarterly Journal of Studies on Alcohol, 5,* 575–619.

Horton, D. J. (1943). The functions of alcohol in primitive societies: A cross-cultural study. *Quarterly Journal of Studies on Alcohol, 4,* 199–320.

Hunt, G., & Satterlee, S. (1986). Cohesion and division: Drinking in an English village. *Man, 21,* 521–537.

Hutchinson, B. (1961). Alcohol as a contributing factor in social disorganization: The South African Bantu in the nineteenth century. *Revista de Antropología, 9,* 1–13.

International Center for Alcohol Policies. (1997). *Safe alcohol consumption: A comparison of nutrition and your health: Dietary guidelines for Americans and sensible drinking* (Report 1). Washington: Author.

International Center for Alcohol Policies. (1998a). *Drinking age limits* (Report 4). Washington: Author.

International Center for Alcohol Policies. (1998b). *What is a "standard drink"?* (Report 5). Washington: Author.

International Center for Alcohol Policies. (1999). *Government policies on alcohol and pregnancy* (Report 6). Washington: Author.

Iontchev, A. (1998). Central and eastern Europe. In M. Grant (Ed.), *Alcohol and emerging markets: Patterns, problems, and responses* (pp. 177–201). Philadelphia: Taylor & Francis.

Isaac, M. (1998). India. In M. Grant (Ed.), *Alcohol and emerging markets: Patterns, problems, and responses* (pp. 145–175). Philadelphia: Taylor & Francis.

Jackson, M. (1977). *The world guide to beer: The brewing styles, the brands, the countries.* Englewood Cliffs, NJ: Prentice Hall.

Jackson, M. 1988. *New world guide to beer.* Philadelphia: Running Press.

Jackson, M., & Smyth, F. (1976). *The English pub.* New York: Harper and Row.

James, W. (1909). *Varieties of religious experience: A study in human nature.* New York: Longmans, Green.

Jankowiak, W., & Bradburd, D. (1996). Using drug foods to capture and enhance labor performance: A cross-cultural perspective. *Current Anthropology, 37,* 717–720.

Jeffers, H. P. (1997). *High spirits.* New York: Lyons and Burford.

Jellinek, E. M. (1960). *The disease concept of alcoholism.* New Brunswick, NJ: Hillhouse Press.

Jernigan, D. H. (1997). *Thirsting for markets: The global impact of corporate alcohol.* San Rafael, CA: Marin Institute for the Prevention of Alcohol and Other Drug Problems.

Jochelson, W. (1906). Kumiss festivals of the Yakut and the decoration of kumiss vessels. In B. Laufer (Ed.), *Boas anniversary volume* (pp. 257–271). New York: Stechert and Co.

Joffe, A. H. (1998). Alcohol and social complexity in ancient western Asia. *Current Anthropology, 39,* 297–322.

Johnson, H. (1994). *World atlas of wine* (4th ed.). New York: Simon and Schuster.

Johnson, H. (1998). *Hugh Johnson's modern encyclopedia of wine* (4th ed.). New York: Simon and Schuster.

Jones, A. W. (1985). Excretion of low-molecular weight volatile substances in human breath: Focus on endogenous ethanol. *Journal of Analytical Toxicology, 9,* 246–250.

Kalin, R., Davis, W. N., & McClelland, D. C. (1966). The relationship between use of alcohol and thematic content of folktales in primitive societies. In P. J. Stone, D. C. Dunphy, M. S. Smith, & D. M. Ogilvie (Eds.), *The general inquirer* (pp. 569–588). Cambridge, MA: Massachusetts Institute of Technology Press.

Kant, I. (1978/1798). *Anthropology from a pragmatic point of view* (trans.). Carbondale, IL: Southern Illinois University Press.

Karp, I. (1970). *Beer-drinking among the Iteso* (Institute for Development Studies Discussion Paper 9). Nairobi: University College.

Karsten, R. (1935). *The headhunters of western Amazonas: The life and culture of the Jibaro Indians of eastern Ecuador and Peru* (Societas Scientiarum Fennica, Commentationes Humanarum Litterarum VII, 1). Helsinki: Centaltryckeriet.

Katz, S. H., & Voigt, M. M. (1986). Bread and beer: The early use of cereals in the human diet. *Expedition, 28,* 23–34.

Kearney, M. (1970). Drunkenness and religious conversion in a Mexican village. *Quarterly Journal of Studies on Alcohol, 31,* 132–152.

Keller, M. (1958). Beer and wine in ancient medicine. *Quarterly Journal of Studies on Alcohol, 29,* 153–154.

Keller, M. (Ed.). (1965). *A cross-cultural study of drinking* (Supplement 3). New Haven, CT: Quarterly Journal of Studies on Alcohol.

Keller, M., McCormick, M., & Efron, V. (1982). *A dictionary of words about alcohol* (2nd ed.). New Brunswick, NJ: Rutgers Center of Alcohol Studies.

Kennedy, J. G. (1978). *Tarahumara of the Sierra Madre: Beer, ecology, and social organization.* Arlington Heights, IL: A H M Publishing.

Klausner, S. Z., Foulks, E. P., & Moore, M. H. (1979). *The Inupiat, economics and alcohol on the Alaskan North Slope.* Philadelphia: Center for Research on the Acts of Man.

Kortteinen, T. (Ed.). (1989). *State monopolies and alcohol prevention* (Monograph 181). Helsinki: Social Research Institute of Alcohol Studies.

Kunitz, S. J., & Levy, J. E. (1994). *Drinking careers: A twenty-five-year study of three Navajo populations.* New Haven: Yale University Press.

LaBarre, W. (1948). *The Aymara Indians of the Lake Titicaca plateau, Bolivia* (Memoir 68). Menasha, WI: American Anthropological Association.

Lalander, P. (1997). Beyond everyday order: Breaking away with alcohol. *Nordisk Alkohol et Narkotikatidskrift, 14,* 33–42.

Leacock, S. (1964). Ceremonial drinking in an Afro-Brazilian cult. *American Anthropologist, 66,* 344–354.

Lebot, V., Merlin, M., & Lindstrom, L. (1992). *Kava: The Pacific drug.* New Haven, CT: Yale University Press.

Ledermann, S. (1956). *Alcool, alcoolisme, alcoolisation: Donées scientifiques de caractére physiologique, economique et social* (Travaux et Documents de l'Institut d'Etudes Démographique 29). Paris: Institut d'Etudes Démographique.

Leis, P. (1964). Palm wine, illicit gin, and the moral order of the Ijaw. *American Anthropologist, 66,* 828–838.

Leland, J. H. (1976). *Firewater myths: North American Indian drinking and alcohol addiction* (Monograph 11). New Brunswick, NJ: Rutgers Center of Alcohol Studies.

LeMasters, E. E. (1975). *Blue collar aristocrats: Life-styles at a working-class tavern.* Madison: University of Wisconsin Press.

Lemert, E. M. (1964). Forms and pathology of drinking in three Polynesian societies. *American Anthropologist, 66,* 361–374.

Lemu, B. A. (1992). *Islam and alcohol.* Alexandria, VA: Al Saadawi.

Lesko, L. H. (1977). *King Tut's wine cellar.* Berkeley, CA: B.C. Scribe.

Levin, J. D. (1990). *Alcoholism: A biopsychosocial approach.* New York: Hemisphere.

Levine, H. G. (1992). Temperance cultures: Concern about alcohol problems in Nordic and English-speaking countries. In M. Lader, G. Edwards, & D. C. Drummond (Eds.), *The nature of alcohol and drug related problems* (Society for the Study of Addiction Monograph 2) (pp. 15–36). Oxford: Oxford University Press.

Levine, M. E., Duffy, L. K., & Bowyer, R. T. (1994). Fatigue, sleep, and seasonal hormone levels: Implications for drinking behavior in northern climates. *Drugs and Society, 8,* 61–70.

Levy, J. E., & Kunitz, S. J. (1974). *Indian drinking: Navajo practices and Anglo-American theories.* New York: Wiley.

Lolli, G. (1963). The cocktail hour: Physiological, psychological, and social aspects. In S. P. Lucia (Ed.), *Alcohol and civilization* (pp. 183–199). New York: McGraw Hill.

Lolli, G., Serriani, E., Golder, G. M., & Luzzatto-Fegiz, P. (1958). *Alcohol in Italian culture: Food and wine in relation to sobriety among Italians and Italian Americans* (Monograph 3). New Haven, CT: Yale Center of Alcohol Studies.

Lowe, G. (1994). Pleasures of social relaxants and stimulants: The ordinary person's attitudes and involvement. In D. M. Warburton (Ed.), *Pleasure: The politics and the reality* (pp. 95–108). Chichester, UK: Wiley.

Lurie, N. O. (1971). The world's oldest on-going protest demonstration: North American Indian drinking patterns. *Pacific Historical Review, 40,* 311–332.

Lutz, H. F. (1922). *Viticulture and brewing in the ancient Orient.* Leipzig: J. C. Heinrichs.

MacAndrew, C., & Edgerton, R. E. (1969). *Drunken comportment: A social explanation.* Chicago: Aldine.

MacPhail, A. P., Simon, M. O., Torrance, J. D., Charlton, R. W., Bothwell, T. H., & Isaacson, C. (1979). Changing patterns of dietary iron overload in Black South Africans. *American Journal of Clinical Nutrition, 32,* 1272–1278.

Madrigal, E. (1998). Latin America. In M. Grant (Ed.), *Alcohol and emerging markets: Patterns, problems, and responses* (pp. 223–261). Philadelphia: Taylor & Francis.

Madsen, W., & Madsen, C. (1969). The cultural structure of Mexican drinking behavior. *Quarterly Journal of Studies on Alcohol, 30,* 701–718.

Mahar, H. (1999). Personal communication; 10 March.

Mahmood, C. K. (1997). Hinduism in context: Approaching a religious tradition through external sources. In S. D. Glazier (Ed.), *Anthropology of religion: A handbook* (pp. 305–318). Westport, CT: Greenwood.

Mäkelä, K. (1987). Attitudes and opinions. In J. Simpura (Ed.), *Finnish drinking habits: Results from interview surveys held in 1968, 1976, and 1984* (vol. 35) (pp. 167–184). Jyväskylä Finnish Foundation for Alcohol Studies.

Mäkelä, K., Arminen, I., Bloomfield, K., Eisenbach-Stangl, I., Bergmark, K. H., Korube, N., Mariolini, N., Olafsdóttir, H., Peterson, J. H., Phillips, M., Rehm, J., Room, R., Rosenqvist, P., Rosovsky, H., Stenius, K., Swiatkiewicz, G., Woronowicz, B., & Zieliński, A. (1996). *Alcoholics anonymous as a mutual-help movement: A study in eight societies.* Madison: University of Wisconsin Press.

Mäkelä, K., Room, R., Single, E., Sulkunen, P., & Walsh, B. (1981). *Alcohol, society, and the state* (vol. 1: A Comparative Study of Alcohol Control). Toronto: Addiction Research Foundation.

Mancall, P. C. (1995). *Deadly medicine: Indians and alcohol in early America.* Ithaca, NY: Cornell University Press.

Mandelbaum, D. G. (1965). Alcohol and culture [with comments by V. S-Ehrlich, K. Hasan, D. Heath, J. Honigmann, E. Lemert, & W. Madsen]. *Current Anthropology, 6,* 281–294.

Mangin, W. (1957). Drinking among Andean Indians. *Quarterly Journal of Studies on Alcohol, 18,* 55–66.

Marlatt, G. A., & Rohsenow, D. (1980). Cognitive processes in alcohol use: Expectancy and the balanced placebo design. In N. Mello (Ed.), *Advances in substance abuse: Behavioral and biological research* (Vol. 1) (pp. 159–199). Greenwich, CT: JAI Press.

Mars, G. (1987). Longshoreman drinking, economic security, and union politics in Newfoundland. In M. Douglas (Ed.), *Constructive drinking: Perspectives on drink from anthropology* (pp. 91–101). Cambridge: Cambridge University Press.

Mars, G., & Altman, Y. (1987). Alternative mechanism of distribution in a Soviet economy. In M. Douglas (Ed.), *Constructive drinking: Perspectives on drink from anthropology* (pp. 270–279). Cambridge: Cambridge University Press.

Marshall, M. (1979a). *Weekend warriors: Alcohol in a Micronesian culture.* Palo Alto, CA: Mayfield.

Marshall, M. (Ed.). (1979b). *Beliefs, behaviors, and alcoholic beverages: A cross-cultural survey.* Ann Arbor: University of Michigan Press.

Marshall, M. (Ed.). (1982). *Through a glass darkly: Beer and modernization in Papua New Guinea* (Monograph 18). Boroko: Institute of Applied Social and Economic Research.

Marshall, M., & Marshall L. B. (1975). Opening Pandora's bottle: Reconstructing Micronesia's early contacts with alcoholic beverages. *Journal of the Polynesian Society, 84,* 441–465.

Martinic, M. (1998). The implications for measurement and research. In M. Grant & J. Litvak (Eds.), *Drinking patterns and their consequences* (pp. 221–240). Washington: Taylor & Francis.

Mass Observation. (1943). *The pub and the people: A work town study.* London: Victor Gollancz.

Maula, J. (1990). Research in production and consumption of alcohol in Tanzania: Background, issues, and prospects. In J. Maula, M. Lindblad, & C. Tigerstedt (Eds.), *Alcohol in developing countries* (pp. 193–205). Helsinki: Nordic Council for Alcohol and Drug Research.

Maula, J. (1997). *Small-scale production of food and traditional alcoholic beverages in Benin and Tanzania: Implications for the promotion of female entrepreneurship* (vol. 43). Helsinki: Finnish Foundation for Alcohol Studies.

Maynard, E., Frøland, B., & Rasmusssen, C. (1965). *Drinking patterns in highland Ecuador.* Ithaca, NY: Cornell University Department of Anthropology.

McClelland, D. C., Davis, W. N., Wanner, E., & Kalin, R. (1972). *The drinking man.* Glencoe, IL: Free Press.

McCrady, B.S., & Miller, W. R. (Eds.). (1993). *Research on Alcoholics Anonymous: Opportunities and alternatives.* New Brunswick, NJ: Rutgers Center of Alcohol Studies.

McGee, R. J. (1990). *Life, ritual, and religion among the Lacandon Maya.* Belmont, CA: Wadsworth.

McGovern, P. E., Fleming, S. J., & Katz, S. H. (Eds.). (1996). *The origins and ancient history of wine.* Amsterdam: Gordon and Breach.

McKinlay, A. P. (1948). Ancient experience with intoxicating drinks: Non-classical peoples. *Quarterly Journal of Studies on Alcohol, 9,* 388–414.

McKinlay, A. P. (1951). Attic temperance. *Quarterly Journal of Studies on Alcohol, 12,* 61–102.

Medicine, B. (1997). Personal communication, 22 July.

Medina, E. (1995). Chile. In D. B. Heath (Ed.), *International handbook on alcohol and culture* (pp. 31–41). Westport, CT: Greenwood.

Meister, K. (1999). *Moderate alcohol consumption and health.* New York: American Council on Science and Health.

Merlan, F. (1998). *Caging the rainbow: Places, politics, and aborigines in a North Australian town.* Honolulu: University of Hawaii Press.

Midanik, L. T., & Clark, W. B. (1994). The demographic distribution of U.S. drinking patterns in 1990: Descriptions and trends from 1984. *American Journal of Public Health, 84,* 1218–1222.

Midanik, L. T., Tam, T., Greenfield, T. W., & Caetano, R. (1996). Risk functions for alcohol-related problems in a 1988 U.S. national sample. *Addiction, 91,* 1427–1437.

Midgley, J. (1971). Drinking and attitude toward drink in a Muslim community. *Quarterly Journal of Studies on Alcohol, 32*, 148–158.

Mitchell, J. C. (1956). *The Kalela dance: Aspects of social relationships among urban Africans in Northern Rhodesia*. Manchester, UK: Manchester University Press.

Mitra, B. R. (1873). Spirituous drinks in ancient India. *Journal of the Asiatic Society* (Bengal), *43*, 1–23.

Modi, J. J. (1888). *Wine among the Ancient Persians*. Bombay: Bombay Gazette Steam Press.

Mohan, D., & Sharma, H. K. (1995). India. In D. B. Heath (Ed.), *International handbook on alcohol and culture* (pp. 128–141). Westport, CT: Greenwood.

Moore, M. H., & Gerstein, D. R. (Eds.). (1981). *Alcohol and public policy: Beyond the shadow of prohibition*. Washington: National Academy Press.

Morris, C. (1979). Maize beer in the economics, politics, and religion of the Inca Empire. In C. Gastineau, W. Darby, & T. Turner (Eds.), *Fermented food beverages in nutrition* (pp. 21–34). New York: Academic Press.

Moskalewicz, J. (1997). Personal communication; 13 June.

Moskalewicz, J., & Zieliński, A. (1995). Poland. In D. B. Heath (Ed.), *International handbook on alcohol and culture* (pp. 224–236). Westport, CT: Greenwood.

Muokolo, A. (1990). Alcohol and its main functions in the Congo. In J. Maula, M. Lindblad, & C. Tigerstedt (Eds.), *Alcohol in developing countries* (pp. 127–133). Helsinki: Nordic Council for Alcohol and Drug Research.

Murray, O. (1983). The Greek *symposion* in history. In E. Gabba (Ed.), *Tria Corda: Scritti in onore di Arnaldo Momigliano* (pp. 257–272). Como Italy: Edizioni New Press.

Musto, D. (1987). *The American disease: Origins of narcotic control* (Rev. ed.). Oxford: Oxford University Press.

Nahoum-Grappe, V. (1995). France. In D. B. Heath (Ed.), *International handbook on alcohol and culture* (pp. 75–87). Westport, CT: Greenwood.

Nash, J. (1972). The devil in Bolivia's nationalized tin mines. *Science and Society, 36*, 221–233.

Nason, J. D. (1975). Sardines and other fried fish: The consumption of alcoholic beverages on a Micronesian island. *Journal of Studies on Alcohol, 36*, 611–625.

Natera, G. (1995). Mexico. In D. B. Heath (Ed.), *International handbook on alcohol and culture* (pp. 179–189). Westport, CT: Greenwood.

National Highway Traffic Safety Administration. (1994). *Traffic safety facts, 1993: Alcohol*. Washington, DC: U.S. Department of Transportation, National Center for Statistics and Analysis.

Nelson, G. K., Novellie, L., Reader, D. H., Reuning, H., & Sachs, H., (1964). *Psychological, nutritional, and sociological studies of Kaffir beer*. Pretoria: Johannesburg Kaffir Beer Research Project, South African Council for Scientific and Industrial Research.

Netting, R. M. (1964). Beer as a locus of value among the west African Kofyar. *American Anthropologist, 66*, 375–384.

Neve, R. J. M., Lemmens, P. H., & Drop, M. J. (1997). Gender differences in alcohol use and alcohol problems: Mediation by social roles and gender-role attitudes. *Substance Abuse and Misuse, 32*, 1439–1460.

Ngokwey, N. (1987). Varieties of palm wine among the Lele of the Kasai. In M. Douglas (Ed.), *Constructive drinking: Perspectives on drink from anthropology* (pp. 113–121). Cambridge: Cambridge University Press.

Nyberg, K., & Allebeck, P. (1995). Sweden. In D. B. Heath (Ed.), *International handbook on alcohol and culture* (pp. 280–288). Westport, CT: Greenwood.

O'Brien, J. M. (1980). The enigma of Alexander: The alcohol factor. *Annals of Scholarship, 1*, 31–46.

O'Brien, J. M., & Seller, S. C. (1982). Attributes of alcohol in the Old Testament. *Drinking and Drug Practices Surveyor, 18*, 18–24.

Oldenburg, R. (1997). *The great good place* (Rev. ed.). New York: Marlowe.

Onselen, C. (1976). Randlords and rotgut, 1886–1905: An essay on the role of alcohol in the development of European imperialism and South African capitalism. *History Workshop 2:* entire issue.

Oshodin, O. G. (1995). Nigeria. In D. B. Heath (Ed.), *International handbook on alcohol and culture* (pp. 213–223). Westport, CT: Greenwood.

Osservatorio Permanente sui Giovani e l'Alcool. (1998). *The Italians and alcohol: Consumption, trends, and attitudes* (Quaderni dell' Osservatorio 11). Rome: Vignola Editore.

Pack, A. J. (1982). *Nelson's blood: The story of naval rum*. Annapolis, MD: Naval Institute Press.

Pan, L. (1975). *Alcohol in Colonial Africa* (Monograph 22). Helsinki: Finnish Foundation for Alcohol Studies.

Park, J. (1995). New Zealand. In D. B. Heath (Ed.), *International handbook on alcohol and culture* (pp. 201–212). Westport, CT: Greenwood.

Parker, D. A., & Harman, M. S. (1978). The distribution of consumption model of prevention of alcohol problems. *Journal of Studies on Alcohol, 39*, 377–399.

Parker, R. N. (1995). *Alcohol and homicide: A deadly combination of two American traditions*. Albany: State University of New York Press.

Partanen, J. (1979). *On national commodity consumption patterns and the use of alcohol* (Report 129). Helsinki: Social Research Institute of Alcohol Studies.

Partanen, J. (1990). Abstinence in Africa. In J. Maula, M. Lindblad, & C. Tigerstedt (Eds.), *Alcohol in developing countries* (pp. 70–85). Helsinki: Nordic Council for Alcohol and Drug Research.

Partanen, J. (1991). *Sociability and intoxication: Alcohol and drinking in Kenya, Africa, and the modern world* (Volume 39). Helsinki: Finnish Foundation for Alcohol Studies.

Patnaik, N. (1960). Outcasting among oilmen for drinking wine. *Man in India, 40*, 1–7.

Pedlow, G. (1998). Alcohol in emerging markets: Identifying the most appropriate role for the alcohol beverage industry. In M. Grant (Ed.), *Alcohol and emerging markets: Patterns, problems, and responses* (pp. 333–351). Philadelphia: Taylor & Francis.

Peele, S. (1987). The limitations of control-of-supply models for explaining and preventing alcoholism and drug addiction. *Journal of Studies on Alcohol, 48*, 61–77.

Peele, S., & Grant, M. (Eds.). (1999). *Alcohol and pleasure: A health perspective*. Washington, DC: Taylor & Francis.

Pernanen, K. (1974). Validity of survey data on alcohol use. In R. J. Gibbins et al. (Eds.), *Research advances in alcohol and drug problems* (vol. 1) (pp. 355–374). New York: Wiley.

Pernanen, K. (1991). *Alcohol in human violence*. New York: Guilford Press.

Pertold, O. (1931). The liturgical base of mahuda liquor by Bhils. *Archiv Orientalni (Prague), 3*, 400–407.

Pirazzoli-t'Serstevens, M. (1991). The art of dining in the Han period: Food vessels from Tomb no. 1 at Mawangdui. *Food and Foodways, 4*, 209–219.

Plange, N-K. (1998). Social and behavioral issues related to drinking patterns. In M. Grant & J. Litvak (Eds.), *Drinking patterns and their consequences* (pp. 89–102). Washington, DC: Taylor & Francis.

Plant, M. (1997). *Women and alcohol: Contemporary and historical perspectives*. London: Free Association Books.

Plant, M. A. (1995). The United Kingdom. In D. B. Heath (Ed.), *International handbook on alcohol and culture* (pp. 289–299). Westport, CT: Greenwood.

Platt, B. S. (1955). Some traditional alcoholic beverages and their importance in indigenous African communities. *Proceedings of the Nutrition Society, 13*, 115–124.

Platt, B. S., & Webb, R. A. (1946). Fermentation and human nutrition. *Proceedings of the Nutritional Society, 4*, 132–140.

Popham, R. E. (1978). The social history of the tavern. In Y. Israel, H. Kalant, R. Popham, W. Schmidt, & R. Smart (Eds.), *Research advances in drug and alcohol problems* (vol. 4) pp. (225–302). New York: Plenum.

Pozas, R. (1962). *Juan the Chamula: An ethnological re-creation of the life of a Mexican Indian* (trans.). Berkeley: University of California Press.

Prakash, O. (1961). *Food and drinks in ancient India: From earliest times to c. 1200 A.D.* Delhi: Munshi Ram Manohar Lal.

Prescott, C. A., & Kendler, K. S. (1999). Age at first drink and risk for alcoholism: A noncausal association. *Alcoholism: Clinical and Experimental Research, 23*, 101–107.

Prestwich, P. E. (1988). *Drink and the politics of social reform: Antialcoholism in France since 1870*. Palo Alto: CA: Society for the Promotion of Science and Scholarship.

Productschap voor Gedistilleerde Dranken. (1997). *World drink trends*, (1997 ed.). Henley-on-Thames, UK: NTC Publications.

Rätsch, C. (1994). The mead of inspiration: And magical plants of the ancient Germans. In R. Metzner (Ed.), *The well of remembrance: Rediscovering the earth wisdom myths of Northern Europe* (pp. 279–295). Boston: Shambhala Press.

Read, K. E. (1980). *Other voices: The style of a male homosexual tavern*. Novato, CA: Chandler and Sharp.

Reed-Danahay, D. (1996). Champagne and chocolate: Taste and inversion in a French wedding ritual. *American Anthropologist, 98*, 350–361.

Rehm, J., Ashley, M. J., Room, R., Single, E., Bondy, S., Ferrence, R., & Giesbrecht, N. (1996). On the emerging paradigm of drinking patterns and their social and health consequences. *Addiction, 91*, 1615–1622.

Robbins, M. C., & Pollnac, R. B. (1969). Drinking patterns and acculturation in rural Buganda. *American Anthropologist, 71*, 276–284.

Robbins, R. H. (1973). Alcohol and the identity struggle: Some effects of economic change on personality structure. *American Anthropologist, 75*, 99–122.

Robinson, J. (1986). *Vines, grapes, and wine*. New York: Alfred A. Knopf.

Robinson, J. (1994). *Oxford companion to wine*. New York: Oxford University Press.

Roebuck, J. B., & Frese, E. (1976). *The Rendezvous: A case study of an after-hour club*. New York: Free Press.

Room, R. (1976). Ambivalence as a sociological explanation: The case of cultural explanations of alcohol problems. *American Sociological Review, 41*, 1047–1065.

Room, R. (1984a). Alcohol and ethnography: A case of "problem deflation"? [with comments by M. Agar, J. Beckett, L. Bennett, S. Casswell, D. Heath, J. Leland, J. Levy, W. Madsen, M. Marshall, J. Moskalewicz, J. Negrete, M. Rodin, L. Sackett, M. Sargent, D. Strug, & J. Waddell]. *Current Anthropology, 25*, 169–191.

Room, R. (1984b). Alcohol control and public health. *Annual Review of Public Health, 5*, 293–317.

Room, R. (1990). Measuring alcohol consumption in the U.S.: Methods and rationales. In L. Kozlowski, H. M. Annis, H. D. Cappell, F. B. Glaser, M. S. Goodstadt, Y. Israel, H. Kalant, E. M. Sellers, & E. R. Vingilis (Eds.), *Research Advances in Alcohol and Drug Problems* (vol. 10) (pp. 39–80). New York: Plenum.

Room, R. (1991a). Cultural changes in drinking and trends in alcohol problem indicators: Recent U.S. experience. In W. B. Clark & M. E. Hilton (Eds.), *Alcohol in America: Drinking practices and problems* (pp. 149–162). Albany: State University of New York Press.

Room, R. (1991b). Measuring alcohol consumption in the U.S.: Methods and rationales. In W. B. Clark & M. E. Hilton (Eds.), *Alcohol in America: Drinking practices and problems* (pp. 26–50). Albany: State University of New York Press.

Room, R. (1991c). Social science research and alcohol policy making. In P. M. Roman (Ed.), *Alcohol: The development of sociological perspectives on use and abuse* (pp. 315–339). New Brunswick, NJ: Rutgers Center of Alcohol Studies.

Room, R. (1992). The impossible dream? routes to reducing alcohol problems in a temperance culture. *Journal of Substance Abuse, 4*, 91–106.

Room, R. (1993). Epidemiological research on drinking patterns and problems. *Tijdschrift voor Alcohol, Drugs, en andere Psychotrope Stoffen, 19*, 195–217.

Room, R. (1997). Alcohol, the individual, and society: What history teaches us. *Addiction, 92* (Suppl. 1):S7–S11.

Room, R., Janca, A., Bennett, L. A., Schmidt, L., & Sartorius, N. (1996). WHO cross-cultural applicability research on diagnosis and assessment of substance abuse disorders: An overview of methods and selected results. *Addiction, 91*, 199–220.

Rossow, I. (1996). Alcohol-related violence: The impact of drinking pattern and drinking context. *Addiction, 91*, 1651–1661.

Roth, H. L. (1896). *The natives of Sarawak and British North Borneo* (vol. 1). New York: Truslove and Comba.

Rutter, O. (1929). *The pagans of North Borneo*. London: Hutchinson and Co.

Sadoun, R., Lolli, G., & Silverman, M. (1965). *Drinking in French culture* (Monograph 5). New Brunswick, NJ: Rutgers Center of Alcohol Studies.

Saggers, S., & Gray, D. (1998). *Dealing with alcohol: Indigenous usage in Australia, New Zealand, and Canada*. Cambridge: Cambridge University Press.

Sangree, W. H. (1962). The social functions of beer drinking in Bantu Tiriki. In D. J. Pittman & C. R. Snyder (Eds.), *Society, culture, and drinking patterns* (pp. 6–21). New York: John Wiley.

Sargent, M. J. (1967). Changes in Japanese drinking patterns. *Quarterly Journal of Studies on Alcohol, 28*, 709–722.

Schiøler, P. (1995). Denmark. In D. B. Heath (Ed.), *International handbook on alcohol and culture* (pp. 52–61). Westport, CT: Greenwood.

Schulenberg, J., O'Malley, P. M., Bachman, J. G., Wadsworth, K. N., & Johnston, L. D. (1996). Getting drunk and growing up: Trajectories of frequent binge drinking during the transition to young adulthood. *Journal of Studies on Alcohol, 57*, 289–304.

Scott, C., & Reicher, S. (1998). The inter-group dynamics of collective football "crowd violence." *Sociology, 32*, 353–378.

Seller, S. (1984). Attributes of alcohol in the New Testament. *Drinking and Drug Practices Surveyor, 19*, 18–22.

Shen, Y., & Wang, Z. (1998). China. In M. Grant (Ed.), *Alcohol and emerging markets: Patterns, problems, and responses* (pp. 123–143). Philadelphia: Taylor & Francis.

Shklovsky, I. W. (1916). *In Far North-East Siberia*. London: Macmillan and Co.

Sidorov, P. I. (1995). Russia. In D. B. Heath (Ed.), *International handbook on alcohol and culture* (pp. 237–253). Westport, CT: Greenwood.

Simmel, G. (1949). The sociology of sociability. *American Journal of Sociology, 55*, 254–261.

Simpura, J. (Ed.). (1987). *Finnish Drinking habits: Results from interview surveys held in 1968, 1976, and 1984* (vol. 35). Jyväskylä: Finnish Foundation for Alcohol Studies.

Singer, M. (1986). Toward a political-economy of alcoholism: The missing link in the anthropology of drinking. *Social Science and Medicine, 23*, 113–130.

Singh, G. (1989). Epidemiology of alcohol abuse in India. In R. Ray & R. W. Pickens (Eds.), *Proceedings of the Indo-U.S. Symposium on Alcohol and Drug Abuse* (Publ. 20) (pp. 3–12). Bangalore: National Institute of Mental Health and Neurosciences.

Single, E., Beaubrun, M., Mauffret, M., Minoletti, A., Moskalewicz, J., Moukolo, A., Plange, N. K., Saxena, S., Stockwell, T., Sulkunen, P., Suwaki, H., Hoshigoe, K., & Weiss, S. (1997). Public drinking, problems and prevention measures in twelve countries: Results of the WHO project on public drinking. *Contemporary Drug Problems, 24*, 425–448.

Single, E., & Leino, V. E. (1998). The levels, patterns, and consequences of drinking. In M. Grant & J. Litvak (Eds.), *Drinking patterns and their consequences* (pp. 7–24). Washington, DC: Taylor & Francis.

Single, E., & Pomeroy, H. (1999). Drinking and setting: A season for all things. In S. Peele & M. Grant (Eds.), *Alcohol and pleasure: A health perspective* (1999), Philadelphia: Taylor & Francis.

Single, E., & Storm, T. (Eds.). (1985). *Public drinking and public policy*. Toronto: Addiction Research Foundation.

Single, E., & Wortley, S. (1993). Drinking in various settings: Findings from a national survey in Canada. *Journal of Studies on Alcohol, 54*, 590–599.

Skog, O-J. (1983). *The collectivity of drinking cultures: A theory of the distribution of alcohol consumption* (SIFA Monograph 69). Oslo: National Institute for Alcohol Research.

Smart, R. G. (1997). Trends in drinking and patterns of drinking. In M. Grant & J. Litvak (Eds.), *Drinking patterns and their consequences* (pp. 25–41). Washington, DC: Taylor & Francis.

Smith, C., & Hanham, R. (1982). *Alcohol abuse: Geographic perspectives.* Washington, DC: Association of American Geographers.

Smith, G. (1995). *Beer: A history of suds and civilization from Mesopotamia to Microbreweries.* New York: Avon.

Smith, M. J., Abbey, A., & Scott, R. O. (1993). Reasons for drinking alcohol: Their relationship to psychosocial variables and alcohol consumption. *International Journal of Addictions, 28,* 881–908.

Snyder, C. R. (1958a). *Alcohol and the Jews: A cultural study of drinking and sobriety* (Yale Center of Alcohol Studies Monograph 2). Glencoe, IL: Free Press.

Snyder, C. R. (1958b). Culture and Jewish sobriety: The ingroup-outgroup factor. In M. Sklare (Ed.), *The Jews: Social patterns of an American group* (pp. 560–594). Glencoe, IL: Free Press.

Sobell, L. C., Sobell, M. B., Toneatto, T., & Leo, G. I. (1993). What triggers the resolution of alcohol problems without treatment? *Alcoholism: Clinical and Experimental Research, 17,* 217–224.

Sonnenstuhl, W. J. (1996). *Working sober: The transformation of an occupational drinking culture.* Ithaca, NY: ILR Press.

Sournia, J-C. (1990). *A history of alcoholism.* Oxford: Basil Blackwood.

Spalding, J. (1988). *Blithe spirits: A toast to the cocktail.* Washington, DC: Alvin Rosenbaum Projects.

Spradley, J. P. (1970). *You owe yourself a drunk: An ethnography of urban nomads.* Boston: Little, Brown.

Spradley, J. P., & Mann, B. J. (1975). *The cocktail waitress: Woman's work in a man's world.* New York: John Wiley and Sons.

Staden, H. (1928/1559). *The true story of his captivity.* London: George Routledge & Sons.

Steinkraus, J. H. (1979). Nutritionally significant indigenous foods involving alcoholic fermentation. In C. Gastineau, W. Darby, & T. Turner (Eds.), *Fermented food beverages in nutrition* (pp. 36–57). New York: Academic Press.

Stewart, O. C. (1964). Questions regarding American Indian criminality. *Human Organization 23,* 61–66.

Stivers, R. (1976). *A hair of the dog: Irish drinking and American stereotype.* University Park: Pennsylvania State University Press.

Stout, D. B. (1948). The Cuna. In J. H. Steward (Ed.), *Handbook of South American Indians* (Bureau of American Ethnology Bulletin 143, vol. 4) (pp. 257–268). Washington, DC: Smithsonian Institution.

Stross, B. (1967). The Mexican cantina as a setting for interaction. *Kroeber Anthropological Society Papers, 37,* 58–89.

Sulkunen, P., Alasuutari, A., Nätkin, R., & Kinnunen, M. (1997). *The urban pub.* Helsinki: National Research and Development Centre of Welfare and Health.

Suuronin, K. (1973). *Traditional festive drinking in Finland according to responses to an ethnographical questionnaire* (Report 76). Helsinki: Social Research Institute.

Syott, C., & Reicher, S. (1998). How conflict escalates: The inter-group dynamics of collective football crowd "violence." *Sociology, 32,* 1–25.

Taussig, M. T. (1980). *The devil and commodity fetishism in South America.* Chapel Hill: University of North Carolina Press.

Taylor, W. B. (1979). *Drinking, homicide,and rebellion in colonial Mexico.* Stanford: Stanford University Press.

Thompson, E. P. (1967). Time, work-discipline, and industrial capitalism. *Past and Present 38,* 56–97.

Thornton, M. A. (1987). *Sekt* versus *schnapps* in an Austrian village. In M. Douglas (Ed.), *Constructive drinking: Perspectives on drink from anthropology* (pp. 102–112). Cambridge: Cambridge University Press.

Turner, C. (1990). How much alcohol is in a "standard drink"? An analysis of 125 studies. *British Journal of Addiction, 85,* 1171–1175.

Uitenbroek, D. G. (1996). Seasonal variation in alcohol use. *Journal of Studies on Alcohol, 57,* 47–52.

U.S. Department of Agriculture and Department of Health and Human Services. (1995). *Nutrition and your health: Dietary guidelines for Americans* (4th ed.). Washington, DC: U.S. GPO.

U.S. Pharmacopeial Convention. (1995). *United States Pharmacopeia* (1995 ed.). Rockville, MD: Author.

Vaillant, G. E. (1983). *The natural history of alcoholism.* Cambridge, MA: Harvard University Press.

Vaillant, G. E., & Milofsky, E. S. (1982). The etiology of alcoholism: A prospective viewpoint. *American Psychologist, 37,* 494–503.

Vittetoe, K. W. (1995). Honduras. In D. B. Heath (Ed.), *International handbook on alcohol and culture* (pp. 110–116). Westport, CT: Greenwood.

Vogt, I. (1995). Germany. In D. B. Heath (Ed.), *International handbook on alcohol and culture* (pp. 88–98). Westport, CT: Greenwood.

Vroublevsky, A., & Harwin, J. (1998). Russia. In M. Grant (Ed.), *Alcohol and emerging markets: Patterns, problems, and responses* (pp. 203–222). Philadelphia: Taylor & Francis.

Waddell, J. O. (1975). For individual power and social credit: The use of alcohol among Tucson Papagos. *Human Organization, 34,* 9–15.

Waddell, J. O. (1979). Alcoholic intoxication as a component of the Papago Indian system of experiential reality. *Journal of Ultimate Reality and Meaning, 2,* 4ff.

Wagner, D. (1997). *The new temperance: The American obsession with sin and vice.* Boulder, CO: Westview.

Wallace, A. F. C. (1969). *The death and rebirth of the Seneca.* New York: Knopf.

Warner, J. (1997). The sanctuary of sobriety: The emergence of temperance as a feminine virtue in Tudor and Stuart England. *Addiction, 92,* 97–111.

Warner, J. (1998). Historical perspectives on the shifting boundaries around youth and alcohol: The example of pre-industrial England, 1350–1750. *Addiction, 93,* 641–657.

Washburne, C. (1961). *Primitive drinking: A study of the uses and functions of alcohol in preliterate societies.* New York: College and University Press.

Wassén, S. H. (1972). Ethnobotanical follow-up of Bolivian Tiahuanacoid tomb material, and of Peruvian shamanism, psychotropic plant constituents, and espingo seeds. In *Annual report of Göteborgs Etnografiska Museum* (pp. 35–52). Årstryck, Sweden: Göteborgs Etnografiska Museum.

Waugh, A. (1968). *Wine and spirits.* New York: Time/Life.

Wechsler, H., Davenport, A., Dowdall, G., Moeykens, B., & Castillo, S. (1994). Health and behavioral consequences of binge drinking in college: A national survey of students at 140 campuses. *Journal of the American Medical Association, 272,* 1672–1677.

Wechsler, H., Dowdall, G., Davenport, A., & Rimm, E. B. (1995). A gender-specific measure of binge-drinking among college students. *American Journal of Public Health, 85,* 982–985.

Wechsler, H., Moeykens, B., Davenport, A., Castillo, S., & Hansen, J. (1995). The adverse impact of heavy episodic drinkers on other college students. *Journal of Studies on Alcohol, 56,* 628–634.

Weibel-Orlando, J. (1986). Women and alcohol: Special populations and cross-cultural variations. In National Institute on Alcohol Abuse and Alcoholism (Ed.), *Women and alcohol: Health-related issues* (Research Monograph 16) (pp. 161–187). Rockville, MD: National Institute on Alcohol Abuse and Alcoholism.

Weiner, M. A. (1977). *The taster's guide to beer: Brews and breweries of the world.* New York: Macmillan.

Weiss, S. (1995). Israel. In D. B. Heath (Ed.), *International handbook on alcohol and culture* (pp. 142–155). Westport, CT: Greenwood.

Westermeyer, J. J. (1971). Use of alcohol and opium by the Meo of Laos. *American Journal of Psychiatry, 127,* 1019–1023.

Westermeyer, J. J. (1974). "The drunken Indian": Myths and realities. *Psychiatric Annals, 4(11),* 29ff.

Wilkinson, A. (1985). *Moonshine: A life in pursuit of white liquor*. New York: Knopf.

Willems, E. (1980). *Followers of the new faith: Culture change and the rise of Protestantism in Brazil and Chile* (Rev. ed.). Nashville, TN: Vanderbilt University Press.

Williams, D. M. (1998). Alcohol indulgence in a Mongolian community of China. *Bulletin of Concerned Asian Scholars, 30*, 13–22.

Williams, G. C., Stinson, F. S., Stewart, S. L., & Dufor, M. C. (1995). *Apparent per capita alcohol consumption: National, state, and regional trends* (Division of Biometry and Epidemiology, Alcohol Epidemiology Data System Surveillance Report 35). Bethesda, MD: National Institute on Alcohol Abuse and Alcoholism.

Williams, S. E. (1980). The use of beverage alcohol as medicine, 1790–1860. *Journal of Studies on Alcohol, 41*, 543–566.

Wilsnack, R. W., & Wilsnack, S. C. (Eds.). (1997). *Gender and alcohol: Individual and social perspectives*. New Brunswick, NJ: Rutgers Center of Alcohol Studies.

Wolcott, H. F. (1974). *African beer gardens of Bulawayo: Integrated drinking in a segregated society* (Monograph 10). New Brunswick, NJ: Rutgers Center of Alcohol Studies.

World Health Organization. (1997). *Manual of the International Statistical Classification of Diseases, Injuries, and Causes of Death* (10th ed.). Geneva: Author.

World Health Organization, Regional Office for Europe. (1993). *European Alcohol Action Plan* (EUR/ICP/ADA 035). Copenhagen: Author.

Wright-St.Clair, R. E. (1962). Beer in therapeutics: An historical annotation. *New Zealand Medical Journal, 61*, 512–513.

Xiao, J. (1995). China. In D. Heath (Ed.), *International handbook on alcohol and culture* (pp. 42–50). Westport, CT: Greenwood.

Yamamuro, B. (1958). Notes on drinking in Japan. *Quarterly Journal of Studies on Alcohol, 15*, 491–498.

Yawney, C. D. (1969). Drinking patterns and alcoholism in Trinidad. *McGill Studies in Caribbean Anthropology Occasional Papers, 5*, 34–48.

Yguel, J. Luciani, S., Duflo, B., M'Bamerzoui, C., Bard, D., & Gentilini, M. (1990). Consumption of alcoholic drinks in three different parts of Cameroon. In J. Maula, M. Lindblad, & C. Tigerstedt (Eds.), *Alcohol in developing countries* (NAD Publication 18) (pp. 113–126). Helsinki: Nordic Council for Alcohol and Drug Studies.

Zinberg, N. E. (1984). *Drug, set, and setting: The basis for controlled intoxicant use*. New Haven: Yale University Press.

Zingg, R. M. (1942). The genuine and spurious values in Tarahumara culture. *American Anthropologist, 44*, 78–92.

Index

Aaron, P., 38
Abbey, A., 61
Abel, E. L., 24
Abipone people, 29, 39, 76, 171
Aboriginal Australians, 57, 89, 115 (*See also* Australia)
Absenteeism, 163
Absolute alcohol, 36, 102 (*See also* Per capita consumption)
Abstainers, 31, 71, 93–100, 123, 180–182
  alcoholics, 95–96, 181
  Austria, 100
  Buddhist, 94, 98
  Canada, 93, 99
  Chile, 94
  China, 94
  Christian, 81, 94, 98–99, 122 (*See also* Fundamentalism)
  defining, 93–94
  Denmark, 94
  Finland, 99
  France, 100
  Germay, 100
  Great Britain, 100
  Hindu, 94, 98
  intolerance, 96
  medical reasons, 96–97
  Mexico, 94
  Muslim, 94, 97–98 (*See also* Islam)
  Norway, 99
  Poland, 93
  religious, 94–95, 97–99
  suspicion of, 81, 100, 172
  Sweden, 99
  U.S., 93, 99–100
  Zambia, 94

Abstinence, 58, 93–100 (*See also* Temperance movements)
Abuse, alcohol. *See* Alcohol abuse
Accidents, 79, 128 (*See also* Costs of drinking; Driving while impaired)
Acculturation, 68–69, 183–185 (*See also* cultural groups by name)
Acuda, W., 2, 13, 25, 53, 94, 139, 186
Adams, W. R., 30, 86, 149
Addiction. *See* Dependence
Additives, 170–171
Adolescence, 25, 79
Adolescents. *See* Youth
Advertising, 39
Afghanistan, 37
Africa, 23, 28, 47, 49, 52–53, 121, 142, 151, 184–186 (*See also* countries and cultures by name)
  beverage types, 139
  central, 143
  court, 58–59, 186
  eastern, 83, 142–143
  historical patterns, 62
  medicine, 178
  north/northern, 22, 32, 145
  southern, 49, 53, 119, 187
  sub-Saharan, 13, 142–143, 148, 173, 179, 187
  western, 143–144
African Americans, 75, 87, 89
Afterlife, 20, 28, 139
Age, 66, 76–82, 177
Aged. *See* Elderly
Aggression. *See* Violence
Ainu people, 20–21, 125–126
"Air-rage," 60